Destiny's Child

ADVANCE PRAISE FOR THE BOOK

'A blend of sweeping historical narrative and moving personal history, Raghu and Pushpa Palat's *Destiny's Child* recounts the fascinating life of Parukutty Neithyaramma of Cochin. Her story, one characterised by a deep involvement in public life and an unshakeable strength of will, is told here in rich detail and readable prose.'—Shashi Tharoor, Indian parliamentarian, writer and former UN Under Secretary General

'*Destiny's Child* is an intimate portrait of a remarkable, complicated, even controversial political figure—a woman who was not meant to wield power, but who claimed it for herself and made history. Packed with family memories, and honest in acknowledging the many shades to Parukutty Neithyaramma's personality, this book tells a story that is long overdue.' —Manu Pillai, author and historian

'Thoroughly researched and charged with emotion and detail, *Destiny's Child* brings to life Parukutty Neithyaramma and her world. In writing this deeply personal history of a long-forgotten queen, Raghu and Pushpa Palat have brought to us a gripping tale of the politics, culture, and personalities that shaped Cochin in the early twentieth century. From the intrigues of the royal household to entanglements with foreign powers and the protocol of the court, *Destiny's Child* is packed with engaging and thought-provoking details that animate Parukutty in a manner that has been done for few Indian queens.'—Anirudh Kanisetti, Author of *Lords of the Deccan*

Destiny's Child

The
undefeatable reign
of **Cochin's**
Parukutty
Neithyaramma

RAGHU PALAT
PUSHPA PALAT

PENGUIN
VIKING
An imprint of Penguin Random House

VIKING

USA | Canada | UK | Ireland | Australia
New Zealand | India | South Africa | China

Viking is part of the Penguin Random House group of companies
whose addresses can be found at global.penguinrandomhouse.com

Published by Penguin Random House India Pvt. Ltd
4th Floor, Capital Tower 1, MG Road,
Gurugram 122 002, Haryana, India

Penguin
Random House
India

First published in Viking by Penguin Random House India 2022

10 9 8 7 6 5 4 3 2 1

ISBN 9780670096305

Typeset in Adobe Caslon Pro by Manipal Technologies Limited, Manipal
Printed at Replika Press Pvt. Ltd, India

www.penguin.co.in

In worship we dedicate this book to
Chottanikkara Bhagavathy

We write this book to introduce our granddaughter
Nivaya
to her ancestry

The only person you are destined to become is the person you decide to be.

Ralph Waldo Emerson

Contents

Preface

On opposite sides of the massive hall at Parukutty Neithyaramma's palace in Trichur, Ratna Vilas, were larger than life paintings of Maharaja Sir Rama Varma XVI G.C.I.E., the first hereditary Maharaja[1] of Cochin and Parukutty Neithyaramma, his consort—the lady who was the power in the state of Cochin during the period her husband was the Maharaja. In this portrait, she is dressed in a simple white sari but adorned with heavy jewellery. She is wearing large star-shaped diamond ear studs, a huge diamond solitaire nosepin and rows of emerald, ruby and gold necklaces around her neck. On her wrist she has several gold and diamond bangles. However, what arrests the attention is her commanding, unflinching gaze that demands both respect and fealty. It is the gaze of a person born to lead.

From the time I was born till her passing away, I lived with her at her houses in Trichur and Coonoor. I was very close to her, especially as she was my great-grandmother and I was her first great-grandson. Our bond was doubly close as I was her great-grandson from both sides of my family—my father's and my mother's—my parents being first cousins. My father was the son of the elder of her two daughters—Ratnam Amma Palatt. My father, being her first grandchild, was her favourite, and so she insisted on bringing him up herself at the Hill Palace in Thrippunithura. My mother was the eldest child of Parukutty Neithyaramma's younger son, Aravindaksha Menon. Both my parents were born and raised at the magnificent 52-acre Hill Palace.

Parukutty with co-author Raghu Palat in Coonoor

I had, in my childhood, heard stories of the extensive terraced lawns, resplendent with bright blooms, of gurgling fountains and clear ponds. The massive palace interiors, though filled with ancient relics and great paintings, were for my father, the hub of several of his childish escapades. It was, therefore, not surprising that once the palace was converted into a museum, my father refused to visit it. When I asked him to take me around what was once his home, he would wistfully explain that he did not have the heart to see it shorn of its glory and wished to remember it as he had once known it.

By all accounts, the diminutive, 4 feet 9 inches tall, plump Parukutty Neithyaramma was a stern and ruthless individual, who had grown men quaking in their boots when she so much as raised an eyebrow. She was not approachable to most people, and on the whole, everyone fearfully stayed away from her unless summoned. She was not a demonstrative woman, though I do believe that she was very fond of her family, and I, as her great-grandson, stand testimony to this. We spent long hours together chatting at her home in Trichur, especially in the early mornings and in the afternoons over tea when she would ply me with ghee-roast dosas, coconut addas and stories. Others too were recipients of her generosity of spirit. On the death of her mother, Parukutty Neithyaramma stepped in and took on the responsibility of bringing up her only brother, Govindan. Her eldest son, V.K. Raman Menon or Akkan as he was known, was her favourite child, and she indulged him to a fault. There was literally nothing she would not do for Akkan. When the First World War broke out, Akkan was studying for a doctorate in Heidelberg, Germany. Fearing for his safety and wanting him back home safe, she went so far as to even petition the Pope in

Rome, and it was only through His Holiness' intervention that she finally managed to get her son freed and deported to Switzerland and then on to England. Unfortunately, both her brother and this son broke her heart when they sued her for the partition of the family property—the property that she had carefully built and husbanded. Many, many years later, Akkan wandered into his mother's home in Coonoor. He was a broken man, frail and despondent. All the money he had gleaned from her had been frittered away, and he arrived in a torn dirty, white cotton suit, unshaven, unkempt and shod in a worn-out pair of unpolished brown shoes. With absolutely no hesitation and holding no grudges about having been dragged to court and for having caused her so much grief, Parukutty Neithyaramma welcomed her prodigal son back home with open arms and asked him to stay with her. It is, of course, another story that a few days later Akkan's son came and took his father back with him, and perhaps this final separation once again broke a mother's heart.

Her largesse extended to my father, and the closeness she felt with him is apparent in that my father would call Parukutty Neithyaramma, Amma and the Maharaja Achan, and his own parents he referred to more formally and in Western terms as Mamma and Pappa. When Parukutty Neithyaramma's husband, the Maharaja, passed away, she left Cochin and travelled to Lausanne, Switzerland, taking my father along with her. There she enrolled him at the world-renowned and prestigious Institut Le Rosey in Rolle. My father received the finest education of the time and was educated at establishments that were the schools for princes and titled aristocracy. In fact, the Shah of Iran, Mohammad Reza Pahlavi, was his schoolmate at the

Institut Le Rosey. After spending two years in Switzerland and another in England, Parukutty Neithyaramma returned home to Cochin but only after enrolling my father at yet another prestigious English public school—Charterhouse in Godalming, Surrey, England.

To me she will always be my doting great-grandmother whom I called Valiamma, mother's elder sister, for no other reason than that is what everyone, including my mother, called her.

Perhaps it was a vestige of a bygone colonial era that my great-grandmother instead of the traditional Malayalee mundu wore gold raw silk frocks when in Coonoor and in the latter part of her life. That to my young and rather untrained eye seemed very glamorous. She was certainly not beautiful but had a face, dominated by a large nose, that arrested attention. She had a perfect set of teeth, gleaming white and symmetrically arranged. Yet, she never ever used toothpaste. Instead of toothpaste, she cleaned her teeth with a black powder called mukkeri and, thereafter, rubbed the teeth with ginger. Whether this was the reason she never ever visited a dentist and had teeth that could have cracked a nut till the day she died is something I will never know. She was a strict vegetarian. My parents were not. At Ratna Vilas, my father had to set up a separate kitchen a distance away from the main kitchen to have his chicken and meat dishes cooked. As her cook Achuthan Nair was not permitted to cook non-vegetarian food, my father hired a person named Gopalan who had cooked at the Majestic Hotel in Coimbatore and knew how to cook Western cuisine. Unfortunately, being an ezhava, Gopalan was considered an untouchable by the upper echelons of society in Cochin.

To circumvent this and to make him acceptable, my father decided to call him Gopalan Nair. I am sure Valiamma knew of this deception, but my father was her favourite and could do no wrong.

My great-grandmother was remarkably insightful and had an acutely sharp intellect. I would watch her handle her property matters with ease and not even the wiliest of men could get anything past her. Even in the dusk of her life, no one really approached her unless summoned, and I believe most people were uncomfortable in her presence.

By the time I was born, Parukutty Neithyaramma's husband, the Maharaja, had long since passed away; but she still continued to command people as she had once done in the royal palaces, and everyone would scuttle off to do her bidding.

She was also quite serious. I cannot recall her bursting into spontaneous laughter at any time or indulging in small talk. Her conversations were usually advice on what one should do and how one should conduct oneself.

She was very frugal too. I remember once my grandfather, Aravindaksha Menon—her son—had purchased an expensive watch. Valiamma, as was her habit, asked him the price. He quoted a figure which was less than half its cost. She castigated him and told him that he had paid too much. At Vishu and other festivals, we would wend our way to her for the traditional vishu kayneetam. She would greet us and give us a rupee. Not a paisa more.

Following the death of the Maharaja, Parukutty Neithyaramma moved out of the palace at Thrippunithura and into the palatial Ratna Vilas at Trichur, which she had built for her retirement. In fact, my earliest memory of her is at Ratna Vilas, her massively large home. It was dusk and she had summoned a Velichhappad. The Velichhappad was to my young mind quite a frightening person dressed in red; his body smeared with ashes and turmeric. He had long curly hair and a sickle-shaped sword. The Velichhappad danced in a frenzy, yelling incomprehensible words. After a time, he took the curved sword that he had been waving around and slashed his forehead. Then, loudly proclaiming the words of the goddess, he fell to the ground exhausted. I have always suspected that perhaps the poor Velichhappad, not having bargained for having to prance so vigorously through such an extensive mansion, must have decided to cut the ceremony short with a dramatic gash to his head, a loud proclamation and a collapse to the floor that could be attributed to the force of the Devi sapping him of all energy, thereby ending his ordeal in a very credible manner. I must have been about three years old at the time, but I still remember the Velichhappad's tantric dance and the blood oozing from his forehead as if it had happened just yesterday.

Parukutty Neithyaramma was a very devout woman and next to the hall in Ratna Vilas was her prayer room—a huge room with many, three-to-four-feet-high, clay idols of our gods and goddesses. Among the idols lay a pair of padukas, single-pronged wooden sandals, that had once belonged to Parukutty Neithyaramma's father. Since we always took off our slippers before entering the prayer room, as a child, I had been intrigued as to why these padukas were not only permitted into the prayer room, but even designated a prominent position. Much later, I learnt that Parukutty Neithyaramma idolized her father, and believed it was he who had made it possible for her to reach the highest echelons of power.

She would, often intone 'Amme save me' or 'Amme I am tired'. This, I later realized, was her calling out to the Chottanikkara Bhagavathy to whom she was devoted. Throughout her life, she maintained that it was Bhagavathy's blessings that had brought her power and position.

Behind her house in Ratna Vilas was a temple—Kulasshery. At this temple, in memory of her husband, she had a shrine for Hanuman and a bhajan room built. She also donated money for a fund, the interest of which would pay for its upkeep.

In the summer months, she would leave the plains and travel to Coonoor in the Nilgiris, where she had a charming, large colonial home—Homedale—and tea estates that her son Aravindaksha Menon looked after. At that time and until my mother died when I was nine, I would stay at 'Grange', another of her sprawling bungalows where my parents lived but would visit Valiamma at Homedale nearly every day. It was at Homedale that she passed away on 25 February 1963. I was at boarding school at the time at the nearby Lawrence School in Lovedale and I was brought back from school. I remember being taken to the room that she spent the day in—her drawing room where she was laid in state on her divan. This is etched in my memory as it was the first time I had seen the body of a person who had passed away. She looked peaceful, as though asleep, and very regal. Later, after her daughters, Ratnam and Vilasini, arrived along with their husbands, we, along with my grandfather and father, were driven to one of her estates—RV (named after her husband, the Maharaja)—and she was cremated there.

I have grown up talking to Parukutty Neithyaramma, hearing innumerable stories about her from my parents and family and from those who worked for her or knew her. My maternal grandmother, Malathy Menon, her daughter-in-law, once told me that though she lived at the Palace too, she only got to meet her mother-in-law rarely and on festivals such as Onam and Vishu. I also had occasion to meet varied people who came to pay their respects to her, and I watched and learnt as she disposed of matters effectively one after another. Then there were the juicy tales of palace intrigues and conspiracies that were often the gossip of old retainers that were later reconfirmed by the family.

Valiamma had played a significant role in my early years and influenced me in many ways. But it was not till much later in my life that I began to once again connect with this remarkably powerful woman who had loved me through my most formative years. My daughter Nikhila, after my elder daughter Divya's marriage, out of the blue evinced interest in her roots and it was with her and my wife, Pushpa, that we embarked on a journey down memory lane.

Our first stop naturally was the Dutch Palace at Mattanchery, the erstwhile capital of Cochin State, where the coronations of the rulers of Cochin State including that of my great-grandfather had taken place. In the palace, among the portraits of the rulers of Cochin was a large portrait of my great-grandfather Maharaja Rama Varma XVI. We walked past the Durbar Hall and memories of the many stories I had heard about coronations tumbled back. Nikhila wished to take pictures of her great-great-grandfather but as photography was not permitted, we waited until we met someone of authority who not only granted us permission to take pictures but welcomed us back to his office where we shared a cup of tea as he regaled us with stories of the rule of my great-grandfather and his consort. I was amazed and humbled by the fact that so many years later, here was a man who knew so much more than me about my ancestry.

It was much the same when we visited the Hill Palace in Thrippunithura where the Cochin Rajas and Maharajas lived. When they came to know who we were, the museum authorities were welcoming and graciously allowed us into rooms that were generally closed. I imagined that among these were perhaps the rooms my father and mother had been born in. They permitted us to take photographs, though photography is not permitted within the palace. Thereafter, we have visited the Hill Palace on many occasions and the respect that we are greeted with on every occasion speaks volumes for the admiration and regard the people still hold for Maharaja Rama Varma XVI and Parukutty Neithyaramma.

As a part of delving into the past, I met Thampurans in Thrippunithura. It was when I introduced myself that it began to dawn on me that my Valiamma was truly a remarkable woman. In fact, they referred to Maharaja Rama Varma XVI as the 'Neithyaramma's Thampuran', affirming that she was the power at the time. Four decades after her death, these princes spoke her name in hushed tones—with respect coupled with what I interpreted as both fear and dislike. As they spoke of her, it became apparent that Parukutty Neithyaramma was undoubtedly a powerful entity in her own right, a force to be reckoned with, and this in an age when consorts were relegated to the shadows with neither voice nor authority.

The credit for this book must go to my co-author—my wife Pushpa. When she heard the stories of my great-grandmother, she insisted that they must be told. A compelling story of a young girl married at the age of fourteen to a man seventeen years older than her, who, challenging convention, rose to rule a state. This is the story of a girl destined to be a ruler. It is the remarkable story of a strong woman, unafraid to break norms, and who, against all odds, rose to rule a state, and ruled it impressively well. This is the story as I know it from my memories and those of her immediate and closest family, and from stories that she herself told me.

This is the story of Parukutty Neithyaramma—a woman no man could gainsay.

Raghu Palat
Mumbai

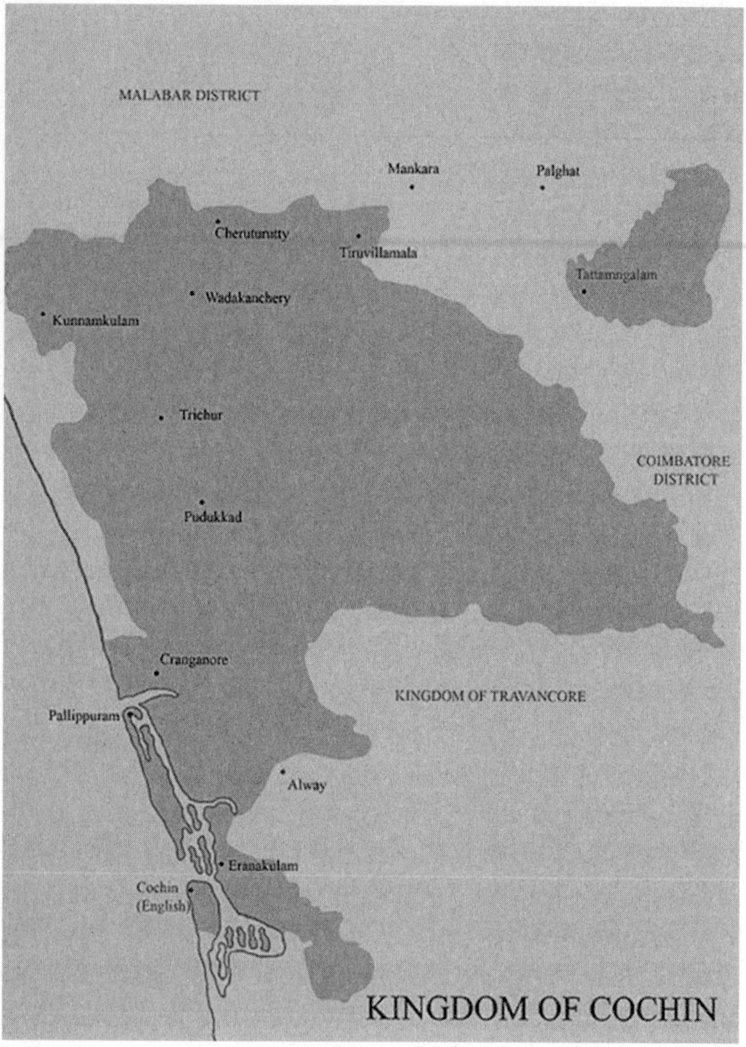
MALABAR DISTRICT
Mankara
Palghat
Cherutunstty
Tiruvillamala
Tattamngalam
Wadakanchery
Kunnamkulam
Trichur
COIMBATORE
DISTRICT
Pudukkad
Cranganore
KINGDOM OF TRAVANCORE
Pallippuram
Alway
Eranakulam
Cochin
(English)
KINGDOM OF COCHIN

FAMILY TREE

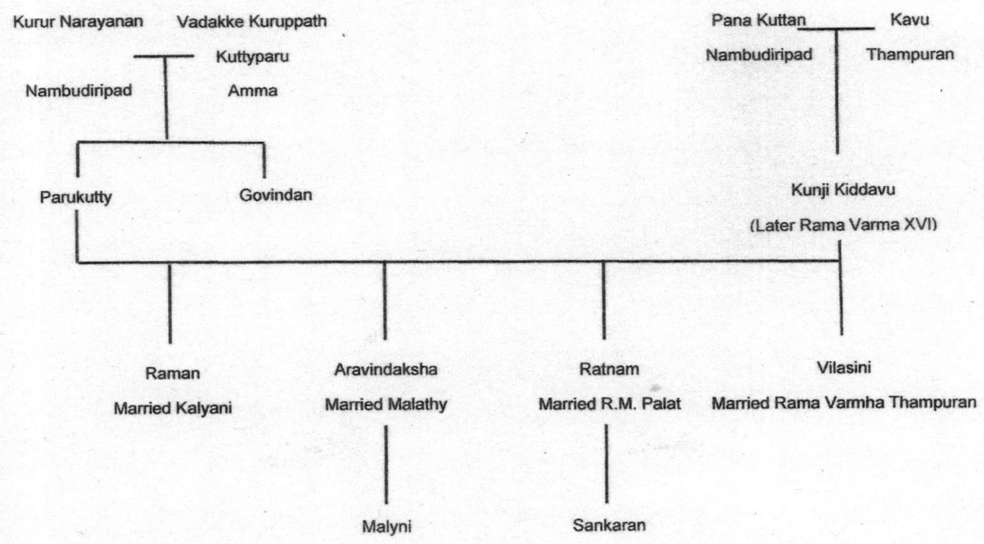
Kurur Narayanan
Nambudiripad
Vadakke Kuruppath
Kuttyparu
Amma
Parukutty
Govindan
Pana Kuttan
Nambudiripad
Kavu
Thampuran
Kunji Kiddavu
(Later Rama Varma XVI)
Raman
Married Kalyani
Aravindaksha
Married Malathy
Malyni
Ratnam
Married R.M. Palat
Sankaran
Vilasini
Married Rama Varmha Thampuran

Residents, Agents to Governor General and Diwans

During the Reign of Rama Varma XVI

Residents

1913–1915	A.T. Forbes
1915–1916	R.A. Graham
1916	A.R. Cummins (Acting)
1916–17	H.L. Braidwood
1917–1920	H.H. Burkill
1920–1923	C.W.E. Cotton

Agents to the Governor General

1923–1926	C.W.E. Cotton
1926–1926	H.A.B. Vernon
1926–1928	C.W.E. Cotton
1928–1929	C.G. Crosthwaite
1929–1930	A.N.L. Cater
1930–1932	H.R.N. Pritchard

Diwans

1914–1919	J.W. Bhore
1919–1922	T. Vijayaraghavacharya
1922–1925	P. Narayana Menon
1925–1930	T.S. Narayana Iyer
1930–1935	C.G. Herbert

Authors' Note

The Thampurans or princes of Cochin were named Rama, Ravi or Kerala. The reason was that it is propagated that the rulers of Cochin were suryavanshies—descendants of Surya, the sun god, and that they descended from Luv, the son of Lord Rama—hence the names Ravi and Rama. The third son was named Kerala as the rulers of the land of the Cheras. To avoid confusion, they were, therefore, known by a nickname or by a distinguishing factor. As the Rajas in this book were both named Rama, the earlier Raja has been mentioned initially as Raja Rama Varma XV and later after his abdication as the abdicated Raja. The Thampuran whose consort the protagonist of this book Parukutty was, is mentioned as Kunji Kiddavu, which was his pet name. After he ascended the throne, he is mentioned as Raja Rama Varma XVI, and later, on his elevation to being a hereditary Maharaja, as Maharaja Rama Varma XVI.

The many anecdotes about Parukutty and Kunji Kiddavu recounted in this book are from stories that Parukutty herself related to her great-grandson, the co-author of this book and the memories of his grandparents, parents, uncles, aunts, cousins and old palace retainers who lived and interacted with Maharaja Rama Varma XVI and his consort Parukutty Neithyaramma. These stories are detailed and extensive as these are first-hand reports of people who had lived through the Maharaja's reign and because these are stories of people the co-author Raghu Palat and later co-author Pushpa Palat have personally interacted with. In writing this book, some scenes have been recreated based on these incidents. In addition, certain events have been expanded to bring alive the time and breathe life into some of the individuals whose paths crossed that of the Neithyaramma.

The references to caste in this story are not comprehensive as the Kerala caste system was extremely complex and totally different from that followed in any other part of India. In the early twentieth century, the period covered in this book, the Varna system of four castes—brahmins, kshatriyas, vaishyas and sudras—had little currency in Kerala. In Kerala, however, there were among the Hindus roughly 420 castes or jatis and each caste had strict codes of conduct regarding touching, speaking, eating, marrying and more. Deviating from these norms was simply not tolerated and could, in some instances, result in being expelled from the jati. In this book, we have focused on the Nambudiris—the brahmins, the Thampurans and Thampurattis—the royal family and the Nairs—the landlords and warriors. The Nambudiris were at the pinnacle of the caste hierarchy and regarded everyone else as sudras. Kerala, at that time, can only be described as priest-ridden and priest-dominated. The word Nambudiri or Nambuthiri is believed to be a compound of two words 'Nampu' and 'thiri'. 'Nambu' means sacred or trustworthy and 'thiri' means light. The suggestion or implication of the name is that the nambudiri is a sacred light. It is at such a time when caste barriers were sacrosanct and rigidly enforced that Raja Rama Varma entered into a sambandham with Parukutty, and later ascended the throne. Parukutty, defying all norms, made her mark as one of the most powerful, feared and benevolent rulers of Cochin.

In order to create the ambience of the time, we have used terminology of the period and many words are in Malayalam. These words are explained in the Glossary.

The images in this book are either from open resources or from family albums.

1

Divine Intervention

The twenty-fifth day of November 1914 promised to be a cool and pleasant day. Dawn was just breaking and the sun was gently peeking around the horizon. Parukutty, having bathed in the kolam attached to her residence, lined her eyes with kohl, combed her tresses and carefully appraised her reflection that gleamed off the long free-standing mirror in her dressing room. Her vermillion red brocade blouse was in sharp contrast to her crisp ivory, gold bordered mundu. Her long, wavy, black hair, freshly washed, lay open at her shoulders, still damp. The scent of fresh jasmine mixed with the aroma of herb-infused coconut oil wafted in the breeze behind her. Parukutty Amma wore a thick gold chain around her neck, on which dangled a delicate thali. Higher up, her neck was adorned with a traditional Kerala choker of chunky gold hung with several deep green, emerald mango pendants. On both her wrists she wore a dozen gold bangles each. On her ring finger she had a large navratna ring and in her earlobes were round diamond studs. Dangling from the top of her ears were thick, heavy, gold loops. Parukutty had always had a penchant for jewellery, and every night as she set aside her day's jewels, she carefully selected pieces for the next morning's visit to the temple. Satisfied with her mirror reflection, she smiled to herself and set off on her daily visit to the Chottanikkara BhagavathyTemple.

The highlight of Parukutty's day was her visit to the Chottanikkara Bhagavathy Temple.

Legend has it that the area around the temple had once been a dense jungle infested with yakshis and rakshas, where wild animals roamed free. The only inhabitants in the forest were some wandering nomads and sages in meditation. Most people avoided this area for fear of being attacked by wild animals or robbers. Unmindful of the dangers, a man named Kannappan lived in the forest along with his only daughter, Thevi. Kannappan was obsessed with the belief that he must sacrifice a cow every day in order to attain great physical prowess. A ruthlessly cruel man, he stole cattle from the nearby villages in order to perform his daily sacrifice. One day, while returning after stealing two cows, he chanced upon a young calf that had strayed into the forest. Kannappan picked up the tiny animal with the intent of offering it as sacrifice. But when his daughter Thevi saw the beautiful calf, she fell in love with it and begged her father to spare the calf's life. Kanappan's only weakness was his love for his daughter. He could not deny her anything. He succumbed and allowed her to keep the calf.[1]

However, one day, as a consequence of his despoiling the countryside, Kannappan was unable to find a single cow. He consequently decided to kill the calf. Thevi would not permit this. Hugging the calf closely, she firmly told her father that if he wished to sacrifice the calf, he must kill her too. Kannappan had no alternative but to relent. From that day forth, it is said that Kannappan was a transformed man. He began to care for and love not just his daughter but the calf too. Gradually, he became less cruel. Unfortunately, a few years later, his daughter died. The calf became his only solace. Years passed, and one night, Kannappan dreamt that there was a divine being beside the calf that had now become a cow.[2]

Awaking with a start, he rushed to the cowshed. There he was surprised to find that where the cow had been tethered was a large stone and right next to it was a rock. It is said that he saw a vision that told him it was Goddess Lakshmi and Lord Narayana that had taken abode in his shed. From then on, Kannappan's devotion increased and he lived out his life as a most pious man.[3]

Much after Kannappan's time, his cottage, the shed and its surroundings were overgrown with thick grass and a forest of tamarind trees. One day, many years later, a Pulayi girl was cutting grass. Seeing a raised stone, she decided to sharpen her sickle on it. To her absolute horror, the stone began to spout blood. Hearing her screams, those in the vicinity rushed to the spot. They found the girl to be in a trance. After the initial consternation, it was decided that a pious person must be asked to determine the cause for this strange occurrence. It so happened that a holy man, Edattu Nambudiri, was in the vicinity, on his way to a nearby village. The Nambudiri was apprised of the unusual happening. Intrigued, he agreed to take a look at the stone. As the holy man approached the stone, he saw a divine glow and sensed the presence of Adiparashakti. He immediately performed a puja and made an offering to the deity. Edattu Nambudiri advised the locals that should they worship the mother goddess they would prosper and no harm would come to them. This marked the origins of one of the most venerated temples of Kerala. It is believed that the sanctum sanctorum of Chottanikkara Bhagavathy is the place where

Kannappan's cottage was once located. The Sreemoolasthanam is where his cowshed was situated.

The magnificent present-day Chottanikkara Temple built in the Vishwakarma wooden sculpture style is a far cry from Kannappan's tiny cowshed. The divine power in the idol is believed to be a combination of the Goddesses Saraswathy, Lakshmi and Kali. And with them at all times is the divine power of Lord Vishnu. The goddess is worshipped in three different forms—as Saraswathy in the morning, draped in white; as Lakshmi at noon, draped in crimson; and as Maha Kali in the evening draped in blue. The prayer 'Amme Narayana, Devi Narayana, Lakshmi Narayana, Bhadre Narayana' pays obeisance to all three and Lord Vishnu, whose idol is placed to the right of the Bhagavathy.

As Parukutty sat in the bullock cart that would take her to the Chottanikkara Temple, she smiled to herself recalling a fond childhood memory. At fourteen, still a child, she had been married to a man seventeen years older than herself. Parukutty was then very childish in many ways. She would often pester her husband for things that took her fancy, and gold and gems ranked high on her wish list. Whenever the goldsmith visited the house with his bag of treasures, Parukutty would rush off to her husband and plead, most endearingly, for at least one or two of the ornaments. Her ever doting husband, who usually indulged his child-bride, finally reached the point when he found her demands getting far too excessive. One day, impatient with her and in a moment of annoyance, he brusquely fobbed her off saying rather curtly, 'I'm not so rich that I can keep buying you expensive baubles. You go every day to worship the Bhagavathy. Ask her for anything you desire and don't come to me.' The innocent Parukutty took her husband's suggestion very seriously and thereafter she spent many hours letting Chottanikkara Bhagavathy know of all her desires. Though it had been several years since then and Parukutty had outgrown her insatiable appetite for jewellery, she still visited the Bhagavathy and confided in the goddess.

The bullock cart now stopped at the western nada of the temple. Parukutty alighted and walked in through the giant temple doorway. As was customary, she walked down the steps to pay obeisance to Goddess Kali before returning to pray to her beloved Bhagavathy. The temple was relatively empty. A few of the regulars were taking their pradishnams around the temple. She entered alone and stood with hands folded, head bowed in deep reverence. Standing before the exquisite idol, Parukutty mentally chanted the Lalita Sahasranamam. Once she had completed the stotra, she prostrated before the goddess and moved to her customary place in a small enclave by the sanctum sanctorum that gave her an unrestricted view of the goddess. She was so regular and constant about her routine at the temple that even the spot at which she sat was always left vacant for her. In later years that spot came to be known as 'Parukutty's space'. Seated in the padmasana position, she shut her eyes and continued with her prayers and meditation. In the quiet and stillness around her, Parukutty felt an all-encompassing peace. Her prayers completed, she stepped out of the enclave and walked around the temple compound three times.

On her way out, as was her custom, she walked across to the priest to prostrate before him, receive his blessing and the temple prasad. The priest blessed her and after handing over the prasad to Parukutty enquired, 'So you have moved house?' Parukutty, surprised at this question, replied that they had certainly not changed residence. The priest looked puzzled and replied, 'Oh I thought you had moved out of that house'.

Parukutty was a bit bewildered and confused as to why the priest should pose such a strange question. Quickly putting it out of her mind, she walked back to the bullock cart to head home, absorbed in thoughts of the many chores she had to complete that day. Never in her wildest dreams could she ever have imagined that there was truth in the words of the priest—it was not just her home but her whole life that had changed.

2

Inhaling the Future

It had been over eight hours and the bouts of pain kept getting worse. The frequency had increased and the intervals between spasms were getting shorter and shorter. Yet, the contractions were neither strong enough nor frequent enough for the old, obese midwife Bala. She sat on the wooden palaga, coolly sipping jaggery-sweetened tea and enjoying an ela full of stewed nendrapazham much to the annoyance of the young mother. Vadakke Kuruppath Kuttyparu Amma, affectionately called Chinnammu, was in the throes of a painful childbirth. Bala kept reassuring her that it would soon be over and once the baby was in her arms, she wouldn't even remember the pain. Chinnammu raised her eyebrows in complete disbelief. Once again, though writhing in agony, she tried to compose herself but could not hold back a loud moan. The older woman hobbled out to the adjoining corridor that surrounded the nadumittam, where on the parapet a large copper vessel of water had been placed. Picking up one of the kindis set alongside, she filled it with water, poured it on her hands and washed them thoroughly. Then returning to the bedroom she went across to

Chinammu. The expectant mother was lying on a high, flat, wooden bed covered with just a thin mattress—certainly not the most comfortable for one whose body was being wracked by an excruciating backache, in addition to the labour pains. As another contraction took hold of her, she clutched tightly the carved circular columns on the side of the bed and dug her nails deep into the wood. Bala gave her a concerned look and then prying Chinammu's legs apart she peered below. Chinammu's frustrations increased. Pregnancy brought with it nothing but pain and ignominy. But there was no denying the midwife's expertise. Bala had been summoned because she was reputed for the ease with which she handled deliveries and because she had a reputation of not losing any of the babies or mothers during childbirth—a far too common occurrence at the time. So, despite the pain, it was a relief for Chinammu that she was in very competent hands.

It had been a difficult pregnancy. Chinammu had retched for the entire nine months. The smell of pappadums had made her vomit so violently that she would need to lie down every afternoon to rest and recover; but no one in this large tarwad would even consider a meal without pappadums. Her legs had swollen up; her belly was so huge that she had even suspected she might be delivering twins. She had hardly had a night of uninterrupted sleep in the interminably long nine months and by all accounts had been irritable and short with most of her extended family. Now, here she was, moments, or would it be hours, away from the birth of her first child.

Her sambandhi, Kurur Narayanan Nambudiripad,[1] scion of the ancient family from the village Adat that had the honour of anointing the chiefs of Palakkad, was outside, terribly nervous and anxious about the delivery. He paced around restlessly. There had been so many horror stories about how both mother and child had died in childbirth. Try as he might, he failed to dispel these thoughts of gloom. He knew his wife to be a strong woman and he now prayed to Lord Krishna to give her all the fortitude she would need to see her through this, the final stages of her pregnancy. He was also excited, in anticipation of the birth of their very first child. Secretly, he hoped it would be a girl.

Behind the locked bedroom door, the now exhausted Chinammu could think of nothing but the end of this terrible ordeal. Shutting her eyes tightly, Chinammu began praying to the Lord of the famed Vadakunnathan Temple, Lord Shiva and to Vaishnavi Devi[2] of the Parmekkavu Temple for a quick and safe delivery. Her silent prayers to the deities, who were so dear to the entire Vadakke Kuruppath tarwad, eased her pain and brought back a semblance of serenity.

It was believed that Chinammu's tarwad, the Vadakke Kuruppath tarwad, owed its prosperity to the Lord of the renowned Vadakunnathan Temple. According to family lore, the large padinjare chira near the temple was swept daily and kept clean by a young woman. Apart from being the public bathing pond, this was where devotees would bathe before entering the sacred interior of the temple. One day, two Nambudiris came to have a bath at this chira. One of them had a diamond ring which he carefully removed and placed beside his clothes on the steps of the chira. After their bath, the two Nambudiris got dressed and left, forgetting all about the ring that had been placed on the steps. It was only much later that the Nambudiri noticed the ring missing from his finger. He rushed back to the chira but alas, in spite of a thorough search, the ring could not be found. A number of people had gathered to help the Nambudiri in his search. It was at this time that the cleaning woman returned to the chira steps. Realizing what all the commotion was about she looked around and noticed that a cow had laid some fresh dung on one of the steps. Knowing that it hadn't been there when she had last cleaned, she suggested that they look under the dung. Sure enough, hidden under the cow dung was the gleaming, precious, diamond solitaire. Delighted and overwhelmed by the integrity of the cleaning woman, the Nambudiri gifted her a house close to the pond.

It was from this pious cleaning woman that the Vadakke Kuruppath tarwad emanated. The house gifted by the Nambudiri grew to become the tarwad's ancestral house and came to be known as Padinjare Shrambi. The family prospered—advancing from the lower rungs of the temple pond to palaces.

In the years that followed, the women of the family became sought after for sambandhams from powerful Nair houses such as the Paliath Achans of Chendamangalam (the hereditary prime ministers of the state of Cochin), the Ambat family of Chittur, the Kizhekepat family and others. The women had sambandhams even with princes of the royal houses of Kerala, including with Cochins's most famous Raja, Sakhtan Thampuran, who ruled from 1790 to 1805. It was with this tarwad that Kurur Narayanan Nambudiripad entered into an alliance by establishing a sambandham with the tall, fair, porcelain-featured, exquisitely beautiful, Vadakke Kuruppath Kuttyparu Amma.

As Narayanan Nambudiripad continued to pace the grounds, he could clearly hear Chinammu's heart-wrenching screams. Black thunder clouds had begun to darken the skies, adding to his sense of foreboding. Feeling totally helpless, he went into the tiny prayer room of the house and began fervently chanting the Vishnu Sahasranamam. It was a further four hours of labour before Bala put a healthy, tiny, screeching, pink-purple, cuddly little infant gently into Chinammu's outstretched arms—her firstborn. The gusty first cry of the infant could be heard clearly above the roar of thunder and the clatter of the torrential monsoon downpour as it crashed down upon the parched earth. Much to Chinammu's surprise, just as Bala had said, within moments of the baby being placed in her arms, all the pain, the irritation and the rigours of the tedious nine months were forgotten. All she felt was a peaceful bliss as the baby, with eyes shut tightly, lay its head close to her heart—a girl child had been born to the Vadakke Kuruppath tarwad.

As per custom, Narayanan Nambudiripad left after the birth of his daughter and returned to his mana promising to come back shortly.

Twenty-eight days later, at her Iruvathetta, a black thread was tied around the child's waist and a black dot of kohl was marked on her chin to ward off all evil. She was bedecked in gold aranjanam, gold bangles and a gold chain with a Vishnu pendant around her neck. The vellaku was lit and the entire family gathered to thank the lord for the gift of a healthy, happy baby.

The infant lay on her father's lap, her eyes wide open and listened intently as he whispered her name, Parukutty, three times in her right ear while covering her left ear with a fresh green betel leaf. Considering the tarwad's affinity to Lord Shiva and to Parmekkavu Devi, it was but no surprise that the little girl was named after Goddess Parvathy, the consort of Lord Shiva.

The large Vadakke Kuruppath tarwad welcomed the new addition to the family. Parukutty was showered with an abundance of love and affection and was constantly transferred from one set of arms to another as a host of uncles, aunts and cousins took turns in admiring the newborn.

Parukutty was born under the astrological star of Pooyam on the twenty-second day of the month of Mithunam in the

Malayalam year 1050.[3] The family astrologer predicted that she would be famous, powerful, highly respected and have stanam.[4] At the time, no one paid much attention to this as most astrologers had a tendency of making such predictions on the birth of a child.

3

Exhaling the Past

Parukutty never left Chinammu's side. She couldn't bear even a moment apart from her Amma. When Chinammu supervised the cooking, Parukutty was comfortably perched on her hip. When she threaded flowers for the temple, Parukutty slept blissfully on her lap. Chinammu would even have the baby accompany her to the kolam when she went for her bath. It was no wonder then that the child could swim almost as soon as she could walk.

By the time she was two, Parukutty's baby babble had progressed to intelligible words. Thereafter, she badgered her mother with constant demands and endless questions. 'Amma where is Achan?' Chinammu would patiently reply, 'Child he lives at his mana.' Her curiosity piqued, Parukutty would ask, 'Why does he live at his mana and not with us?' Chinammu would sigh and reply, 'Because that's the way it is with us Nair tarwads.' Never one to accept something she didn't quite understand, Parukutty would continue relentlessly, 'Then why can't we go live with him.' Exasperated, Chinammu would sternly respond, 'Because we can't and that's it. Now stop bothering me; I have a hundred jobs left to finish this morning and here I am wasting my time answering your pointless questions.' Totally upset with her mother's rude dismissal, Parukutty would end up throwing a screaming tantrum. Much to the family's disapproval, Chinammu's daughter seemed to have quite a temper. She was clearly stubborn and headstrong. While her female cousins were demure and spoke only when spoken to, Parukutty was loud and vocal and always determined to have things her own way. Though her mother cossetted and indulged her, the rest of the family, despite their love for her, was not as tolerant as Chinammu. The elders in the family would often chide Chinammu saying, 'Why do you encourage her unnecessary curiosity about matters that do not concern a child? It's high time you taught her to behave like our other children. Have you ever heard them question us? They do as they are told and behave properly. Not so your daughter, who goes around saying all the wrong things at the wrong time. She is getting rebellious, and we warn you, if you don't do something about this now, you will regret it'.

There were days when Chinammu would feel concerned and worried hearing her family's dismal forecasts, and when Narayanan, her sambandhi, did visit her, she would broach her concerns to him. He would cheerfully dismiss all her fears. In fact, he often boasted that unlike other girls, his daughter was intelligent enough to ask questions. He passed off her obstinacy as having a decisive nature and the confidence to assert her will.

Whenever he did visit, which was fairly often, Parukutty would spend hours with him, bombarding him with a multitude of questions. Patiently, her father would answer each one, marvelling at his daughter's astute intelligence which certainly belied her age.

Narayanan believed in the ancient sciences and took to heart the astrologer's prediction that Parukutty would one day occupy an important position. Even though the prediction had seemed a little far-fetched, he felt that it could do no harm to prepare Parukutty for a world beyond her tarwad. As she grew, he spoke to her at length of worldly matters. Unmindful of protests from the family and Chinammu, who felt 'children should be children', Narayanan would continue to discuss matters of importance with his daughter and make sure she grasped the details clearly. He sincerely believed that his daughter was meant for greater things and that it was his job to prepare her for her future.

When Parukutty was ten years old, her father delighted her with the news that in a few months she would have a sibling. Narayanan could barely contain his own excitement. He had loved every moment he had spent with his daughter and looked forward to the second child not just for himself but for Parukutty too, who he knew had always longed for a sister or brother of her very own. Parukutty loved her cousins but a sibling of her own was something she had always dreamed of.

When Chinammu gave birth to a healthy baby boy, Parukutty was beside herself with joy. However, her euphoria was short-lived. Shortly after childbirth, Chinnammu was stricken with acute sepsis to which she succumbed.[1]

Narayanan was devastated. He did not know how to break the news to his daughter but he knew he must. Lifting the tiny boy in his arms, he took him to his chechi in the hope that the sight of the infant would soften the blow and make the devastating news more bearable for Parukutty. Parukutty, who had been waiting impatiently, rushed up to him as he opened the door. Then looking up at her father's face she stopped short, sensing that something was dreadfully wrong. Narayanan knelt down, still carefully cradling the baby and nodded to Parukutty to come closer. As she did, she saw the tears well up in her father's eyes. She had never seen him cry before and at that moment, she knew her mother had left them. She ran up to her achan and hugged him tightly around his neck, placing her head gently on his shoulders. Then letting go, she sat down on the cold floor next to her father. She stretched out her arms for her little baby brother and once he was safely on her lap, she looked up at her father with such deep abiding love that her father knew that both he and his newborn son would be fine. Parukutty would make sure they were.

Parukutty was never the same after that tragic day. Her mother's death had a significant impact on her. Overnight, a carefree ten-year-old child transformed into a child-woman. She turned more silent, more serious and more introverted. Her happiest moments were when she fed, played with or sang to her baby brother. This was her brother and the ten-year-old willingly shouldered the responsibility of his care. So much so that she vowed to herself that Govindan, her brother, would never feel the absence of a mother. She would make sure that he was loved and cared for all his life.

Parukutty missed her mother. She had always accompanied Chinammu to the Parmekkavu Devi Temple. After the period of pela, she resumed her temple visits but now with the rest of her family—her aunts and cousins. She had hoped that this might ease some of the pain and loneliness she felt but somehow it was never the same. She missed holding her mother's hand as they walked to the temple. When she put her cupped palm forward for the prasad, it was not her mother's bemused and loving eyes that now looked back at her. She missed the scolding her mother used to give her when she used her mundu pallu to wipe the sweat off her face. She would laugh and run off ahead as her mother grumbled about how naughty her daughter was. Now all that she was left with were memories. Parukutty became quieter—sadder. She doted on her young brother Govindan but being ten years younger he was not much of a companion. She felt very alone. Her amma had been her confidante, her security, her go-to person. As she was a motherless child, the elders, particularly her aunt Narayani Amma, now showered her with more attention and affection but even this did not seem to ease the loss. Try as they might, the sorrow Parukutty felt on losing her mother just seemed to envelop her. Parukutty was grateful for the love and care her extended family showered on her and would never forget this. Many years later, Parukutty would reciprocate their love and care in ways that the family had never imagined possible.[2]

Narayanan could not but notice how lonely and unhappy his daughter was and it worried him. He visited the tarwad as often as he could and spent time with her. He had always observed that, unlike the other girls in the family, Parukutty showed no inclination towards cooking or home management. In fact, she dismissed this aspect altogether.

Narayanan, on his visits, would give her a handful of pice exhorting her to keep these safe and to tell him when he visited next how much she had collected. This invariably brought a smile to her face and a sparkle to her eyes, and Narayanan once again would get a glimpse of the Parukutty she once was. Parukutty guarded these coins carefully—hoarding them and frequently counting them—never parting with even a single pice. Whenever her achan visited, she would take out her cache and show it to him proudly. She always knew exactly how much she had collected. This invariably brought a proud, indulgent smile on Narayanan's face and he would then give her a few more pice. Perhaps it was these early experiences of monetary acquisitions that grew into Parukutty's obsession with jewellery and later with her constant desire to gain and hoard financial assets.

As Parukutty approached her teens proposals started coming in for sambandhams. Those were the days of early relationships. If it was considered to be a suitable suitor and the proposal happened to come from a prestigious tarwad, the family astrologer was summoned and jadhagams were matched. Not till the horoscopes matched perfectly was any sambandham considered.

As her aunts had daughters of their own and were busy arranging fitting matches for them, they spared little time looking for a sambandhi for Parukutty. As Parukutty entered her teens, Narayanan began to fret about a match suitable for his daughter. In a year or two, it would become impossible to find a good match. Narayanan knew that it would not be easy to find a match for his daughter. She would be a total misfit in a conservative, traditional tarwad house. At her tarwad home, Parukutty had been indulged and for the most part had lived her life on her own terms. Yet she had never quite recovered from her mother's death. There was a sadness about her that Narayanan had never been able to quite erase. Narayanan wanted his daughter to be happy. He couldn't see Parukutty living her life merely looking after the home and family and waiting for conjugal visits from her Nair or Nambudiri sambandhi. He remembered too the astrologer's prediction that she would have a stanam.

To reassure himself and to be doubly sure, he brought the well-known and highly respected astrologer Sreedhara Panicker from Pattancheri near Chittur to Trichur. The learned astrologer, after reading her jadhagam, agreed that Parukutty's was an unusual horoscope and that she was very blessed. When Narayanan pressed him for more details, he agreed to do a prashanam. After doing the prashanam, Panicker made certain calculations and then drew on the ground the position of the planets on that day in relation to their position at the time of her birth. Then, after a short prayer, he threw a handful of cowrie shells within the chart that he had drawn on the ground. He was immersed in thought for a while. He even went to another room to go through some texts. On his return, he continued with some more calculations. Then, finally turning to Narayanan, Sreedhara Panicker said, 'I have not seen such a strong jadhagam. Your daughter is blessed. After her sambandham, her life will take a new course. She will hold an important and prestigious position. Fame and fortune will be hers. She will earn respect and will change the lives of many. She will make a name for herself.'

Sreedhara Panicker's predictions strengthened Narayanan's resolve to find a match for Parukutty that would allow her to live up to her predicted potential. But this would mean taking her out of her present circumstances. He began to seriously contemplate on how he was to go about facilitating Parukutty's destiny. He knew it would not be easy to battle conventional norms. The strict tradition-bound society of the time would be up in arms at any hint of a break away from accepted practices. Nairs' marumakkatayam dictated that the girl even after the sambandham remain in her mother's tarwad and that her progeny belong to the matriarch's tarwad. This would mean that Parukutty would remain in the home that she had been born in and like the rest of her cousins take on her share of household responsibilities. Narayanan knew that though Parukutty loved her family, the tarwad home held many sad memories of her mother and these were crushing her. He was also convinced that she would wither away in a traditional household. He knew she needed to be free of such shackles. There were other hurdles too—Nair girls could not leave their tarwads without forfeiting their right to return to the tarwad.[3] If Parukutty was to live outside of the tarwad, it meant she would never ever again have access to her birth home. This was indeed a difficult imposition to force on any girl. Added to all this was the fact that girls needed the permission of the Karnavan to travel from their ancestral house. Yet Narayanan Nambudiripad resolved that he would find a way to free Parukutty.

4

Sambandham

Narayanan Nambudiripad, a man of substantial wealth, enjoyed the privilege of travelling frequently and extensively within the Kingdom of Cochin and British Malabar. He had made several visits to Madras too. Being of a pleasant nature and from a respected landed family, Narayanan had easy access to the higher echelons of society. He had over the years of travel acquired many friends. One of his closer friends was Prince Rama Varma of Cochin. The prince's father, Kuttan Nambudiripad of Pana Mana, was related to him. As the princes of Cochin could only be named Rama, Ravi or Kerala and it was difficult to distinguish one from another, they were also given another name. Prince Rama Varma of Cochin was known as Kunji Kiddavu.

Kunji Kiddavu was educated and well-read. Apart from achieving a high degree of scholarship in Sanskrit, he had expertise in the Vyakarana, Nyaya and Vedanta philosophy. He was also well-versed in English. An avid reader, he was greatly influenced by Herbert Spencer's *Study of Sociology* and John Stuart Mills's *Political Economy*. These were his favourite texts. He had a deep understanding of economics and political science, and harboured a love for Western literature and science.[1] Being of a scholarly bent, he had studied Ayurvedic medicine, specializing in the treatment of snakebites through reading books such as *Lakshamrutham*, *Narayaniyam*, *Samgraham*, *Jolsnika*[2] and other books relating to cases of poisoning.[3]

The prince was also athletic. When he was young, he spent a considerable period of time at Chowara, about 17 miles away from Thrippunithura. At Chowara, he gained great expertise in boat racing. He was also an excellent rider and had a string of horses.[4]

Kunji Kiddavu was keen on agriculture, and after he had finished his schooling, devoted a great deal of time in studying the land to make it more productive. He successfully converted a lot of land that was thought to be barren to fertile land.[5]

Like all the other princes of Cochin, Kunji Kiddavu also received an allowance to look after his needs from a fund known as the Palli-Ara Muthalpidi. Many of the princes would squander their allowance on frivolous pursuits and sensuous pleasures. Not Kunji Kiddavu. Prudent in his spending—even miserly—the prince would lend the surplus money after expenses to farmers on interest, holding their property as security. An astute financier, he would not lend the money until he had first inspected the property and ensured that the title deeds to the land were clear and without encumbrances. He used his savings and the interest he received to buy property, much to the disdain of the other princes who felt it was beneath them to indulge in business and property dealings. Worse still, Kunji Kiddavu, putting his Ayurvedic medicinal expertise to good use, would, in his professional capacity, treat patients of snakebites. This provided him with an additional income. Earning a living and engaging in a profession were considered infra dig among the royals.

Perhaps it was this spirit of confidently flaunting his individuality that appealed to Narayanan and they grew to become close friends. Whenever Narayanan met the prince, they would have long and spirited discussions on finance and agriculture. Often Narayanan would pick Kunji Kiddavu's brains to find solutions that could be effectively implemented on his own family estates. Gradually, it dawned on him that Kunji Kiddavu would make an ideal partner for Parukutty as they had such similar personalities—both being highly individulistic, confident and opinionated. Besides, as the prince was forward-thinking and broadminded, an unconventional girl like Parukutty would be a good match for him. However, Kunji Kiddavu, being at the time sixth in line to the throne with no prospects of position or power, was unlikely to offer Parukutty the elevated status the astrologer had predicted. After careful consideration, Narayanan concluded that this alliance with a prince was the best he could arrange for Parukutty. It would give her some stanam—standing in society—and being broadminded and educated, Kunji Kiddavu would be able to appreciate and acknowledge Parukutty's intelligence and financial acumen.

Finding a suitable opportunity, Narayanan broached the idea with Kunji Kiddavu. Kunji Kiddavu was at first taken aback. He was seventeen years older than Parukutty and more of a companionable age to her father, who was his friend. It was also not normal for a father to suggest a liaison for his daughter. However, Narayanan's persuasive skills prevailed and Kunji Kiddavu agreed to accompany him to Trichur to meet Parukutty before coming to a final decision. The prince, quite dubious about this proposal, made the proviso that no one should know the purpose of his visit.

At Trichur, Kunji Kiddavu stayed at the Elaya Thampuran Palace, the abode of the heir apparent. He spent the first few days getting to know the township of Trichur. The prosperity of the little town impressed him. Like all devout Malayalees, Kunji Kiddavu visited the temples and prayed at the holy Vadakunnathan Temple and the Parmekkavu Devi Temple every day. One morning, as he completed his prayers and was leaving the temple, he noticed a group of ladies entering the Devi Temple. He was told they were from the Vadakke Kuruppath tarwad. The ladies were, of course, going about their regular morning ritual of offering obeisance at their local temple. Curiosity got the better of him and he stopped to look at the group, but as there were several young women and he did not know what Parukutty looked like, he walked away. Being a prince, he could not strike up a conversation with the Nair ladies. However, he did visit Narayanan's father at the Kurur mana.

The palace at Trichur

Narayanan's father was absolutely delighted at this honour. Kunji Kiddavu had lunch at the mana and returned to Trichur late in the evening. He was glad to have visited Narayanan's home. He had also accompanied Narayanan's elder brother and father to some nearby holdings to get a better understanding of the Kurur estates.

Parukutty was very surprised when her father asked her and her brother Govindan to accompany him to the palace at Trichur.[6] Having never been to a palace, Parukutty was very excited. The palace was about two kilometres away from the Kuruppath tarwad house.

When they arrived at the palace, Kunji Kiddavu was sitting in the veranda.[7] Narayanan, Parukutty and Govindan walked down the length of the veranda. When they reached the prince, Narayanan introduced them.

Parukutty looked at the prince resting his tall frame on a cane easy chair. He had a serious face and piercing eyes. His hair was completely grey. With a smile on his lips, he asked Parukutty in a serious, commanding voice what her name was. Parukutty hesitantly folded her hands in a namaste and inclining her head mentioned her name. Kunji Kiddavu repeated this with her brother too. After that, turning to Parukutty he asked her whether she enjoyed music and singing. Before Narayanan could say anything, Parukutty looking directly at him said, 'I was taught music by Nemmara Gopalakrishna Bhagvathar[8] and I enjoy listening to music, but I am far more interested in matters happening around us.'

This was an unexpected but refreshing response, and Kunji Kiddavu laughed. He then asked Parukutty to go to the end of the veranda and walk back again.[9] Puzzled, she did so, assuming that Kunji Kiddavu wanted to speak privately to her father and wished her to be out of earshot. Much to her chagrin, she was to later learn that Kunji Kiddavu had wanted to get a good look at her and the walk down the length of the veranda had provided him that opportunity.

Kunji Kiddavu instantly took a liking to Parukutty. A good judge of character, he sensed that she was extremely intelligent, confident and also unafraid. The manner in which she looked at him candidly and answered with no hesitation and complete self-assurance was certainly refreshing. She was not about to let her father speak on her behalf, and the prince had a new respect for this young girl. Most other women, even those several years older than Parukutty, would, in all likelihood, have either looked down shyly, giggled self-consciously or been too awestruck to say anything.

But being a prince, Kunji Kiddavu did not want to betray his interest right away and thereafter continued to talk exclusively with Narayanan. He spoke of his impressions of Trichur and of his meeting and conversation with Narayanan's father. Parukutty listened intently, fascinated by an outsider's view of her hometown. When it was time to leave, Parukutty and her brother politely thanked the prince and bid their farewell.[10]

Parukutty and Govindan were thrilled to have visited the palace. None of their cousins had done so and after they returned home, they regaled the rest of the family with several stories of the palace and the prince, some of the stories being slightly enhanced.

Narayanan was busy travelling for the next few days, and when he returned to Trichur, he found that the prince had returned home. Not one to leave a matter so important unresolved, he went to Thrippunithura to meet Kunji Kiddavu. Kunji Kiddavu, when they met, smiled at him and said that he would be happy to enter into a sambandham with Parukutty. Narayanan was delighted.

Now that this was settled, Narayanan returned to Trichur and met the Karnavan at the Vadakke Kuruppath tarwad and told him the happy news. The Karnavan was delighted. It was prestigious for the family to have a member enter into sambandham with a prince. Not so Parukutty. Though she was impressed by the prince, as far as she was concerned, he was an old man with white hair. She did not want him. Her father spent much time trying to explain to her that this was a good alliance. She stormed. She ranted. She yelled that she wanted no sambandham. In the end, she relented and gave in as she reasoned that her father would only do what was best for her.

However, as the sambandham was with a Thampuran, there was no fanfare or ceremony. It was simply understood that the prince will enter into a consensual relationship with Parukutty. There was no indication that she would leave the tarwad house. However, Narayanan was so happy that he had goldsmiths make her some exquisite jewellery—a diamond necklace, several bracelets, broaches and gold necklaces.

A few months passed and there was no word from Kunji Kiddavu. Nor was there any indication that he planned to visit, even though during this time several Thampurans who had entered into sambandhams with Nair ladies in Trichur had been to Trichur.

In those days, caste was all important.[11] The Thampurans were considered as kshatriyas while Nairs were considered sudras.[12] Thus, even touching a Nair—even the one the Thampuran was in a relationship with—required the Thampuran to have a bath thereafter to purify himself. Hence, any kind of proximity between a Nair girl and her Thampuran sambandhi was usually restricted to cohabitation at night. In the morning, the Thampuran had to have a purifying bath before returning to his palace. Additionally, the Thampurans were not allowed to have any physical contact with a Nair sambandhi during the time she had her monthly periods, while she observed pela for a dead relative or during childbirth. Consequently, Nair sambandhis lived in a house separate from their Thampuran sambandhis. Thampurans were in the enviable position of bearing no financial responsibility for their Nair sambandhis, and yet, enjoyed the rights to visit them as often as they wished.[13]

If Kunji Kiddavu would not visit Trichur, then Narayanan wanted Parukutty to move to Thrippunithura. However, that was far from easy. If a Nair lady left her tarwad house, she could not return. Nor could she claim a share in its wealth.[14] As a consequence, no Nair lady had, till then, ever left her tarwad house to reside with a prince in Thrippunithura.

Narayanan thought this over and discussed this with a few other Nambudiripads, and came up with a solution. He went to the Karnavan of the Vadakke Kuruppath tarwad and told him that he wished to take his daughter to meet the Raja in Thrippunithura. The Karnavan could not refuse this and gave his consent.[15] Narayanan called Parukutty and shared with her his thoughts. Parukutty loved her father and trusted him implicitly. She told him that she would do whatever he thought was best.

Narayanan and Parukutty, with two maidservants, departed in the morning by a vallam to Thikkakara, about 13 kilometres from Thrippunithura, and from there by bullock cart to Thrippunithura.[16] This was the best way as the roads were not particularly good or comfortable. However, the going was slow and tedious. It was evening by the time they reached Thikkakara. Another bumpy bullock cart ride took them to Thrippunithura. For Parukutty, the long ride was exciting. She had never travelled before, and she soaked in the sights and sounds, and true to her nature asked her father a million questions about all that she observed.

On arrival, Narayanan took Parukutty directly to Kunji Kiddavu's palace.[17] Kunji Kiddavu, on returning home, was surprised to see his friend waiting for him. Narayanan told him that he had come with his daughter. Kunji Kiddavu was in a quandary. This was totally unexpected. There were no Nair sambandhis staying with Thampurans in their palaces in Thrippunithura.

Nothing could be more overwhelming for a young fourteen-year-old than to be transported into another town where she knew no one and where there was no one to even guide her. And nothing could be more crushing than knowing that the person whom she was to live with was not only surprised but horrified at her arrival. All she had was an implicit faith in her father and a belief that he would not do anything that could harm her. In this faith lay Parukutty's confidence. Somehow, she knew that she was going to be alright.

5

Taking up the Gauntlet

Parukutty had been disheartened when, after her sambandham, Kunji Kiddavu had not visited her at all. At first, she had attributed it to him being busy. However, as the months passed and she saw her cousins speaking of their sambandhis' visits, and seeing how happy they were, she was a little sad. She wondered whether there was something wrong with her. It was while she was in this unhappy state that her father had told her of his plans to take her to Kunji Kiddavu in Thrippunithura.

On hearing the news, Parukutty, after the initial trepidation, was both excited and delighted. Much like most other young girls, she began to fantasize about being a princess—wearing priceless kasavu mundus, with an assortment of precious jewels to pick and choose from and with handmaids to oil and comb her long tresses. She pictured herself being waited upon hand and foot by a retinue of palace staff—her every wish their command. It was with stars in her eyes that young Parukutty left her tarwad home to begin a life that would be unlike anything she had known so far.

Parukutty at Thrippunithura

Nothing had quite prepared her for her welcome at the palace. Kunji Kiddavu had been taken aback at her arrival at his palace and as this was quite contrary to tradition, he was unsure of what to do. Fortunately, Narayanan had taken Kunji Kiddavu's father Pana Kuttan Nambudiripad into confidence. As no Nair sambandhi had ever resided with a Thampuran, Pana Nambudiripad suggested that Parukutty could stay in the outhouse of the palace. Kunji Kiddavu consented, especially as Narayanan was a dear friend of his. And also, he did not know what else to do.

Kunji Kiddavu sent his staff to accompany Parukutty to the outhouse. To her absolute horror, the outhouse was in a state of total disrepair. It was not furnished. It was also quite dirty as it had not been swept. Holding her mundu indelicately above her ankles, she had stepped into the outhouse and retreated in horror. Wrinkling her nose in distaste she said, 'I absolutely will not live in this dirty house even for a night. I do not wish to stay on in Thrippunithura. Take me back to Trichur.' Her eyes welled up with tears as she saw all her dreams and fantasies crumble.

She shook her head vigorously. Then wiping off her tears with the back of her arm, she turned to face Kunji Kiddavu and repeated this time quite firmly, 'I did not come all this way to live in this wretched outhouse'. Her innate stubborn streak had kicked in and now neither her father nor Kunji Kiddavu could persuade her otherwise.

As she glared at the two older men standing before her, she noticed that Kunji Kiddavu seemed bemused and even a little impressed by her obstinate stance. She had a manner of speaking that did not permit anyone to gainsay her.

The prince took a good look at his bride. Not even five feet tall, this fourteen-year-old with flowing black hair that came down to her knees was striking in appearance. She had a presence that arrested attention. Her self-confidence belied her age and sheltered upbringing. He noticed that her large eyes that looked directly at him reflected her innate intelligence. The prince was bemused at the young girl's audacity. Her fearlessness and frankness drew Kunji Kiddavu's admiration. Parukutty certainly wasn't one to allow anyone, not even a prince, to dictate terms to her. Seeing how adamant she was and considering how young she was, Kunji Kiddavu gave in. Kunji Kiddavu became the first prince to permit his Nair sambandhi to stay with him in his palace at Thrippunithura.[1]

On that eventful day, Parukutty, without even realizing it, had by moving into the palace with her sambandhi destroyed a centuries-old tradition. What was worse, barely into her teens, she had brought upon herself the derision of the elders.

The conservative Nairs and Nambudiris were appalled by her move into the palace of a Thampuran. The moment she stepped in through the giant doorway of Kunji Kiddavu's palace, she earned herself the ignoble honour of being the first Nair sambandhi of a prince to ever live with him.[2]

The news rocked Thrippunithura. Normally, Parukutty would have been mocked as a loose girl foisted on a Thampuran. However, here the circumstances were different. The father, a Nambudiripad—the highest of the Malayalee brahmins—himself had brought and left her at the palace, signifying parental blessing.

Up until then, Nair women had submissively acquiesced to living apart from their partners—the princes. Being considered of lower caste to the Thampurans, they were expected to be grateful for an alliance with a prince even though it was without the privilege of living with him. The fourteen-year-old Parukutty had flouted all social dictates. She had aroused the derision and anger of the Thampurattis, who instantly ostracized and condemned her. After all, it was only royal-born princesses who were entitled to live in the palaces, not upstart Nair girls.

Where Parukutty had dreamt of days of leisure and ease, she was now expected to follow a strictly regimented lifestyle dictated by the customs and protocol of royalty. As the sambandhi, her responsibilities included the supervision of all the household chores. Having entered his home, she had the added duty of ensuring that Kunji Kiddavu was well cared for. Just fourteen, she was entirely unprepared for her new life. At her tarwad home, she had had the luxury of childhood. At the palace, she was hurled into adulthood. At the tarwad, being a motherless child, her extended family had indulged her and she had been relieved of most of the routine housework. Here, she was expected to run the household. Fortunately, she had been accompanied by two trained staff members who were competent and could manage most of the heavy load of housework. While her staff managed most of the routine housework, Parukutty took upon herself the responsibility of looking after Kunji Kiddavu's requirements. Though he was a complete stranger to her, Parukutty sensed that he was a good and kind man. Instinctively she knew he would protect her. Despite the initial reception, she knew she was safe. She quickly understood his habits and his needs, and provided for them, endearing herself even more to Kunji Kiddavu.

Apart from managing the household, she was expected to conform to the life at Thrippunithura. This she was glad to do as she saw this as a means of getting to know her peers in town and making friends.

The main temple in Thrippunithura, the Poornathrayeesa Temple, played a big part in the life of all the royals. One of the customary practices of the royal family members—the Thampurans and Thampurattis—was their daily visits to Poornathrayeesa Temple, whose main deity was Maha Vishnu. This famous temple was frequented by the royal family and the upper-crust Nambudiris. The Thampurattis would awake early each morning, bathe and enter the temple precincts during Brahma Muhurta, which was usually around 4.30 a.m. Their prayers and archana completed, they would return to their palaces by around 6 a.m. Parukutty, who was deeply religious, used to make daily visits to Trichur's Parmekkavu Temple with her aunts and cousins, though never at such an early hour. Yet, being young and adventurous she was open to and excited about this new experience.

Every day she awoke at the crack of dawn, bathed and went to the temple. The royal ladies were not forthcoming in their welcome of Parukutty. In fact, it was just the opposite. They ignored her and would, when she arrived, point her out and whisper to each other, 'That's the one—that's Kunji Kiddavu's.' They avoided her. They slighted her. They wickedly sniggered both in front of her and behind her back. In loud stage whispers they'd say, 'Her family got so desperate that after saddling her onto Kunji Kiddavu they even brought her to his palace and dumped her there!' Yet, all their vile comments, though within earshot of Parukutty, were never mentioned openly as it was Parukutty's father, an esteemed Nambudiripad, who had decided to leave her with her sambandhi. This meant that she had parental consent. They knew too that Kunji Kiddavu's father Pana Nambudiripad was also complicit. Not even the royal ladies were brave enough to provoke the ire of these two powerful Nambudiripads. None of these women were bothered about the hurt, sadness and humiliation they were causing a young child.

After several attempts to 'fit in' and 'adjust', Parukutty, upset by the attitude of the ladies and to avoid encountering them, decided that she would not go to the Poornathrayeesa Temple in the mornings like the others. Instead, she decided to go to the Chottanikkara Temple, a few kilometres from her residence. With her very first step into Chottanikkara began her lifelong devotion to Chottanikkara Bhagavathy—a devotion that would see this 'destiny's child' through her innumerable highs and lows. Every morning as the Thampurattis left for Poornathrayeesa Temple, Parukutty would take a bullock cart and head to Chottanikkara, another act that astounded the Thampurattis. They were incensed at Parukutty's audacity.[3]

Parukutty also faced derision from her own Nair community. Whereas Parukutty lived with her spouse at his palace, other Nair women who had sambandhams with royalty lived apart from their sambandhis in their own tarwads. Naturally, they disapproved of one of their own being singled out for special privileges and having the courage to do something they did not dare to. To assert their disapproval and perhaps because they were decidedly envious of her, they blatantly ostracized her. They made sure none of them ever invited her to any of their homes. Not just that, at every opportunity, they ridiculed her, even making fun of the way she dressed. Though hurt by their constant taunting, defiantly Parukutty vowed she would one day be better than all of them. She would make each one of these ladies regret that they had ever slighted her.[4]

So deep were the wounds of those early years that even as an octogenarian, Parukutty, when recounting stories of her life to her great-grandson would appear sad as she said, 'You have no idea of the bad things they said about me. But I always considered it beneath my notice.'[5]

Parukutty had the strength of resilience. No matter how bad it got, her never-say-die attitude had her determined to make the very best of the life that her father had chosen for her. She set about adapting herself to the expectations of her new home.

Kunji Kiddavu was, at the time, the sixth prince in the line of succession to the musnad. He had no official responsibilities. Being several years older than her, he felt very protective towards her and referred to her affectionately as 'Paati'—a corruption of Parukutty. It was often said that the only two who mattered to him were Paati and Patti—his pet German shepherd. With time on his hands, Kunji Kiddavu took on the role of mentor and teacher. Apart from music that she had learnt from Nemmara Gopalkrishna Bhagvathar, Parukutty knew how to read and write Malayalam. Kunji Kiddavu was keen to educate Parukutty and taught her Sanskrit and introduced her to Malayalam literature.[6] He was delighted to discover that Parukutty was an eager learner, had a quick mind and a sharp intellect. She would question him, causing him to brush up on his own knowledge in order to make sure he could answer her many queries.

Shortly after their sambandham, Kunji Kiddavu, not wanting to leave her alone in a hostile environment, took Parukutty on a trip he had to make to Madras. On arrival, Kunji Kiddavu met acquaintances there, including the Raja of Pudukottai and his wife. The Rani of Pudukottai, Brihadambal Rajamani Bayi, had two daughters of her own. Her daughters were now grown up and married. The Rani's maternal instincts were aroused by this shy, young girl who listened more than she spoke and quietly absorbed everything she heard—a young girl who seemed determined to live up to the expectations of her newly acquired stature. The Rani took an instant liking to Parukutty and decided to make her comfortable on this, her first trip away from her home state. She asked Kunji Kiddavu to send Parukutty to the Pudukottai Palace every morning while he was away at meetings. Parukutty happily spent time with the Rani.[7]

When he had some free time, Kunji Kiddavu would take Parukutty on drives to the beach and around the countryside. Parukutty had never experienced anything like the big city life of Madras. The fancy well-stocked shops, the busy thoroughfares and diversity of people left Parukutty wide-eyed with amazement. The Madras trip also brought the couple far closer to each other. Without hangers-on, Parukutty was able to enjoy Kunji Kiddavu's full attention. The more they discovered each other, the more they realized that their sambandham was truly one blessed by the heavens.

Parukutty revelled in the attention. One day, when Parukutty was riding with the Rani in her carriage, they passed the bookshop Higginbothams on Mount Road. The Rani pronounced the name slowly but deliberately. Parukutty marvelled at the Rani's fluency in English. She too wanted to be able speak the language.[8] However, before she could find out from the Rani how she too could pick up the language, Kunji Kiddavu's work in Madras ended and they returned to Thrippunithura. The trip had been so exciting but, for Parukutty, it had ended all too quickly. Parukutty was sad to lose the companionship of the Rani and hated giving up the exhilarating city life. Madras was so vibrant and there was so much to see and do, quite unlike sleepy Thrippunithura. And it was not so strait-laced, custom-bound and intolerant.

The Rani had left an indelible impression on young Parukutty. She was determined to speak English as the Rani did. Wasting no time at all, Parukutty, on their journey back, expressed her desire to Kunji Kiddavu, 'Did you hear how well the Rani of Pudukottai spoke English? Not only does she speak the language, she can read and write it. We passed a big bookshop and she read its fancy name out to me quite effortlessly. I was so impressed. I too wish to learn English.' At that time, Kunji Kiddavu had mumbled an incomprehensible reply and had gone back to checking his work files. Perhaps because it was still fairly early in their sambandham Kunji Kiddavu had thought that her desire to learn English was just a passing fancy. But barely had they reached home than Parukutty began badgering him to arrange a tutor for her English lessons. It slowly began to dawn on Kunji Kiddavu that Parukutty was like no other girl or woman he had ever known. With unconcealed admiration he said, 'I will arrange for you to learn English, but I think it is even more important that you learn mathematics and agriculture as this will help you assess our income and manage our estates."[9]

As she heard him speak, Parukutty was instantly transported to her early childhood days and her father's visits. He would give her a pice, encourage her to save and then proceed to discuss finance with her. Here was Kunji Kiddavu offering her the opportunity to hone her skills and contribute with her inputs in handling their finances. In that one moment, Parukutty fell in love with Kunji Kiddavu. Here was a man who was strong enough to welcome a true partnership with a woman. With a beaming smile that was as clearly visible on her lips as in her sparkling eyes, she replied, 'I would be delighted to study all the subjects you recommend. Thank you. I will study hard and make you proud of me.'

Kunji Kiddavu, true to his word, engaged an excellent tutor—Ramanarayana Iyer—to teach her English and Tamil, and she quickly gained fluency in both these languages.[10]

As part of her education, every morning after Parukutty returned from the temple, Kunji Kiddavu would take her to the fields to watch the farmers. He wanted her to see how fields were ploughed, how much manure was used, how paddy was planted and how it was nurtured. He would also take her to the plantations of pepper, cardamom, coconuts, mango and other fruits. He had her visit the nurseries to see how the saplings were cared for, how they were planted and looked after. She was very happy to do this and, encouraged by Kunji Kiddavu, asked questions and cleared her doubts. The haughty Thampurattis were stunned. It was unheard of for a lady to plod through fields, associate with farmers and talk about matters so mundane as produce and yields.[11]

In the afternoons, after lunch and a short nap, Kunji Kiddavu and Parukutty would head for the study. There, surrounded by ceiling-high shelves of thick leather-bound volumes of every subject conceivable, Kunji Kiddavu would teach her mathematics. Being especially adept at finance and knowing this to be a subject that had always interested Parukutty, he introduced her to the magic of interest rates. He talked to her about economics and how to best manage pecuniary matters.[12] A quick learner and familiar with money, Parukutty swiftly assimilated all that he taught. Encouraged by her enthusiasm for learning, Kunji Kiddavu, being well educated and a scholar versatile in Sanskrit, moved on to teaching Parukutty Sanskrit and the Hindu scriptures. Kunji Kiddavu, being very disciplined, set up a regular schedule and would painstakingly teach young Parukutty. The couple bonded through these lessons and Kunji Kiddavu's respect and admiration for Parukutty grew, as did Parukutty's respect and admiration for Kunji Kiddavu.

There was much that Parukutty learnt from the prince. These study sessions marked the beginning of a very special connection between the couple, which developed into a deep trust and acceptance of each other's decisions. Parukutty now completely understood why her father had picked Kunji Kiddavu as her partner and why he had felt it prudent to leave her all alone in a new town with a man she had only met for a couple of hours.

Kunji Kiddavu's eclectic knowledge of subjects extended to Gawli Shastra too. In the Cochin of yore and even in some parts of Kerala today, Gawli Shastra or lizard astrology is a practice that several Malayalees rely on. Kunji Kiddavu was well-versed in Gawli Shastra. Hearing the clicking of a lizard, he could accurately foretell what was to happen. He could often, after listening to the sounds of a lizard, tell Parukutty to begin mixing certain herbs as a person, who required to be treated with that particular concoction, would be arriving shortly.[13]

Quite unlike the other sambandhis of his time, Kunji Kiddavu was totally unconventional in his relationship with his sambandhi. He took her on long rides by bullock cart around Thrippunithura, which Parukutty immensely enjoyed. One of the reasons he did this was to visit those farmers who had taken loans from him, to ascertain how they were doing and whether they were in a position to repay the loans. Here too, Kunji Kiddavu was breaking tradition: not only did Thampurans not lend money to farmers, very few actually owned lands. They depended on the allowance they received from the palace. It was unheard of for the few that did own land to visit their lands. They entrusted their kariastans to oversee their estates. The crafty kariastans often took advantage of the princes' indolence and siphoned off huge sums of money for themselves. The unsuspecting and trusting princes ended up getting far less than they were actually due. Unlike all the other Thampurans, not only did Kunji Kiddavu visit his properties regularly, he also insisted on a proper site inspection should a farmer approach him for a loan. This was to ensure that the money was being put to good use. Only after evaluating the farmer's proposal did he provide the loan. To her delight, Kunji Kiddavu included Parukutty not only in the visits but encouraged her to assess property matters and valued her inputs.

Those were supremely happy years for young Parukutty. In the second year of their marriage, the couple was blessed with a son, whom they named Raman. A few years later, Raman was followed by another son, Aravindaksha, and then Parukutty gave birth to two daughters, Ratnam and Vilasini.

This was also the time when Kunji Kiddavu climbed up the accession ladder to become the Elaya Raja (heir apparent), the second-oldest Thampuran of the family and next in line to the musnad.

The family before Kunji Kiddavu ascended the throne

6

Coming into One's Own

The Cochin Thampurans lived a life of privilege. At the age of five, they began their education at the palace school known as the Residential Palace—a school exclusively for the princes of the royal family. Though the school provided boarding facilities, the majority of the princes preferred to live in the comfort of their own palaces, enjoying the company and security of home life with their parents and family. The royal education commenced with being initiated into the mysteries of the Malayalam alphabet.[1] Tutors were engaged to teach the princes English, Mathematics and Sanskrit. Those interested were also taught riding and taken on hunts. The expenses of their schooling and of the residential facilities were derived from the income of a fund known as the Palli-Ara Muthalpidi, which was created to look after the welfare of the Thampurans for as long as they lived.

The Palli-Ara Muthalpidi estate and the Amma Raja estate were established by Raja Rama Varma XII in 1843[2] to provide for the maintenance of the members of the Cochin royal family. Whereas the Palli-Ara Muthalpidi estate was for the maintenance of the princes, the Amma Raja estate was for the maintenance of the princesses. Raja Rama Varma XII had set up the Amma Raja estate by giving property worth Rs 200,000 to the female members of the family. The Amma Raja estate was managed by the Senior Rani, the oldest Thampuratti. The remainder of his properties, Raja Rama Varma XII constituted as a separate estate for the Thampurans, thus, creating the Palli-Ara Muthalpidi properties.[3] The Palli-Ara Muthalpidi properties were under the direct management of the incumbent ruler and it was customary for the Raja, when he ascended the musnad, to add his private properties to the estate.

On completion of their education and at around fifteen or sixteen years of age the princes were invested with the sacred thread, the poonul, at the Upanayanam-cum-Samavarthanam ceremony.[4] Thereafter, each Thampuran was given a palace to reside in and an allowance from the state to take care of his expenses.[5] In fact, Thampurans were provided for from birth till their death. In addition, as a Thampuran rose in rank and seniority,[6] his allowance was increased.

The princes used their allowances for their various outgoings. As the allowances were generous, they could, if they chose to, make savings or investments from these allowances. Most of the Thampurans 'cut their coat according to the cloth' and lived within their allotted allowances. However, there were some who were extravagant—frittering away their allowances on horses, women and other sensuous pursuits.

Unfortunately, most of the Thampurans had very little interest or competence in financial matters. The management of the properties owned by the Palli-Ara Muthalpidi and Amma Raja estates was left in the hands of kariastans. Mismanagement and unscrupulous practices resulted in the princely estates running into huge deficits. Added to this was the fact that Cochin was not a wealthy state. Prior wars and mismanagement had entirely depleted the treasury. Corruption was rampant throughout the state.

Raja Rama Varma XV,[7] who had ascended the throne in 1895, was determined to no longer allow Cochin's financial affairs to remain submerged in this quagmire of mismanagement. At the time of his birth in 1853, the royal family comprised just twenty-three members. However, by the time he was coronated in 1895, the family had expanded to over 150 members.[8] Income from the two estates had become woefully inadequate. As a consequence, the estates experienced shortages to the extent that salaries had not been paid for over ten months.[9] Yet, despite the financial crunch, the royal allowances of the princes and princesses remained intact and constant. The Raja found it increasingly difficult to meet the financial needs of the family.

Despite the fact that many of the Thampurans were derisive of Kunji Kiddavu's interest in such plebeian matters as managing his own allowances and lands, his reputation for successfully growing his wealth and his income had spread. The Raja too was aware of Kunji Kiddavu's financial acumen and prowess. Faced with the indomitable task of reviving the estates, he decided to enlist Kunji Kiddavu to assist in their management.

Raja Rama Varma XV invited Kunji Kiddavu to the palace. When Kunji Kiddavu arrived at the Hill Palace, the Raja's Sarvadhikariakar met him at the entrance. Addressing him with due formality, he requested Kunji Kiddavu to accompany him directly to meet the Raja. 'His Highness is expecting you and awaits you in the study,' he said, as he politely gestured toward the direction they should go in. The Sarvadhikariakar respectfully followed just a few steps behind.

Kunji Kiddavu had visited the palace before. The palace, a magnificent piece of architecture which is still standing, has long corridors with floors of gleaming black and white checkered English tiles and wide balconies with large windows, allowing in an abundance of sunlight. All around the expansive structure lie acres of green foliage—a grand palace fit for a king. Years later, Parukutty, reminiscing with her great-grandson, would recall that Kunji Kiddavu had strangely always felt, even on his earliest visits to the palace, very much at home. Whereas she, gauche at the time, had felt awed by its eminence.

The Raja's private study was located alongside the audience chamber. The Sarvadhikariakar stretched out his arm towards the door on the left, indicating to Kunji Kiddavu that they had arrived at the study. Kunji Kiddavu entered the large study that was dominated by a rosewood carving of the crest of the Cochin Royal family on the wall facing the doorway. Inside, the Raja was seated at the far end on a long settee and was reading some papers. When Kunji Kiddavu came in, the Raja smiled and thanked him for seeing him at such short notice. Then, rising from the leather settee, he moved across to his desk. His ever-attentive Sarvadhikariakar quickly pulled out the ornate silver chair placed at the centre of the heavy rectangular mahogany desk. Once the Raja was comfortably seated, he beckoned for Kunji Kiddavu to take the seat across from him. Kunji Kiddavu walked across to the three leather upholstered high-backed chairs that were placed across from the Raja's silver one and sat directly opposite the Raja.

The Raja began by making a few polite enquiries about Kunji Kiddavu's health and his most recent activities. Then, almost abruptly, the Raja switched the conversation to matters that were at that time uppermost in his mind. He expressed his concerns about the state of the Amma Raja and the Palli-

Ara Muthalpidi estates. Being a prince himself and aware of the increasing size of the royal family, Kunji Kiddavu was not surprised when the Raja informed him of the condition of the estates' finances. The Raja picked up a couple of files from the pile on the table. Opening some of the files, he handed them over to Kunji Kiddavu to show him various income and expenditure figures. He gave Kunji Kiddavu a detailed account of the estates' financial situation. He also brought to Kunji Kiddavu's notice that the number of royal family members had increased substantially since he had taken over the throne. Whereas in 1853 the family had only 23 members by 1899, the number of royal family members had grown to 150[10]—comprising 81 females and 69 males.[11] The senior rani or Amma Thampuran's responsibility consisted of 21 ladies, 13 grown-up girls between the ages of fifteen and twenty-one, and 26 girls and 21 boys below the age of fifteen. They were maintained by a monthly stipend of Rs 3,200 from the Sircar[12] plus the annual income of Amma Raja's estate, which at the time, amounted to Rs 27,000 a year. Additionally, a sum of about Rs 1,000 and another of Rs 6,650 were spent on Government taxes, temples and charities. With 81 beneficiaries, the estate expenses of Her Highness, the Amma Raja, amounted to about Rs 56,000. And also, the kovilakam provided Rs 2,000 per annum for various expenses incurred during the pregnancy of the royal women. This sum had been allocated at a time when there were, on an average, no more than three cases of pregnancies a year, whereas in 1899, during Raja Rama Varma XV's rule, the average was closer to six pregnancies a year.[13]

Naturally, with no growth in income and the steady increase in princely allowances on account of the increase in family members, something had to be done to avert a complete collapse of the estate finances. Once he had completed his financial analysis, the Raja expressed his wish that Kunji Kiddavu step in as the financial administrator of the estates.

Kunji Kiddavu was, at this time, busy managing his own affairs and that of his uncles.

Though he was excited at taking on this challenging responsibility, he paused thoughtfully to evaluate the Raja's request. Intertwining his fingers, he sat back comfortably in his chair in complete silence for a few minutes. For a man who revelled in the business of money and investments, an opportunity to turn around the finances of the two estates was certainly exhilarating. As Elaya Raja, he felt that it was important to understand the estates' finances. He knew he was up to the challenge. Yet, being a man of moderation, he did not wish to raise the expectations of the Raja too much. Nodding his assent, he said to the Raja, 'I do gladly accept this responsibility that you are entrusting to me but this must have the consent and approval of the Amma Raja Thampuran. I assure you of my most sincere efforts in turning around the finances of the two estates. Naturally, there will be some tough decisions to be made and I hope your Highness will support me in these decisions?'

The Raja smiled and assured Kunji Kiddavu that his request had been endorsed by the Amma Raja Thampuran.

The Raja rose from his chair indicating that their meeting was over. It had been a long discussion and had taken all morning. Ringing the silver bell on his desk, the Raja summoned his Sarvadhikariakar and ordered him to escort Kunji Kiddavu out.

Kunji Kiddavu could barely contain his excitement at being recognized for his financial acumen and being handed over the vital responsibility of turning around the estates' finances. All through the ride home, his mind ticked off one by one the various discrepancies he had noticed in the financial figures. He knew he would need to make several changes but he was looking forward to the challenge. He was impatient to get home and inform Parukutty of his new responsibilities. She would be so proud of him and would be completely supportive.

When he reached home, Parukutty was waiting for him. She was very curious about why the Raja had summoned him. Kunji Kiddavu explained at length his meeting with the Raja and exactly what had transpired. She listened intently, occasionally asking questions to fill in the gaps in his narrative. As he had expected, she was as eager as him about starting work on the matter right away. Kunji Kiddavu had a healthy respect for Parukutty's innate financial instincts and her forthright evaluation of members of the family. He heard her out. That night, the couple stayed up late discussing the intricacies of the financial project ahead and the manner in which it should be handled.

Kunji Kiddavu was at the palace early the next morning. He was shown into a basic and functional room at the far end of the palace. This was exactly what Kunji Kiddavu had wished for. He was a simple man; his requirements were minimal and he preferred a work environment that allowed for few distractions. The heavy wooden desk placed in the centre of the room had four drawers on the right side, a footrest below, and the tabletop was covered with green felt cloth. On the table was a glass inkwell, filled to the brim with Prussian blue ink, a wooden hand blotter with a small handle mounted on a curved base with its bottom surface covered with a pad to absorb the wet ink. Also on the table was a narrow silver tray that had just enough space for two pens—one a dip pen and the other a new-fangled fountain pen. At one end of the table lay a bundle of files, each neatly tied in the middle with a red ribbon and labelled according to their contents. Some of these he recognized as having glanced through the previous day, but most he had not seen before. The single window in the room let in a surfeit of light, for which Kunji Kiddavu was grateful as peering for long hours at figures in dimly lit rooms would tire his eyes. He walked around the desk and pulled out the wooden swivel chair—deep brown and upholstered in soft hide—tucked neatly below the desk. It looked decidedly comfortable. Sitting himself down in the chair, he swivelled it around to face the large portrait of Raja Rama Varma XV. Swivelling back, he leaned on the table, his hands clasped tightly ahead of him and fell into deep thought. Once out of his reverie, he took a quick look at his pocket watch and turned to the chief kariastan, who was patiently waiting at the door for orders from him.

He requested the kariastan, 'I would like you to take out from this pile of files all those that pertain to the royal estates. Should there be any other books or files on the estates, I would like you to bring them to me too.'

Kunji Kiddavu had come in prepared with a well-thought-out plan as to how best to handle the mammoth task assigned to him. The royal estates were to be his first area of scrutiny. They were the primary source of income. Hence, it was imperative that he acquainted himself with every detailed bit of information about revenues from the estates.

The kariastan was taken aback by Kunji Kiddavu's request. It was unusual for a prince to inspect something as humdrum as account ledgers. Yet, Kunji Kiddavu seemed rather insistent that he be provided with the books. The kariastan hesitated for a minute or so but when Kunji Kiddavu gave him an enquiring look, he quickly set about doing exactly as he was ordered. Instinctively knowing that looking into the books spelled trouble for many, he rather grudgingly handed over some ledgers, files and loose documents all tied up together in an untidy bundle. This heap of raggedy papers he placed on to the till-now uncluttered table. It was a large pile and Kunji Kiddavu knew that before he could begin examining them, he had the tedious task of sifting through the papers and getting them into some kind of order.

However, it did not take long for Kunji Kiddavu to determine and conclude that the estates were being totally mismanaged. Amounts due were often not collected. There were farmers who had not paid their dues for months and yet no one had bothered to follow up on these dues or even make any attempt to collect the outstanding amounts. There were other farmers who claimed that their crops had been destroyed due to floods or heavy rains, but no attempts appeared to have been made to verify these claims. There were other cases where the estate had paid for sea walls to be built near fields that were by the sea on account of farmers claiming that the sea had destroyed their crops.[14] There were no indications to show that the kariastans had actually attempted to ascertain whether these claims were, in fact, true.

The next day, Kunji Kiddavu summoned the kariastans of the various properties. He directed them to send palace retainers to all the tenants who had been persistently defaulting on their payments. The tenants were to be informed that should they not pay their dues within the month, they would be thrown out of their holdings. The kariastans, realizing that their inefficiency and corrupt practices were about to be exposed, tried desperately to coax and then argue Kunji Kiddavu out of taking such drastic measures. They even brought in others to give credence to their advice. Kunji Kiddavu stood firm. But it tickled his curiosity as to why these hard-nosed, shrewd kariastans seemed to soften when it came to the matter of tenants' dues. A little digging and it came to light that one of the main reasons for this was that managers were known to overlook a tenant's defaults for a 'price'. So, the very next step Kunji Kiddavu took was to reduce the number of kariastans, weeding out the more corrupt ones. He then determined how much each holding had to pay, assigned each of the remaining managers a fixed group of tenants and made the kariastans responsible for ensuring that the dues were collected, and collected on time. For the first time and much to their indignation, the kariastans were made accountable.[15]

The next area that Kunji Kiddavu tackled was the allowances of the Thampurans. If dealing with the kariastans was difficult, dealing with the Thampurans was even more challenging. All the Thampurans received allowances according to their rank, and as they ascended in rank, their allowances increased. As the allowances were not based on need and they were well provided for, none of the Thampurans actually worked. They lived comfortably on their allowances. Kunji Kiddavu rationalized these allowances. He took his suggestions and recommendations to the Raja. The Raja agreed that just because a Thampuran ascended in rank because of the death of a Thampuran senior to him, there was no reason for his allowance to increase.[16]

Kunji Kiddavu recommended that allowances be based on certain fixed criteria. Consequently, the allowances, though fair, were not extravagant. Naturally, this did lead to several princes becoming agitated. Thirteen princes from among the third to the eighteenth prince voiced their grievances to the Raja.[17] The Raja patiently heard them out. Thereafter, he discussed the grievances of the princes with Kunji Kiddavu. Backing his recommendation with actual expense figures, Kunji Kiddavu explained that there was no possibility of sorting out the estates' finances without certain cuts in the princes' allowances. There was no refuting the logic of Kunji Kiddavu. The Raja accepted that, considering the financial crisis, these stringent measures were inevitable. Realizing that it was absolutely necessary to make some hard decisions and unavoidable changes, the Raja wholeheartedly put the weight of his support behind Kunji Kiddavu. The princes could do nothing now but grumble.

With the changes implemented and the estates managed efficiently, there was no longer a deficit. Mr Rajagopalachari, the then Diwan of Cochin, in his memorandum dated 26 January 1900 acknowledging the financial turnaround, gave Kunji Kiddavu great credit for this accomplishment.[18]

Despite his work at the palace, Kunji Kiddavu was not about to ignore the management of his own financial affairs. He continued to acquire lands of his own. Initially, he took over farmlands from those farmers who were unable to repay the loans that he had advanced them. He would then rent these to others or to the same farmers in return for a portion of the produce. With the money he saved, he also began to acquire more property in Thrippunithura, in Trichur—Trichur being Parukutty's hometown—and in other parts of the state. For both Parukutty and Kunji Kiddavu, financial deals were a passion that they enjoyed immensely. They had even made a game of the acquisition of property. Whereas most investors would do a survey of the property and its potential before investing, Parukutty and Kunji Kiddavu had converted the complex arena of financial investment into a sport. It was rather like a reality version of the modern board game of Monopoly. Every so often, Kunji Kiddavu and Parukutty would summon their bullock cart and head out to the villages. Sitting comfortably under the shade of the straw canopy, they would pass the time chatting or quietly gazing out at the verdant green landscape spread out for miles. Cochin's undeniably rich and fertile soil was clearly on display. Besides innumerable paddy fields, swaying coconut palms and banana groves, there were tapioca, pepper and rubber plantations and areca nut, cashew and jackfruit trees too. The sight of nature's bounty never failed to impress Parukutty. Often, she sat with legs dangling out of the cart, eyes shut, enjoying the cool breeze as it wafted past her cheeks. After a while, breaking the silence, Kunji Kiddavu would call out to the bullock cart driver and instruct him to stop.

Kunji Kiddavu and Parukutty would step out and stretch their legs a bit before standing back to admire the farmland on both sides of the dirt road. Kunji Kiddavu would then smile and say, 'It's time for you to decide on our next acquisition Paati.'

There would be an unmistakable gleam in Parukutty's eyes as she smiled back at him and said, 'Yes, let's see what good fortune awaits us this time.'

She would then pace around a bit to find a good-sized stone or rock. Picking it up, she would dust the loose dirt off it. Then, closing her eyes, she would send up a quick prayer to her Devi before tossing it with all her strength in any direction she could, with her eyes tightly shut. Kunji Kiddavu and the cart driver would carefully follow the trajectory of the stone so as not to lose sight of it even for a moment. Then, the three of them would trudge forward in search of the stone. Once they reached the field where the stone had dropped, they would approach the farmer and make him an offer for his land.[19] If the farmer sold it to them, it would become a part of their estate.

The game did not end there. Just as in Monopoly, in this game too, once a property was acquired, it needed to bring in revenues and needed to be built into an even bigger asset. For them, what mattered was not so much about adding to their ever-increasing assets but about figuring out ways and means to maximize their profits on their investment through astute management. They enjoyed their financial game the most when the property had been consistently making losses and they succeeded in making it highly profitable. The bigger the challenge, the more fun the game. There was an undeniable thrill in converting properties from loss-making ones to profit centres. These trips were also an opportunity for them to be together on their own. Within kottakakam, the area in Thrippunithura where their palace was located, they were required to follow the strict caste rules and restricted proximity. Not so when they left the confines of kottekakam.

With Kunji Kiddavu's involvement, the royal finances were shaping up well but the Raja's woes were far from over. Cochin had become a vassal state of the British in 1791, subsequent to which, unfortunately on many occasions, the Cochin rulers had differences of opinion with the British. In most instances, the Rajas could literally do nothing but yield to the British whim in order to retain the throne. Raja Rama Varma XV too was no exception and faced opposition from the British in many instances. In his autobiography, he makes several mentions of when he found his powers curtailed or his reforms delayed such as the Cochin State Tenancy Regulation Bill that was kept pending by the Government of Madras for a very long time.

Though the Raja to all intents and purposes was the absolute monarch, he was obliged to either consult or seek the approval of the British in all matters. The chief executive of the state was the Diwan who was appointed by the Raja, and he was the point of contact for all the ministers of the state and for the British Resident. Though he was supposed to be appointed by the Raja, the Raja had to get the concurrence of the Madras Government before he was appointed, and there were occasions when the Madras Government, as opposed to agreeing with the choice, chose to place one of their own in that position. In short, the Diwan always needed to be someone the

British Government approved of. Raja Rama Varma XV was annoyed when he was informed by the Government of Madras in June 1902 that N. Pattabhirama Rao had been appointed as Diwan as though the Raja could not decide by himself. Later, when Diwan A.R. Banerji's successor had to be chosen in 1914, the Raja had wanted a panel to be constituted to decide on this issue. The Government of Madras rejected this and Mr Joseph Bhore was chosen to succeed Mr Banerji.[20]

The Government of Madras even instructed the Raja on how much the Diwan should be paid. In 1901, in reply to his request to extend his Diwan Rajagopalachari's term with an increment in his pay, the Raja was told by the British Resident that in the opinion of the Government of Madras, Cochin could not afford to pay the Diwan more than Rs 1,200 per month. The Raja says in his autobiography that he was disappointed and annoyed at the Government of Madras dictating as to what he could pay his Diwan, especially as there were clear precedents of Diwans being given higher pay.[21]

Raja Rama Varma XV was unable to do anything directly as everything needed the sanction of the Diwan, even though the Diwan was supposedly his appointee. Many a time, when the Raja required immediate action, he was faced with a Diwan who refused to accede. To make matters even worse, there were times when the Diwan would take action without the concurrence of the Raja. Among the many such instances was one when an excise officer from Madras was appointed without consulting the Raja.[22]

There was an instance when the Raja had arranged for the purchase of an X-ray machine for the treatment of his mother whose leg was injured. The Raja believed the most logical and correct mode of payment would be to debit its cost to the Ernakulam Hospital, as this was where it was to be placed and where it would be used. The Diwan raised this issue with the Chief Medical Officer, Dr Coombes, who felt that there was no need for an X-ray machine in the hospital. The Diwan then told the Raja that he could not recommend charging the hospital and the Raja was forced to pay for it from his personal funds.[23]

It is not surprising then that Raja Rama Varma XV resented the wording of the thittooram that he was required to give on the appointment of the Diwan which stated, 'You are requested to pay an annual subsidy due to the British Government and to perform your duty consulting the British Government in all necessary matters, so as not to affect the friendship and confidence reposed by us on that Government.' This declaration clearly indicated the limitation of the so-called 'sovereign' in absolute terms of real power.[24]

The Raja was being constantly reminded of his subordinate position to the British and he strongly resented this. In 1913, the Raja wrote a private letter to the Viceroy, Lord Hardinge, requesting him to absorb his nephew Kerala Varma in the Indian Financial Services. In this letter, he addressed the Viceroy as 'my esteemed friend'. The Resident, Mr Andrews, and the Governor of Madras took exception to this as lacking in decorum and respect and told him that the Viceroy was not his equal and should be addressed as 'My Lord'. This was in spite of the private secretary to the Viceroy having told him that he may so address the Viceroy.[25]

In another instance, in 1904, after vacationing in the hill station of Kodaikanal, the Raja wanted to purchase a house, then known as Haddon House, using his private funds. The Government of Madras did not permit this.[26] This is an instance highlighting the need of an Indian ruler requiring British permission to even spend his own funds.

To build the Cochin–Shornur Railroad, the Raja wanted to take a loan of Rs 30 lakhs. He had discussed it with the engineers, who agreed that this was a reasonable requirement as the total cost was estimated at Rs 50 lakhs. The Raja asked the British Government to give him a loan at 4 per cent per annum. This was refused. Then, he asked the Government to permit him to take the loan from the Maharaja of Mysore, who was prepared to lend him the money. The Government again refused, stating that it was, in principle, against lending money to ruling chiefs, and also permitting ruling chiefs to borrow from other ruling chiefs.[27] As he was committed to this project and the work was underway, he took loans and even sold 14 of the 15 nettipattams of the elephants of the Poornathrasseya Temple[28] to complete the project.

Several other loans, projects and appointments were opposed by the Diwan and the Resident, and the Raja's frustration was such that he considered abdication several times during his reign.

On 19 November 1913, he finally mentioned this in writing to the Governor of Madras, Lord Pentland, when he stated, 'In the first place, I candidly tell your Excellency that my desire is to retire partly due to the difficulty I feel in carrying out the administration in the face of obstructions unwittingly caused by these long delays.'[29] This letter was penned after a visit to Madras, where he had met both the Governor of Madras and the Viceroy.[30] He even went so far as to mention in an extraordinary issue of the Gazette dated 8 December 1913 that he planned to retire.[31] He had done this earlier too. As early as in 1905, he had written about his intent to retire. In his autobiography, he recounts that around the middle of 1905, he had made a proposal to the Government of Madras to abdicate and retire to private life. He says that he had arrived at this decision after much thought as he found that there was a concerted effort on the part of the Madras Government to thwart him at every conceivable opportunity. Initially, he says, he thought that it was incidental to his position as the ruler and bore the humiliations and aggravations stoically. But then his problems as opposed to reducing only increased. He also found that the attitude of the British Resident became more and more formal and that he no longer received the degree of consideration that he had received from the earlier Residents such as Mr Thompson and Mr Nicholson. The Residents instead of being helpful were critical. He also felt that the quality of those selected to be Residents was not high.[32]

To the British, it appeared that the Raja threatened to abdicate every time he felt his power was curtailed. It was also rumoured that the British were gradually getting tired of his threats.

There were matters that nettled the British too. The Raja had used Germans, whom the British were to go to war with, to build the Parambikulam tramway.[33] He had openly entertained the German Consul Bueler at the Hill Palace. The Germans were being increasingly entertained in the state. The German Consul Bueler had arranged for the German cruiser SMS Gneisenau in 1911 to visit Cochin. Gneisenau was an armoured cruiser of the German Navy, part of the two-ship Scharnhorst class. The Raja went aboard when it docked at Cochin and was shown around by its captain, Von Uddlar. The Raja later gave a tea party to the officers of the cruiser.[34] The German Crown Prince Wilhelm and his wife Duchess Cecilie visited Cochin in 1911 when the prince was on a state visit to India. The Raja entertained them and even threw a garden party for them at the Hill Palace. The Diwan had also entertained them at the Bolghatty Palace. Kunji Kiddavu's daughter Ratnam recalls cuttings of the Kaiser being pasted in books by children in Thrippunithura.[35] In 1907, the German Baron Kauffman visited Cochin as the Raja's guest, spent time hunting in the forests and got a monograph on the Raja written in German on his return. These occurrences horrified the British.

The British Government wanted to ease the Raja into retirement after the First World War broke out because they suspected him of having German sympathies. As Cochin was a strategic port, the British could not afford to have a ruler whose loyalties were suspect. Therefore, the next time the Raja threatened to resign, the British accepted the resignation.

The news was greeted with shock. No king had willingly given up his throne to retire to private life.

Gossip had it that the Raja was as surprised as the rest of his subjects when his resignation was formally accepted by the British Resident. Apparently, the acceptance was done in a manner that the Raja did not expect. At a banquet held on 24 November 1914, the Resident rose and announced that the Raja had decided to abdicate and the Government had agreed to accede to his request. It is believed that this acceptance stunned no one more than the Raja but as he had made the request, he could not do anything but acquiesce[36] and follow that up with a notice in the gazette on the next day.

Whatever be the reason, in a sudden flash of a few moments, the incumbent Raja was relieved of his duties and Kunji Kiddavu quite unexpectedly rose in those few moments from Elaya Raja to become Raja Rama Varma XVI.

Coincidently, just as an astonished Kunji Kiddavu was receiving the news of his sudden elevation, the priest at Chottanikkara Temple while handing over prasad to Parukutty was asking her, 'So, you have moved house?'

When Parukutty, still puzzling over the priest's strange query, reached home, there waiting for her with a copy of the Gazette Extraordinary of that day—25 November 1914—in his hand was Kunji Kiddavu. Taking the paper from him she read aloud, 'It is the desire of His Highness the Raja to abdicate on 22 Vrishchigaom 1090—7th December 1914'.[37]

Parukutty looked up dumbfounded at an equally speechless Kunji Kiddavu.

What was fortuitous about the unexpected abdication of Raja Rama Varma XV was that had he not abdicated, Kunji Kiddavu would never have been crowned Raja as both Raja Rama Varma XV and Kunji Kiddavu died in the same year, just two months apart from each other.

Chottanikkara Bhagavathy's priest had been absolutely right, Parukutty was indeed moving house. She was moving into the magnificent Hill Palace.

7

The Road to Destiny

On 7 December at 12.50 p.m., Raja Rama Varma XV addressed his subjects in the Durbar Hall. His request that he be provided a house befitting his status and a pension had been met. Once his meeting with his well-wishers and subjects was over, he left the magnificent royal palace that had been his home for the past nineteen years.

For Parukutty, Kunji Kiddavu's unexpected elevation to the throne was a benediction from her beloved Chottanikkara Bhagavathy.

The British had accepted Raja Rama Varma XV's resignation with alacrity. They had a very capable successor in Kunji Kiddavu. In fact, Kunji Kiddavu's ability had been recognized as early as in 1901 by the British Resident, G.T. Mackenzie, who in a letter to Mr Winch of the Government of Madras had written, 'The Elaya Raja, the immediate heir, is a man of good physique and of some force of character. He is very frugal and lends his money out at interest.'[1]

It was exactly a week after the erstwhile Raja's abdication on 13 December 1914, at an auspicious hour, that Parukutty and Kunji Kiddavu entered their new home—the Hill Palace. It was a day that would be etched in Parukutty's memory for the rest of her life.

Hill Palace, Thrippunithura

The events of the past few days had seemed almost like a dream and there were times when Parukutty feared waking up to reality. Never had she ever imagined that she would be the consort of the ruler of Cochin. The momentous day arrived. She decided that she would savour each and every bit of that day. Somewhere deep within, she knew that this was her destiny.

Kunji Kiddavu had been a regular at the palace and was quite familiar with its interiors and with the requisite palace etiquette. Parukutty had driven past the palace several times in her bullock cart, en route to the Chottanikkara Bhagavathy Temple but with its high boundary walls and extensive grounds, she had never even had a glimpse of the grand palace. The palace itself, despite being on a hillock, was well hidden from view. Parukutty was looking forward to exploring the grounds, setting up her puja muri and enjoying the regal luxuries that she had once expected when she first entered Kunji Kiddavu's modest palace home.

Unschooled in palace etiquette, she hoped she would not make any gaffes. As a young adolescent bride, she had already borne the brunt of taunts and jibes, and was not looking forward to being criticized for breaking palace conventions too.

However, Parukutty had come a long way from the naive fourteen-year-old who had entered into a sambandham with a man seventeen years her senior—a man who happened to be of royal descent. Thankfully, Kunji Kiddavu had accepted her just as she was—self-willed and opinionated. In fact, he had been her strongest support through the tough adjustment period. Kunji Kiddavu's unflinching defence of his partner had irked many of the members of the royal family. His support had made it easy for her to disregard the rude comments of the Thampurattis. She had quickly learned to steel herself against their harsh opinions. After a while, though not apparent to most people, she no longer bothered with anyone's opinion but her own, Kunji Kiddavu's and her father's.[2] Parukutty was slowly transforming into the tough and often dictatorial woman that she was later reputed to be—the woman everyone learnt to fear.

The days following Raja Rama Varma XV's abdication had passed in a whirl. The entire household was in a flurry of packing their personal belongings and entertaining visitors who had come to congratulate Kunji Kiddavu or curry favour on his elevation. Parukutty had hardly slept or eaten since she had received the extraordinary news. The night before their move to the Hill Palace, Parukutty tossed and turned in bed until finally, giving up on any hope of sleep, she decided to get out of bed well before sunrise. Despite her hectic and busy schedule, Parukutty had no intention of missing out on her daily trip to the Chottanikkara Temple to express her gratitude to the Devi for her extraordinary blessing—her husband being elevated as the ruler of Cochin and she, as his consort, becoming the most powerful woman in the state.

She was bathed and dressed for her temple visit well before Brahma Mahurat—Time of Brahma. She had lit the holy villaku in her puja muri and chanted the Vishnu Sahasranamam. It was still very dark outside when she had completed all her morning rituals. The first of the sun's rays were yet to pierce through the darkness. The moon was clearly visible in all its resplendent glory. Through the window of the puja muri, she could see the stars twinkling merrily as though they too were happy for her. She stepped out of the room and sat for a few moments on the ledge surrounding the nadumittam, taking in the whole house—the Elaya Raja's palace—and reminiscing about the many memorable moments she had spent at this palace.

Later at Chottanikkara, as she prostrated herself before the deity, she prayed that the Devi give her and Kunji Kiddavu the strength and fortitude to rule justly and with integrity.

Despite her reputation as a dominant personality, tough and determined, on that particular day, 13 December 1914, there was no denying that some of Parukutty's bravado seemed to have given way to hints of trepidation.

Once back from the temple, she went to check in on her children, who were excited, even elated, about the move to the palace. A host of visitors were already at home to meet Kunji Kiddavu. She dragged the children, who were beside themselves with excitement, away for a quick breakfast. The cook had already laid out the steaming hot idlis, puttu, and iddiyappams with an assortment of chutneys, sambar and coconut milk. There were nendrapazhams, and steaming hot tea and coffee. As they sat down to eat, she instructed her staff to provide the visitors with some tea and refreshments. The breakfast, for the most part, was eaten in silence. For Parukutty, it was important that they sit together as a show of support for each other on this very momentous occasion. She made sure that Kunji Kiddavu was served his breakfast separately. Kunji Kiddavu could not eat with them as conservative traditions forbade a Thampuran from eating with anyone other than other Thampurans or Nambudiris.

As was the norm, the family astrologer had been consulted and he had apprised them of the auspicious time to leave their home and the most favourable time to arrive at the palace. Accordingly, soon after breakfast, the family left for the Amma Thampuran's palace to receive her blessing before heading off to the Hill Palace. As a matrilineal family, having descended from the niece of Cheraman Perumal, the blessing and acceptance of the Amma Thampuran was deemed necessary before being recognized and accepted as the Raja. Custom too dictated that the Amma Thampuran as the head of the royal family had the authority to appoint or dismiss the king.[3]

It was late morning by the time Parukutty, Kunji Kiddavu and three of their children, Aravindaksha, Ratnam and Vilasini arrived at the Hill Palace otherwise known as the Kanakakkunnu Palace. Raman, their eldest son, could not be included on this important family occasion as he was away in Heidelberg, Germany, pursuing a doctorate.

The palace, about 2 miles from Thrippunithura town, is perched on a small hillock and set on an expanse of 52 acres. It commands an impressive view of the countryside. The property was originally purchased in 1855 from the Kokkara

Nambudiri by the then Raja of Cochin, Ravi Varma. Successive rajas had added and embellished the building. At the time of Kunji Kiddavu's accession, the royal residence was a blend of an ettukettu building with several blocks that housed the poomukham, the homappura, the madappally, the oottupura, the Hanuman temple and many other minor rooms with two central nadumittams. The northern block of the main complex was relatively new, having been completed only fifteen years earlier. Its design was different from that of traditional Malayalee architecture as it had been conceived by European engineers. These included the cabinet hall and the adjoining structure in the central block. There was a unique lift imported from England installed in the cabinet hall connecting the ground floor to the first floor. The cabinet hall had Victorian tiles with floral designs on the floor and a metallic, ornamental ceiling. The royal residence had Italian marble tiles and the royal bedroom had ceramic tiles. The flooring in the other rooms was traditional, made of a mixture of charcoal, lime, plant juices and egg whites, which when polished resembled black marble.[4]

The expansive courtyards allowed for air and light to circulate freely. In one of the courtyards, there was a small temple dedicated to the Payyannur Bhagavathy, the family deity of the Cochin royal family.

As the palace guards opened the large wrought-iron gates to allow their car to enter, the family's excitement heightened. Their two daughters, Ratnam and Vilasini, who were still quite young—about 11 and 9, respectively—could no longer rein in their enthusiasm. They rolled down the car windows, popped their heads out and craned their necks to get a glimpse of their new home as the car drove up the long winding driveway. They passed the extensive terraced gardens that led up to the palace. The girls grew increasingly restless as they were in a tearing hurry to jump out of the vehicle and race up and down the many stone steps. Their mother was quick to give them a stern warning glance indicating quite clearly that it would be prudent for them to behave.

The flowers were in full bloom. Set amidst the multitude of colourful flowers were the most exquisitely carved marble fountains that were sputtering water into their gleaming white round basins. Acres and acres of wooded land could be seen beyond the palace. The children squealed in delight as they sighted an occasional spotted deer, which were known to run free through these grounds.

Aravindaksha, though far more subdued, was also extremely happy that he had managed to stay back for this historic occasion. He had been about to leave for higher studies in Madras, but once his father's royal appointment had been announced, he had decided to delay his departure. He was going to be studying engineering, and here was an opportunity to decipher and study the different architectural blends and structures of the palace. Architecture and engineering being his passions, he was excited to have access to the most famous edifice in the state of Cochin.[5] He keenly absorbed his surroundings, and decided that later during the day, he would explore the palace grounds on his own.

The winding driveway led up to the palace porch. The liveried chauffeur stepped out and held the door open for Kunji Kiddavu and Parukutty. The younger children wiggled out from almost under their parents, much to Parukutty's horror. Aravindaksha, who had been sitting in front beside the chauffeur, had already stepped out.

Awaiting their arrival was Diwan J.W. Bhore, who respectfully and formally welcomed the new Raja and his family. They then proceeded towards the main building. The entrance right up to the main doorway was flanked by a retinue of palace retainers who stood in line, their hands folded in namaskaram with head bowed down and eyes lowered to the ground.

Etched above the giant entrance doorway of the palace was the royal Cochin crest. Parukutty looked up with pride at the all too familiar insignia of the two elephant trunks raised in protection of the kingdom of Cochin and inscribed below was the royal motto 'Honour is our Family Treasure'. Despite having seen the crest so often, this time the pride she felt was extraordinary. She and Kunji Kiddavu would from this day forth be responsible for upholding their family motto. The enormity of that moment in her life engulfed her and Parukutty paused for a few moments, while the rest of her family walked ahead and entered the palace. Standing there, quite still, she looked up again at the royal coat of arms. Then shutting her eyes, she prayed to Chottanikkara Bhagavathy for her blessing in this—the next exciting path she was embarking on. Parukutty then slowly stepped into the Hill Palace—the royal residence that was to be her 'home' for the next 18 years.

The formalities completed, Diwan Bhore took the family around the palace—first to the cabinet room and the public rooms and then to the living quarters. The tour seemed to have taken longer than they realized, as by the time they were shown to their rooms, their personal belongings had already arrived.

Kunji Kiddavu's bedchamber was large and dominated by a four-poster bed. The room was sparsely furnished, with two heavy teak wardrobes and a large mahogany chest of drawers. At the far end, just below an open window, was a midsized study table and a velvet upholstered upright chair. Beside it stood a revolving wooden bookstand that housed an eclectic selection of English first editions, some Malayalam works and some religious chronicles.

Parukutty and the children had separate living quarters. Parukutty's room was a little distant from Kunji Kiddavu's bedchamber. It had a slightly more feminine ambience with an ornately carved rosewood almirah, a four-poster bed with a lace canopy and, rather incongruously, at one end of the room, hanging from the high ceiling, a swing. The swing's polished teakwood base, which gleamed like a mirror, was held up with ornate silver-plated metal chains with intricately carved elephant figurines linking the chains. As it was to be occupied by a woman, the room had several rosewood chests for storage. There was also a comfortable sitting area with a sink-in long settee and two cotton-padded single chairs covered in soft, smooth satin. Though all the furniture was heavy and ornate, the room looked quite uncluttered and spacious.

Aravindaksha who was seventeen at the time was given a suite of rooms in another wing of the palace. The two girls, especially Ratnam, clamoured for a room near him, arguing that she was old enough and mature enough. Parukutty, with a fierce look, silenced her. The two girls were given rooms adjoining their mother's bedroom.

The children were by now hungry and demanded lunch. In the massive dining hall, the gigantic mahogany dining table had been set perfectly with golden plates and tumblers. There was no need for any flatware as this was a typical Malayalee meal that could and should be eaten only with one's fingers. This was the dining ware that was customary at the palace, though they would occasionally use the regular ela. However, it was not every day that they were served such an extensive sadhya. There were so many items that it was almost a valiya sadhya. There was avial with all the seasonal vegetables in an aromatic curd gravy, pungent sambar, kaalan—chockful of tasty yam—the delectable ollan cooked in sweet coconut milk, pumpkin elesheri, zesty thoran and a selection of accompaniments, including puffed-up pappadums, banana and jackfruit chips and fiery mango pickle. The meal ended with a special jaggery payasam[6] and a creamy milk adda payasam. It certainly was a meal for a monarch, thought Parukutty as she licked the last morsels off her fingertips. It was a shame that Kunji Kiddavu had to eat on his own with just the deferential staff waiting on him. The cook had painstakingly made this special meal to welcome the new Raja and it had been well appreciated. However, Parukutty made a mental note to mention to him that this food extravaganza was to be restricted for dining with royal visitors and on state occasions.

The elaborate meal and the tour of the expansive interiors of the palace had taken most of the day. The royal couple had not even managed to traverse the grounds yet. Ratnam and Vilasini had been allowed to explore the front gardens. Accompanied by their nannies, they had had supervised outdoor play time. Their brother, Aravindaksha, lost in his own architectural world of adventure, had roamed into and through all the many parts of the magnificent Hill Palace and its extensive grounds.

Kunji Kiddavu and Parukutty spent the rest of the day busy in discussions with the acting Sarvadhikariakar, P. Damodara Menon, and estate managers who had come to apprise them of matters relating to the palace and the royal estates. What Parukutty appreciated most about Kunji Kiddavu was that he respected her opinions and valued her inputs. He never shied from having her present and participating in all his meetings. In fact, he encouraged it, no matter how many eyebrows it raised. Theirs was a partnership that many could not quite understand and most envied.

Kunji Kiddavu was served a working tea brought in on a silver salver and the discussions continued till late evening.

It had been a long and eventful day, and the royal couple was exhausted.

After the Sarvadhikariakar and estate managers left, Parukutty suggested to Kunji Kiddavu that it would be beneficial to meet as many of their subjects as they could. With Kunji Kiddavu's agreement, Parukutty recalled the Sarvadhikariakar and told him to invite a few prominent citizens whom they had not previously met to the Hill Palace the following day.

Shortly after that, Parukutty joined the children for a light dinner. The gold thalis were replaced by the most exquisite Minton porcelain china embossed with the royal crest. The golden flatware too was embossed with the royal crest. The children gabbled excitedly on about what they had seen and what they planned to do.

The next day, on 14 December, a few important invited citizens arrived at the palace. Kunji Kiddavu and Parukutty met them very informally. Of his meeting with the royal couple Mr T.K. Krishna Menon writes, 'Paid my respects to the new ruler. He has a magnanimous presence. I met the consort as well. She seemed to me to be a great, capable lady. I saw them both for the first time. But both treated me with great kindness.'[7]

A month later, a public meeting was held on 11 January 1915 at Thrippunithura to congratulate Kunji Kiddavu on his accession to the musnad. On this occasion, Parukutty and Kunji Kiddavu met with all the leading citizens of the state of Cochin.

The coronation—the formal installation—was to take place ten days later, on 21 January 1915.

8

The Crowning

The Rajas of Cochin, earlier known as Perumpadappu Swaroopam, had traditionally been coronated in the palace at Chithrakoodam in the Perumpadappu Village of Vanneri (modern day Malappuram). However, at the end of the thirteenth century, this town was conquered by the Zamorin of Calicut and the Perumpadappu Swaroopam was driven out of his capital. He fled to Mahodayapuram, near Cranganore, and established it as his capital. Despite losing their capital, the Rajas continued to be coronated at Chithrakoodam till the end of the seventeenth century, at which time they were stopped from doing so by the Zamorin.

Rama Varma V, who ruled from 1701–21, on his accession, took an oath that he would not wear a crown if the coronation ceremony was not held at Chithrakoodam. Unfortunately, the Cochin Rajas could not recapture the palace and Rama Varma V's successors, respecting his oath never ever wore a crown on their head. Instead, from that time on, the Cochin Rajas at their installation held the heavy gold crown embedded with 69 emeralds, 95 diamonds and 244 rubies on their lap and wore a customized, ornate, bejewelled turban on their head.

The crown of Cochin

On the morning of 21 January 1915, Kunji Kiddavu had a bath early and then attired in white garments—a fine muslin mundu and a simple short-sleeved white shirt—went to the shrine of the family deity, the Pazhayannur Bhagavathy, at the Hill Palace and sought her blessing. Then, along with Parukutty and his children, he was driven down to the Poornathrayeesa Temple for the blessings of Maha Vishnu. After this, they proceeded to the Amma Thampuran Kovilakom, next to the temple, to meet the Amma Thampuran—Kunjippilla Thampuran—who was also Kunji Kiddavu's mother's elder sister, for her blessing. Though Kunji Kiddavu's aunt was very fond of him and would have enjoyed a conversation with her nephew, Kunji Kiddavu could not spend any time with her as he had to go to Mattancherry for his installation as Raja. After he received Amma Thampuran's blessing, the family returned to the Hill Palace.

It was now time for the soon-to-be coronated Raja to be dressed for the part. In his bedchamber his valet awaited his arrival as did a retinue of male staff members, each holding up one piece of his ensemble. Kunji Kiddavu was a man of simplicity and not given to ostentation. Yet, there was a certain decorum and apparel that were de rigueur at the coronation and Kunji Kiddavu willingly subjected himself to their ministrations. The future Raja had been apprised of the protocol and the flow of events by the palace staff. He had also been prepped on the important dignitaries who were to attend the coronation. After a quick study of each of their profiles, Kunji Kiddavu, not wanting to be at loss for words, had meticulously prepared formal greetings and few words of conversation for each of them. Well prepared for the formal ceremony, he was in the process of being garbed in the required regalia. The final ministrations of the undressing and dressing were completed. Kunji Kiddavu was graciously led to the full-length, heavy, gold-framed mirror. His valet, head bowed low, awaited his approval. Kunji Kiddavu nodded his approval. The lace cloth he had on was surprisingly light and comfortable. Above linen trousers, they had donned him in a long coat, heavily embroidered with gold thread. On his feet were handcrafted, embroidered slippers. Around his neck he wore the long and large royal pearl necklace, his wrist was adorned with thick and broad jewel-encrusted gold bangles and on his fingers were an assortment of rings that glittered and gleamed each time he moved his hands. Turning away from the mirror, he strode briskly out of the room.

Parukutty and a few of his nobles were waiting for him in the courtyard. The royal car, a gleaming black Lanchester with the royal crest embossed on both sides and gold-capped headlights, stood ready to take the Raja on this important journey. Its driver, Gopalan Menon, was dressed in white livery with a red sash and a turban on which the brass emblem of the Cochin crest shone brightly. After acknowledging all those present, Kunji Kiddavu got into the open car. Parukutty did not join him as ladies were not permitted to attend the coronation. Aravindaksha got into another car along with the Sarvadhikariakar. Other cars conveyed the villakkars and Kunji Kiddavu's personal bodyguard. The convoy of cars left the Hill Palace at Thrippunithura for the Huzur Jetty in Ernakulam at the auspicious time specified by the royal astrologers. At the Huzur Jetty, they were to take the royal boat to British Mattancherry for the coronation.[1]

All along their route to the jetty, the soon-to-be coronated monarch was cheered on by the local folk who had lined the streets to get a glimpse of their new Raja.

At the jetty, a large crowd had assembled and as Kunji Kiddavu stepped out of his car, the assembly awaiting his arrival raised a great shout of, 'Long life to the Valia Thampuran'.

At the entrance to the Huzur Jetty, in front of an exquisite floral archway bursting with colour and fragrance, there were two detachments of the Nair brigade awaiting their new Raja. Beyond that was a decorated covered walkway that had been especially prepared for the royal procession. At the pier, a crowd of his subjects had gathered, keen to see their new king. He smiled and waved to the mass of happy faces. These were the people of Cochin, and their welfare and responsibility now lay with the new ruler.

Kunji Kiddavu was met at the entrance by the Diwan Peishkar and the president of the Ernakulam town council. They escorted him to the royal longboat moored at the edge of the jetty, bobbing cheerfully on the calm, clear waters as it awaited its royal passenger. The pathway leading to the jetty was covered in new unwashed white cloth. At the waterfront was the commander of the Nair brigade along with a detachment of his soldiers. Escorted by the commander of the brigade and accompanied by the Sarvadhikariakar, Aravindaksha, his bodyguards and the villakkars who had accompanied him, Kunji Kiddavu walked briskly onto the boat, still engrossed in thoughts of the enormity of the task ahead of him. He was solicitously guided to a gilded ornate throne-like chair that had been positioned at the helm of the boat. The oarsmen slowly and expertly manoeuvred the vessel. The royal boat was accompanied by 20 snake boats in which sat the royal musicians playing five instruments—kombu, edakka, thimila, ilathalam and maddalam—the pandivadhyam, the traditional Kerala orchestra.[2]

The procession of beautifully decorated boats sailing in a perfectly symmetrical sequence made an impressive sight as it wended its way across the waters of the massive Vembanad Lake. The Cochin flag with its royal insignia in gold had been hoisted at the top of the mast of the royal boat. The other boats following in coordinated formation too looked festive with buntings in the state colours hanging from the top of the mast to the bow and stern in a triangular arrangement. The boats bobbing along, the flags waving in the breeze and the excited participants of the water parade embodied the joy and happiness of the occasion. The boats sailed gracefully across the lake, bypassing the outlet to the sea, and headed towards Mattancherry, about 8 miles from Ernakulam town in British Cochin.

On arrival at the Dutch Palace jetty in Mattancherry, Kunji Kiddavu was received by the Nambudiri priest of the

Pazhayannur Bhagavathy Temple with ashtamangalam and welcomed with the traditional aarti. In attendance and to greet the new Raja were the Diwan, several noblemen and the chief judge.

From the jetty, Kunji Kiddavu went in procession on foot through a well-decorated covered walkway, on which had been spread a new unwashed white cloth; he was followed by his bodyguard of troopers and two detachments of the Nair brigade with colours flying. Preceding the procession were drummers beating the uruttu chenda, kuzhal and ilathalam. Behind them were Christian musicians playing the violin and the Jonaka Mopillas—Mohammedans of the three streets of Kochangadi—with their drums and pipe music. There were also musicians with the pandivadyam. Adding to the pageantry were Nambudiri priests carrying four deepayeshtis, four silver kuttuvilakkus and changalavattas, with the auspicious palli sanku blown at regular intervals.

The procession halted at the nearby Ariyittuvazcha Kovilakam, the palace where the Ariyittu Vazhchacha ceremony would take place. This was the ceremony prior to the coronation and installation of the Raja.

On entering the palace complex, Kunji Kiddavu went first to the Pazhayannur Bhagavathy Temple in the courtyard, which had been decorated with 2,000 jasmine flowers for this momentous occasion. Standing to the east of the Deepastambham, he prayed to the goddess and made an offering. A man of immense religious faith, Kunji Kiddavu closed his eyes and prayed with passion and sincerity for her blessing as he embarked on his new journey in life.

Completing his prayers, he returned to the entrance of the palace. He climbed a flight of stairs to the north of the shrine and crossing through the room known as the Komalataracha Palli

Ara, the royal room—the ceiling of which was decorated with bell metal bulbs—walked to the southernmost room known as Kootara Machulla Palliyara, a room with a ceiling shaped like a tent. This room was opened only for the installation of the Raja. At the centre of the Kootara Machulla Palliyara was a tall traditional Kerala silver villaku that had been lit with wicks submerged in ghee. On both sides of the lamp were paras, filled with raw rice that had a bunch of areca fronds placed decoratively on top. Besides these paras were large bunches of ripe plantains. Kunji Kiddavu with palms folded in a namaskaram went round the lamp three times. He was then seated on a cot facing the east. The cot was covered with a black blanket which in turn was covered with a white cloth. Above the cot and just above where Kunji Kiddavu was seated was an olakkuda. In consonance with the vow taken, the crown was placed on his lap as Nambudiris performed Vedic rituals. Marking the end of the ceremony, rice grains, the Hindu symbol of auspiciousness and prosperity, were showered on Kunji Kiddavu. All those assembled at the ceremony clapped and cheered as the exquisitely jewelled turban was placed on Kunji Kiddavu's head by the Nambudiri of the Pazhayannur Bhagavathy Temple. Cochin had a new Raja.[3]

After the cheering ended, the Naickeru Veetil Menon,[4] a nobleman, came forward and presented Raja Rama Varma with his nuzzar of a plain gold ring placed on a plantain leaf. Another subject, Mandala Mudalaliyar,[5] then presented his nuzzar of six muris. These were accepted on behalf of the Raja by the Sarvadhikariakar. The other nobles then presented him with nuzzar in the form of gold coins.[6]

After all the nobles had thus promised fealty to the newly coronated Raja, he returned to the Pazhayannur Bhagavathy Temple in the palace where he made an offering of a gold thali, a piece of silk, an offering of 32 puthens and a measure of ghee for lighting the lamps. After worshipping the goddess, he gifted the priest 32 puthens as theertha dakshina.[7]

Kunji Kiddavu then prayed to the various deities at the Paliyaradakavu Temple nearby and at the Azhi Trikkovil Temple dedicated to Lord Vishnu. On completing his prayers, Kunji Kiddavu went to the nearby houses of brahmins to seek their blessings.

The Raja was then taken to the Dutch Palace in an ornate and gilded state palanquin followed by the eminent Nairs—the Paliath Achan, the Kavalappara Nair, the Chondath Mannadiar, the Kuruppath Menon and other citizens—with the Sarvadhikariakar heading the procession, requesting the crowds to give way to the royal palanquin.

The palace had been gifted in 1555 by the Portuguese to the Cochin Raja. In 1663, the entire palace had been renovated and had since then been called the Dutch Palace. This had been the royal seat until the Hill Palace had been constructed. The palace built in strict conformity to thachu sastra faces east and overlooks the backwaters. It is a quadrangular, double-storeyed building built in the traditional nalukettu style. The four separate halls open into a central courtyard. In the centre of this courtyard is enshrined the titular deity of the royal family—Pazhayannur Bhagavathy. Temples dedicated to Siva and Vishnu are situated on the southern side of the palace. There is a high wall enclosing the entire structure. In the upper floor are the coronation hall, council halls and the residential quarters of the royal family. The wooden ceilings are decorated with carved floral designs. The bedchamber has a low ceiling and is covered with murals. The flooring is a mixture of burnt coconut shells, plant juices and egg whites, and looks like shiny black marble. The lower floors house the dining hall and the kitchen. On the western side is a kolam for bathing.[8]

At the entrance to the Dutch Palace, the Diwan, Mr Bhore met the Raja. Raja Rama Varma, followed by the Diwan and other officials, proceeded to the coronation hall for the formal investiture. Aravindaksha was already waiting there, barely managing to conceal his excitement.

In the coronation room, Raja Rama Varma, wearing the bejewelled turban, sat on the royal throne. The ornate, gilded throne with the massive royal banner as its backdrop, the glittering crown on the Raja's lap and the heavy turban on his head with its large precious stones glistening on all sides, was an extravagantly majestic sight. The room was filled with all of Cochin's leading citizens and landowners who were there to declare their allegiance to the new Raja.

Shortly after the Raja and those present at the hall had taken their places, the sound of trumpets heralded the arrival of A.T. Forbes, the British Resident in Travancore and Cochin. Pith helmeted Forbes, resplendent in a white uniform with an array of medals on his chest and a sword strapped to his waist, strode smartly into the coronation room. Removing his helmet, he walked up to the throne and bowed to the Raja. Then moving to the side so as to not have his back facing the Raja, he turned to the assembled personages and formally declared, 'Whereas His Highness Raja Sri Sir Rama Varma, G.C.S.I., G.C.I.E., lately Raja of Cochin abdicated on 22 Vrischigom 1090, corresponding to 7 December 1914, his next cousin the Elaya Raja, Rama Varma, who has been recognised by the Governor General in Council as the lawful heir and successor, is accordingly proclaimed Raja of Cochin, and the inhabitants of Cochin are hereby directed to acknowledge him and obey him as Raja and Ruling Chief of the State.' Kunji Kiddavu ascended the musnad as Raja Rama Varma XVI. [9]

Following this, the people of Cochin presented the newly coronated Raja with a casket and their representative made an address of congratulation. Accepting their tributes, the Raja responded graciously. On the occasion of this coronation, 14 convicts were also released as a mark of clemency.[10]

Once all the formalities had been completed and the newly crowned Raja had met with several of his well-wishers, he, accompanied by Aravindaksha, left the Dutch Palace to head for the jetty to take the boat back to Ernakulam. They were accompanied by the Diwan and leading noblemen. At Ernakulam's Huzur Jetty, a magnificent barouche driven by four horses—two white and two black—awaited him. Father and son settled comfortably in the carriage and began their ride back to Hill Palace. The streets were lined with citizens eager for a glimpse of their new ruler. He travelled in the barouche to Thrippunithura receiving the accolades of his subjects.

Prior to going back to the palace, he stopped at the Poornathrayeesa Temple for the lord's blessings. Raja Rama Varma XVI exited the temple with the enormous responsibilities of a kingdom to rule and a large and diverse populous to govern. He would need the blessing of all the gods to fulfil his duties to his people and to protect his sovereignty.

Well ahead of the coronation and soon after receiving the news of Kunji Kiddavu's elevation to the post of the Raja, Kunji Kiddavu and Parukutty had decided that they must present themselves as accessible to their people. Accordingly, Raja Rama Varma XVI and Parukutty had the Sarvadhikariakar arrange for a garden party on the day following the coronation. The royal couple met each one of their guests, enquired about their concerns and gathered as much information as they could about the welfare of their citizens. Parukutty knew that by getting to know her subjects, especially the women, she would know the mind and the pulse of the nation. She spoke with many of the ladies and invited some of them to visit her at the Hill Palace too.

A garden party at the Hill Palace

Two months later, there was another ceremony at the Dutch Palace. In front of all the nobles, Raja Rama Varma XVI, seated on his throne, summoned Parukutty. She came into the coronation hall and stood in front of him. The monarch too stood up. Then taking a kai vilakku, he raised it above her head and chanting neithyar, he moved it in a circular clockwise motion three times above her head.[11] Then, to everyone's amazement and surprise, he announced that she would be his royal consort, and invited her to stand beside his throne, making it very clear that he would rule the country with her by his side. Never before had any sambandhi of a Thampuran ever been given this kind of pre-eminence. No other Raja had ever taken such a bold stand before. The assembly was aghast at what they had just seen and heard.[12]

What appeared as just a passing whim, a vagary of an infatuated man was, in fact, a very carefully thought-out plan. The British did not recognize sambandham and considered it more of a morganatic marriage. As a consequence, the sambandhi of a Raja was never invited to official meetings nor did they ever meet senior British officials. By declaring Parukutty as his consort, Raja Rama Varma XVI had created universal awareness of their relationship and had legitimized it. The Raja had shrewdly recognized that his elevated position would undoubtedly create a great deal of enmity and machinations, and he needed someone unconditionally loyal to him at his side, someone who was perceptive, pragmatic, authoritative and yet astutely diplomatic—his Paati.

9

A Formidable Team

Raja Rama Varma XVI, as Mr G.T. Mackenzie, the British Resident in Travancore and Cochin, had observed was careful with money.[1] He was frugal and intended now to do for Cochin what he had done for the Amma Raja and Palli-Ara Muthalpidi estates.

Fortunately, as Kunji Kiddavu and Parukutty had for several years been acquiring properties for themselves all over the state and visiting their estates as landowners, they were familiar with most of the state, and many of the landowners and farmers. Furthermore, as Kunji Kiddavu had for the last 16 years been assisting and advising the previous Raja, Raja Rama Varma XV on financial matters, he was well informed on the economy of the state. However, up until now Parukutty had never involved herself in the Cochin state's finances.

Raja Rama Varma XVI and Parukutty knew that they had begun their rule at an extraordinarily difficult time. The country's finances were meagre. The state was in debt. The European war was threatening not only dislocation of commerce and its attendant activities but also possible depression. Therefore, they were conscious of the fact that they must husband the scanty resources and capital of the state and manage it. At the same time, welfare measures for the citizens needed to be instituted to look after their subjects. Apart from all this, they were acutely aware that the British Raj would expect them to contribute to the war efforts, even though it was a European war and had nothing to do with Cochin. Failure to do so could cost them the throne, as had just happened to the abdicated Raja. The British would not hesitate to rid themselves of a sovereign who they felt was not favourable to their demands. They would seek every opportunity and use whatever means they could to rid themselves of a ruler who showed any signs of dissent towards the British Government.

Raja Rama Varma XVI and Parukutty had pragmatically accepted that in order to retain their sovereignty, they had to appear loyal and supportive of the British crown. Parukutty was an ambitious woman. She was not going to provide any occasion for her husband's powers to be wrested from him. Having evaluated the political scenario, she prudently decided that, despite the state being in debt and its finances precarious, they would need to provide a reserve of funds sufficient to fulfil British demands towards their war efforts. This meant that there had to be a trimming of expenses, and until the state was in better financial condition, additional expansions and improvements to the infrastructure could not be considered.

Kunji Kiddavu and Parukutty decided that their focus would be on improving the condition of the people. In order to do so, they would necessarily have to keep a strict control on expenditure, especially expenditure on capital projects.

The war had also caused a huge stress on Cochin's financial resources. Great Britain and Germany had been the state's best customers for coconuts and coconut products. On account of the ongoing war, they had stopped purchasing.[2] This fact is reiterated by Diwan Bhore who in his annual administration report states, 'The European war which broke out just as the year was coming to a close will undoubtedly put a strain upon the state's resources.' He observed that a watchful eye had to be kept on the expenditure.[3]

The bond between Kunji Kiddavu and Parukutty, which was deep, intense and strong, was becoming even more so. They trusted and relied on each other completely. This was unusual in that era as in a matrilineal society even though the family property belonged to the woman, it was generally the male members of the family whose opinions were sought and accepted in important financial and property decisions. In reality, it was the eldest male member of the family—the Karnavan—who was the final deciding authority. This was even more so in the case of rulers of a country. However, Kunji Kiddavu, on account of the trust he had in Parukutty and her political and social acumen made it a point to discuss all matters in detail with her. And decisions were taken only after they had thoroughly debated all aspects of an issue.

Kunji Kiddavu encouraged Parukutty to study the state's finances. Taking this opportunity very seriously, Parukutty in the first few months spent time with the royal estate managers and heads of departments, to understand the financial workings of the state. This, for most of the royal staff, was certainly a departure from regular practice. However, as it had been ordered by the Raja, they acquiesced but not without reservations. She would also be present when the Raja discussed state affairs. Gradually, it became apparent that the consort of the Raja played a definite and important role in state policies. Parukutty, however, in deference to Kunji Kiddavu's position, would always during state meetings remain standing in his presence. She would never speak or express an opinion, unless specifically requested to do so. When she did broach an opinion, she would always clarify that, 'This is just my opinion. It is for His Highness to decide.' This was her practice as she was very aware that even though Raja Rama Varma XVI had declared her his consort, she had no official standing.[4]

On one occasion, the Diwan came to Raja Rama Varma XVI with a query: A prince wished to go to Benaras to study and expected the state of Cochin to finance his education. But the Diwan pointed out that it was customary for the state to pay for a prince's studies only if he went to Madras to study. The Diwan felt that if the state was to fund this prince's studies at Banaras, it might set a precedent. Other future princes might, citing this, ask for funding at educational establishments of their choice in other parts of India. Raja Rama Varma XVI was unsure of the decision he should take. As he pondered the matter, he turned absently to Parukutty and as was his habit casually enquired of her and asked, 'Paati, what do you think?' This was not what was expected of a Raja. There was a hush in the audience room. Unfazed, Parukutty dealt with the Raja's query just as she would any official query. Addressing the Raja with formality she replied, 'Your Royal Highness, it is my opinion that the royal treasury should fund the prince's education. My reasoning being that the prince's enthusiasm to further his education should be encouraged by permitting him to be educated at the institute of his choice. However, Your Highness I am merely presenting my opinion. It is only Your Highness who can make a judicious decision.'

Parukutty had presented her opinion just as the Diwan had presented his. She had spoken as though she was offering an alternative point of view from that of the Diwan for the

Raja to consider, though, in fact, she had cleverly manoeuvred the decision.

In these situations, what worked to Parukutty's advantage was the fact that, as Diwan Sir T. Vijayaraghavacharya had mentioned, 'His Highness conveys his commands in a socratic method.'[5] The Raja's socratic style of speaking, of systematic doubt and questioning and of critical thinking helped at those times when, though he did follow Parukutty's advice, it was not made completely obvious to others since he had also sought the opinions of others.

10

A Legacy of Loans

Cochin was sandwiched between Travancore and British Malabar. The state occupied an area of 1418 square miles, of which 605 square miles comprised forests. The aggregate population at that time was about 1 million, of which 67 per cent were Hindus, 25 per cent Christians and 7 per cent Muslims. More than half the population was engaged in agriculture.[1] For administrative purposes, the state was divided into five taluks—Cochin, Mukundapuram, Trichur, Talapalli and Chittur. The capital of the state was Mattancherry, which was in British Cochin. The Raja's residence—the Hill Palace—was at Thrippunithura.

The total income of the state at the time was Rs 47,06,999 while the expenditure was Rs 44,04,596, leaving a surplus of a mere Rs 3,01,403.[2] Cochin's income was derived mainly from land revenue, excise, timber from the forests and railways. The expenses were on account of medical, sanitation, education, public works and the palace.

Agriculture was the mainstay of the economy and the total area under cultivation was 496,597 acres. The area under coffee cultivation was 2,057 acres and the total yield was 451,660 pounds. The total area under rubber cultivation was 10,513 acres.[3]

Cochin was not commercially developed, and at the time, there were only 15 joint stock companies registered. These related mainly to transportation and spinning and weaving. With regard to medical welfare, there were 10 hospitals, 13 dispensaries and 2 asylums.

At the end of 1914, when Raja Rama Varma XVI ascended the throne, there were 132 Sirkar schools and 158 private schools. There were 23,416 students in Sirkar schools and 40,394 in private schools. The total number of students under instruction was 63,810. Of these, 44,495 were boys and 19,315 were girls. Primary education was given in 1,319 schools. The total number of girls' schools was 60—of which 40 were Sirkar and 20 aided. There was one college with 180 students.[4]

The new Raja and Parukutty made it very clear that their focus would be on the people—on education, hospitals and agriculture—and not on huge capital spending.

The abdicated Raja had tried to develop the infrastructure and industrialize the state. He had undertaken several capital-intensive projects such as the Shornur to Cochin railroad and the Parambikulam Tramway system by which timber could be transported from the forests to the capital.

The Shornur–Cochin Railway was the abdicated Raja's first large project. This railway line was to be laid from the border of Cochin state with British Malabar to Ernakulam, thus connecting Cochin to British Malabar by rail. The initial cost was estimated at Rs 50 lakhs. As the state did not have adequate funds, the Raja could not undertake this without borrowing. He first proposed to borrow Rs 30 lakhs for 10 years at 4 per cent per annum from the British Government, or if the British Government was not prepared to extend the loan, from the Mysore Government. Though Lord Curzon, the Viceroy, sanctioned the railway, he not only refused the loan but did not permit the loan being taken from Mysore either since the British Government was, in principle, against ruling chiefs borrowing from other ruling chiefs. Nineteen miles of the railway from Angamally to Edapally had to pass through the state of Travancore. Hence, to defray some of the cost, Travancore was asked whether they would also like to join Cochin in this venture. Unfortunately for the Raja, Travancore refused. Rama Varma XV, left with no alternative, decided that Cochin would bear the entire cost by availing of a loan. To fund the project, the state notified in the Gazette their requirement of a loan of Rs 10 lakhs at 5 per cent per annum interest.[5] The project was subscribed for by the people of Cochin and the construction was undertaken by the Madras Railway Company.

After the construction began from Shornur, war broke out with South Africa and as a consequence the price of iron and other materials ordered from England for the construction went up, necessitating additional funds.[6] The abdicated Raja had also, much against the will of the princes, sold 14 gold elephant nettipattams that belonged to the Sree Poornathrayeesa Temple and several ornaments that belonged to the Cochin royal family to fund the project.[7] This created agitation among the princes and much unhappiness. The construction took three years as there were several bridges that had to be built, and finally, the metre-gauge railway was opened for goods traffic in June 1902 and for passengers in July 1902. The one-track railway from Shornur to Cochin was about 62 miles long, with a circular track laid at the terminus to enable the train to turn.

The forests at Parambikulam, near Chittur, at the border of Cochin state with British Malabar, were rich in teak, rosewood and other expensive trees. However, it was not feasible to transport these easily to the port for dispatch. J.C. Kohloff, the conservator of the forests of the Cochin state proposed the construction of a tramway. Raja Rama XV agreed and after a feasibility study, construction began in 1905. Tramlines were laid for a total of 49.5 miles and were divided into three sections—the first from Chalakudy for a distance of 21 miles, the second for 6 miles from Kavalai to Pothupara and the third for 22.5 miles from Komalapara to Chinnar. The lines began operation in 1907. The intent was that the wealth from the timber sold would feed the state coffers, catalysing Cochin's transformation into an affluent princely state.

However, this project had been undertaken shortly after the introduction of the Cochin–Shornur Railway which had already cost the state Rs 70 lakhs. The tramway cost the state another Rs 22.5 lakhs.[8] These large expenditures forced the state to take large liabilities in the form of debentures of Rs 20 lakhs and loans of another Rs 10.5 lakhs.[9]

In spite of the already outstanding loans, the abdicated Raja had, just prior to his abdication, approved plans to set up a hydroelectric project by harnessing the waters from the Athirapilly Falls near Cochin—yet another a capital-intensive project.

Consequently, at the time of Kunji Kiddavu's ascension to the musnad, the kingdom had a debenture loan of Rs 10 lakhs. Other liabilities included deposits from the Devaswom,[10] the Town Fund, the Palace Fund and the Provident Fund, aggregating Rs 7,88,654.[11]

As the First World War had just been declared, it was a difficult period. This meant not only losses in trade but shortages in vital commodities as well. In addition, the British war effort had to be bolstered. Not exactly a utopian time for a king to ascend a throne.

The task ahead to reverse Cochin's finances was onerous. Kunji Kiddavu and Parukutty knew that they would have to evolve a very clear plan to reverse Cochin's fortunes. They worked together in earnest and devised a meticulous plan for the state exchequer. Once they had finalized the plan, they knew it was one they could not deviate from.

11

Manoeuvres and Outmanoeuvres

Shortly after his accession to the throne, Raja Rama Varma XVI summoned Diwan Bhore to discuss the economy of the state and to advise him on his views on the administration and what should be done going forward. As a ruler, he intended to be a constitutional monarch and work towards the progress of his people. As a man, he was simple, not given to ostentation, and disliked pomp and pageantry.[1]

The Diwan was effectively the chief executive officer of the state, who was appointed by the Raja to administer his policies. However, as most Diwans were foisted onto the Raja by the Madras Government, many of them acted as a power unto themselves and did what they wanted, as the abdicated Raja had often experienced. Diwan Joseph William Bhore, who was appointed as Diwan of Cochin in 1914, too had been imposed on the abdicated Raja by the Madras Government. Prior to this appointment, Bhore had served as Under Secretary, Government of Madras. Fortunately for the abdicated Raja, Raja Rama Varma XV, Bhore saw eye to eye with him on most of his endeavours.

Joseph William Bhore was a short man, inclined to plumpness. Bald, with a bushy dark brown moustache and deep piercing eyes, he was the epitome of punctiliousness. He was puritan in his ways and stoic in nature. Mr Bhore was not ostentatious, had no expensive habits and was not addicted to any bad habits. He was very disciplined—punctual and systematic in all that he did. Mr I.N. Menon, the abdicated Raja's son, says that as an administrator, he was not officious or sentimental, but was sympathetic and always open to bona fide criticism. Mr Menon's statement clearly indicates that the abdicated Raja and Diwan Bhore had an excellent rapport, in spite of him being appointed by the British, and this is evident in the many letters they exchanged even after Raja Rama Varma XV abdicated.

However, in his description of Diwan Bhore, Mr I.N. Menon does mention, 'Compared and coming immediately after Banerji, Bhore looked like a common place interlude of prose after a piece of impassioned poetry.'[2]

Diwan Bhore was keen on the extension of the forest tramway, the introduction of a hydroelectric scheme and the development of indigenous industries with the application of cheap electrical power, the improvement of agriculture by use of scientific methods, and the extension and improvement of both major and minor means of irrigation, the provision of more hospitals and of more prophylactic measures against the spread of disease, and the preliminary steps in connection with the building of the Cochin harbour.[3]

Bhore was entirely committed to the tramway project. The tramway had opened in 1907. By the end of 1913 the capital and recurring expenditure of the project amounted to Rs 28,17,962. The total value of the forest produce carried by the tramway after deducting the incidental charges such as felling and loading of timber had been Rs 14,87,826. Bhore, himself estimated that by 1919, the gross value of transported forest produce would be around Rs 11 lakhs and that the cost of maintenance during this period would be Rs 6.25 lakhs. Plus, there would be the cost of running the tramline. In short, the tramway would result in recurring expenditure with no real gain. It was estimated that the capital and recurring charges on the one hand and the total value of the produce it would carry after deducting costs on the other would amount to Rs 34 lakhs and Rs 26 lakhs, respectively. In short, this meant the depletion of valuable teak and rosewood from the forests to the detriment of the exchequer.[4] Additionally, Bhore himself stated that the more valuable timber which alone could pay for the tramway would be exhausted in four years. Despite this, Bhore and the abdicated Raja were committed to keep the tramway project running.

With regard to electricity, the erstwhile Raja along with Bhore had planned to harness the strength of the Athirapilly waterfalls near Cochin to supply electricity. To do this, the state would need to take a loan of Rs 35 lakhs. In February 1916, Bhore put up a proposal to take the loan. To support this, he had procured a guarantee from the Tata Group to take up all the electricity produced and had been assured a 9 per cent return. Bhore's submission was that the loan would be at 6 per cent, and consequently, the state would gain a profit of 3 per cent.[5]

Kunji Kiddavu, who was now Raja Rama Varma XVI, having inherited an exchequer crippled by heavy loans in a time of war knew that taking on additional loans for new projects such as the hydroelectric project would further impede the economy. Moreover, he had heard that the British may, should the state be in a financial crisis, take over the state and annex it to British

Malabar. Raja Rama Varma XVI had astutely deduced that the primary reason the Government at Madras and the British Resident made it so difficult for the earlier Raja to govern was that the British eyed Cochin and were keen to annex the state into the Madras Presidency[6] as they had done to Malabar. The Madras Presidency would then have a presence in both the east and the west coasts. Mattancherry, on the west coast, was already a part of British India. The British strategy was to either frustrate the Raja to abdicate or ensure that the state had so much debt that when it seemed that the state could not meet its obligations to foreclose, then take over the state. This is the likely reason that the British did not lend the state money but forced it to take loans at a higher rate from elsewhere to fund its development projects. Perhaps, this might also explain why Bhore was propagating capital-intensive projects.

Savvy to British manoeuvres and politics, Kunji Kiddavu and Parukutty were absolutely clear that until the state was financially secure, no large developments would take place. They would instead pursue those schemes that were for the upliftment of the people, such as the development of agriculture and the building of schools and hospitals.

Raja Rama Varma XVI, who had earlier been assisting Raja Rama Varma XV with his financial matters, was acquainted with Diwan Bhore. He was also aware of the manner of his appointment and the support he had from the Madras Government. Raja Rama Varma XVI realized that it was best not to oppose the Diwan directly on the projects he had initiated during the previous Raja's rule. Instead, he cleverly opted to delay decisions. These delay tactics are recounted by a rather annoyed abdicated Raja in his autobiography. He felt that Raja Rama Varma XVI should have taken his predecessor's advice and supported these projects. Raja Rama Varma XVI, who had excellent financial acumen and had successfully turned around not only the royal estates but also his own personal acquisitions, was not about to take the advice of a ruler who had left him a state in serious financial crisis.

The autobiography of the abdicated Raja Rama Varma XV includes copies of Bhore's letters of April 1918 and May 1918 to him that indicate that though time and again Bhore had written to His Highness, Raja Rama Varma XVI, regarding the tramway extensions and the hydroelectric projects, decisions from the sovereign remained unforthcoming.[7] Bhore wrote to the abdicated Raja on 30 April 1918 that he had taken all the details regarding the tramway extension and the hydroelectric project to Raja Rama Varma XVI in person in order to discuss these projects and answer queries that may arise and answer objections that may be made in order to arrive at a conclusion. He added that after the Raja had heard him for ten minutes, he was asked to return after a fortnight as the Raja was busy with the thalikettu arrangements for his daughters. He stated that the Raja mentioned that should Bhore leave, the schemes that he proposed may fall through. Bhore added, tongue-in-cheek, that the Raja may exult in his departure as that would relieve him of the need to decide on whether to pursue the projects or not.[8]

In another letter dated 14 May 1918, Mr Bhore informs the abdicated Raja that Raja Rama Varma XVI had fixed 13 May 1918 for a full discussion on the projects and had promised that they'd arrive at a conclusion. Bhore met the Raja and had a discussion for two hours after which the Raja told Bhore that he had not seen Bhore's detailed note of July 1917 on the tramway project and that he needed to study it. Diwan Bhore stated that he was more than a little surprised to hear this as he distinctly remembered that he had sent the first copy to the Raja.

On his return to his office, he checked his files and noted that it had been sent to the Raja on 26 July 1917. He added that the Raja was also ambivalent about the hydroelectric project. The Raja felt that Rs 35 lakhs was too large a sum to borrow even though Bhore told him that the Tatas were prepared to give a stamped and registered guarantee to take the power generated and the Cochin Government was assured of a return of 9 per cent per annum. He had submitted that even if an interest of 6 per cent had to be paid on the loan, the state would earn a clear 3 per cent. He concluded the letter in a dejected manner saying, 'Things appear to be no further advanced than they were months ago.'[9]

The delays were in spite of the acting Sarvadhikariakar P. Damodara Menon, who had been Bhore's secretary, recommending the advancement of the schemes.

Parukutty knew that Bhore was in touch with the abdicated Raja and was regularly writing to him and informing him about what was transpiring within the palace. In this he had an able conveyor of news—his former private secretary, Damodara Menon, who was now acting as the Sarvadhikariakar of Raja Rama Varma XVI. The abdicated Raja welcomed this as he was keenly interested in what was happening, at times even writing to the Resident and to the Madras Government on what he felt should be done and on other matters including on policies he did not agree with, even though he had abdicated and it was no longer his responsibility.

Another issue that riled the abdicated Raja was with regard to shares that he had purchased of the Moopley Valley Rubber Company when he was the ruler. The shares were in the name of His Highness Sir Rama Varma, G.C.S.I., Raja of Cochin. The abdicated Raja claimed that they belonged to him and that the dividend should be paid to him. Parukutty took the stand that the owner was the Raja of Cochin. The abdicated Raja filed a case in the Travancore court as the rubber company was headquartered in Travancore. To his chagrin, he lost the case.[10]

It was becoming apparent that though he had abdicated, the former Raja wished to influence all decisions made by his successor.

Further pressure was put on Raja Rama Varma XVI when Bhore went so far as to ensure that his complaint was heard by the Madras Government through a letter written to the Government by Sarvadhikariakar Damodara Menon. In this letter to the Resident Mr Braidwood, Menon wrote, 'It would be difficult to expect Bhore to continue as Diwan if schemes on which he has spent so much time and care are simply shelved without reason.'[11]

Braidwood after talking with Bhore took up the matter with Raja Rama Varma XVI. With quintessential British diplomacy, he began by stating that the British Government was happy to support him in any way he wanted and with all the experts at their command. Continuing, he mentioned that they could not understand why the Raja was so keen to reverse all his predecessor's policies.[12]

Raja Rama Varma XVI in a polite yet firm handwritten note to Braidwood on 11 May 1918 stated that he had been occupied with the thalikettu kalyanams of his daughters. He then continued,

> From the tone of your letter, I am led to believe that you have understood me to be totally against Mr Bhore's schemes and if that is the case, you have been totally misinformed. The resources of my state, in my humble opinion, do not permit me for the time being, to undertake any serious risk. I would prefer to be on the safe side.[13]

Despite concerted efforts by the abdicated Raja and Mr Bhore to pressurize him into taking on additional loans for capital-intensive projects, Raja Rama Varma XVI stood his ground, and insisted that he'd first focus on the state's dwindling finances.

Kunji Kiddavu agreed with Parukutty that as Bhore's term was soon to end, their new Diwan should preferably be an Indian. They also agreed that they should have a new Sarvadhikariakar. The acting Sarvadhikariakar Damodara Menon's loyalty, being Bhore's secretary, lay with the British Diwan. Additionally, Damodara Menon had without the Raja's knowledge on one occasion sent an order to the Thrippunithura Devaswom Inspector. This was inexcusable. Even the abdicated Raja told Kunji Kiddavu that this was a very serious matter, as every order issued from the Sarvadhikariakar's office was in the Raja's name.[14] Menon had sent orders without even bothering to inform the Raja, an offence that should have resulted in his immediate dismissal.

Parukutty spoke to her cousins and they suggested the young lawyer Narayana Pisharody, who was reputed to be hardworking and intelligent, and had a knack of getting on with people. Parukutty asked Pisharody to meet her at the Hill Palace. On the appointed day, Pisharody came. Parukutty met him first. She liked his frank demeanour and questioned him at length on his thoughts on the state, its people and on how he would conduct himself. Satisfied, she took him to Kunji Kiddavu, who agreed that he was the person they were looking for and decided to engage him on a trial basis. It was made clear to Pisharody that apart from his competence, his loyalty was not negotiable.[15]

Raja Rama Varma XVI, when he was heir apparent, had been looking after the management of the Amma Raja estate and the Palli-Ara Muthalpidi estate. The senior Thampuratti

Kunjipilla Thampuran, the Amma Thampuran, who was the Raja's aunt, was 74 years old and not very well. She was extremely happy with the manner Kunji Kiddavu was managing the Amma Raja estate. She decided that as he had been managing the Amma Raja estate even during the reign of the previous Raja, and had been doing so very efficiently, he should continue to manage the Amma Raja estate. The Palli-Ara Muthalpidi in any case was the responsibility of the incumbent ruler as the Karnavan or head of the family. As he had done during the previous reign, Raja Rama Varma XVI continued to manage both the estates. As the Amma Raja estate was for the welfare of the princesses and children, Parukutty took over its supervision while Kunjipilla Thampuran eased herself into retirement. Parukutty thus became the de facto Senior Rani. This shocked and upset the other Thampurattis and the princes. They were horrified that the Nair consort of the Raja had usurped what was the right of the princesses. Unfortunately, their protests fell on deaf ears as Parukutty had the support of not only the sovereign but also the Senior Rani, Kunjipilla Thampuran. Parukutty, of course, had absolutely no qualms about usurping the position. She was confident of running it efficiently.[16]

Shortly after Raja Rama Varma XVI had ascended the throne, the royal couple faced a personal crisis. Their eldest son Raman was in Germany at the University of Heidelberg pursuing a doctorate. As Cochin was part of British India, Raman, as a subject of Great Britain, was regarded as an enemy of Germany and imprisoned. Raman was Parukutty's eldest and favourite child. The news, when it came to Cochin, several months later in October 1915, devastated Parukutty. Both Kunji Kiddavu and Parukutty began to examine ways and means to secure Raman's release. They wrote to the Viceroy and to Sir Chettur Sankaran Nair,[17] who was at that time the only Indian in the

Viceroy's executive council. Sir Sankaran, in turn, approached the Secretary of State for India, Edwin Montagu and sought his intervention. As Britain was in a state of war with Germany, the British officials threw up their hands and said that there was nothing they could do.[18] They even went so far as to say that should they intercede on Raman's behalf, his situation may become even more precarious as the Germans may suspect him of being a spy or a valuable asset of the British. While the Raja and Parukutty were in this quandary, the Governor of Madras invited them to Madras for the opening of the Madras People's Park Fair.[19] It was to raise funds for the war effort and the summons could not be ignored. Parukutty went along with the Raja in December 1915 as she did not want to remain alone in Cochin while she was in such a disturbed state of worry and concern about her son. A visit to Madras would also give her the opportunity to see her second son Aravindaksha, who was studying engineering there. With one son in deep trouble and so faraway, she wanted to reassure herself that her other son was safe and well.

V. K. Raman Menon in Heidelberg, Germany

As this was their first state visit after ascending the throne, Raja Rama Varma XVI and Parukutty went by special train to Madras on 21 December 1915. On their way, at the Mullurkara railway station, the Paliath Valiachan, the head of the Paliath tarwad greeted Raja Rama Varma

XVI with great pomp. Then at Cheruthuruthy, the Nambudiris and the local people met the Raja and his consort with letters of praise. At the Madras station on 22 December 1915, the couple was met not only by representatives of the Governor of Madras but also by several other dignitaries. Led by a Madras High Court advocate, all the Malayalees residing in Madras too came to the station to honour the royal couple.[20]

Raja Rama Varma XVI and Parukutty on the day after their arrival drove to the Government House to call on Lord and Lady Pentland. The Governor, Lord Pentland, and his wife welcomed them and spent a considerable period of time telling them about the fair and carnival that had been organized. Lord Pentland was delighted when Parukutty volunteered to be on the committee along with Lady Pentland. That evening, Lord Pentland returned the Raja's visit. The royal couple was in Madras for a fortnight and had several opportunities to meet the Governor and his wife and get to know them. Raja Rama Varma XVI took advantage of this to apprise the Governor of the situation in Cochin and the assistance he needed.[21]

Parukutty remembered her earlier visit to Madras and one day she had herself driven to Higginbothams on Mount Road. She strode into the shop and browsed through the many books on display and purchased several, not only for herself but for Kunji Kiddavu and her children too. Kunji Kiddavu and Parukutty also went with Aravindaksha to his college and met his teachers. The couple took this opportunity to meet various dignitaries such as the Maharaja of Bobbily, the Raja of Tanjore, Pandit Madan Mohan Malaviya, the Raja of Ramnad and the Raja of Vengitagiri.[22]

While in Madras, the Governor, Lord Pentland, aware of their plight regarding their eldest son, suggested that as the Pope was neutral, they should try and get him to intercede on

Raman's behalf. This seemed a good idea and after discussing this suggestion threadbare, Kunji Kiddavu and Parukutty decided to seek an audience with Giovanni Aelen, the Archbishop of Mylapore, in Central Madras.

A meeting was arranged and the Archbishop, when they met him at his palace, was most cordial.[23] He heard their concerns, sympathized with them and promised to approach the Vatican through the Patriarch of the East Indies at Goa, Maleus de Oliveira Xavier. This effort was not in vain and in March 1916, the Secretary of State to the Pope, Cardinal Pierro Gasparri telegrammed to say that Raman had been freed and that he had crossed the border to Switzerland.[24] Parukutty was ecstatic. She was a little disappointed though that Raman had elected to remain in Switzerland to complete his doctorate, and then proceed to England instead of directly returning home. She comforted herself that this was the best option as it was no longer safe to travel from Europe to India.

12

A Study Tour

The Viceroy had summoned the ruling princes and chiefs for a conference in Delhi on 30 October 1916. The intent of the meeting was to get the rulers to reaffirm their support to the British in the World War and secure their commitment of men and money. Raja Rama Varma XVI decided that he would seize this opportunity to visit other states and get to understand the manner these states were being governed. Additionally, as he had not visited north India till then, he was keen to see as much as he could.

He, along with Parukutty, Diwan Bhore and his staff, left by special train for Madras on 8 October 1916. He stayed in Madras for two days and then departed for Bombay. In Bombay, he spent a few days meeting the Governor and other officials. Parukutty and he also visited several historical monuments. He visited the harbour and while there boarded a ship owned by the Madras Hospital. The Gaekwad of Baroda was a friend of theirs, and Parukutty and the Raja visited Baroda as guests of the Gaekwad, where they were welcomed with great pomp and ceremony. On the way, they stopped at Billimora, where they visited a candle factory. The Gaekwad shared their interest in education, and Parukutty and the Raja were taken on a tour of a few schools. They continued their travels from Baroda to Delhi travelling through Ahmedabad and Ajmer. At Ajmer, the royal couple visited the prestigious Mayo College that had been founded for the education of princes. Raja Rama Varma XVI and Parukutty arrived in Delhi in the early hours of 30 October 1916, the day of the conference, and were met with much ceremony by a representative specially appointed by the Government of India. Later that day, Raja Rama Varma XVI attended the conference with Parukutty, who was among the few royal ladies permitted to be present. Raja Rama Varma XVI made his presence felt and pledged to support the King Emperor in every way he could.[1] Later, at the party thrown by the Viceroy at the Viceregal Palace, the Raja and Parukutty used this opportunity to acquaint themselves with several other rulers. In these modern times, this would have been referred to as networking.[2]

The Raja and Parukutty, after the conference, visited places of historical importance in Delhi such as the Red Fort, the Old Fort and Humayun's Tomb, spending their evenings in the company of other rulers and important personages. On 6 November, they travelled from Delhi to Agra. At Agra, they marvelled at the pristine beauty of the Taj Mahal, the muscular strength of the Agra Fort and the classic city of Fatehpur Sikri. After that they went to Benares and bathed in the Ganges and prayed at the Kashi Vishwanath Temple. They travelled to Sarnath and paid homage to Gautama Buddha. They then went to Allahabad and dipped into the waters at the Triveni Sangam. From there they proceeded to Calcutta. At Calcutta, they spent a few days and then began their return journey to Madras, stopping on the way at Rambha in Orissa, Waltair

Maharaja of Baroda on a visit to Cochin

and Vijayawada. They returned to Cochin on 29 November 1916, having been away for nearly two months. Both Parukutty and the Raja agreed that this trip had been a great experience, as apart from meeting and entering into friendly terms with several princes, they learnt novel ideas of governance and gained an understanding of the people of the rest of India.

On their return, the Kochi Mahajana Sabha presented the royal couple a letter of praise,

> We were awed and filled with wonder as we heard of your detailed and marvellous travels . . . Getting a golden opportunity to not only visit historically significant places and community welfare organizations, but also getting to know and discuss issues of great significance with other kings and prominent members of the British empire, would indeed be of great benefit to us and this kingdom as a whole.

The Raja, in reply, said, 'This trip has greatly helped me in gaining new knowledge in the field of ruling policies and occupational possibilities. I am sure that this knowledge has heightened my hope for a brighter and better future for all of us.'[3]

13

Save and Splurge

During the initial years of his reign, Raja Rama Varma XVI wished to be seen as pro-British. Both Parukutty and the Raja felt this would be prudent while they established and strengthened their position.

The royal family at the Hill Palace

The British expected the rulers to support them in the First World War with men and money. Unfortunately, Raja Rama Varma XVI had no troops he could send to fight in the World War. In 1791, during the Mysore wars, the then East India Company entered into a treaty with the then Raja of Cochin, by which Cochin became a tributary to the East India Company. That Raja agreed to pay a subsidy of Rs 1 lakh per annum for protection.[1] By this treaty, the Cochin army had to be disbanded. At the time, the understanding was that there would be British troops stationed in Cochin for protection against invaders. However, during the abdicated Raja's reign in August 1900, in spite of objections, the troops were withdrawn as there was trouble in China. Even though at that time an assurance was given that another detachment would be sent soon, it was not.[2] When the First World War broke out, the Nair Brigade had dwindled to 25 officers and 244 men.[3] Yet, in spite of this, Raja Rama Varma XVI ensured that 581 combatants and 493 non-combatant recruits were sent to join the Imperial Forces.[4]

Just before the war several German dignitaries had visited Cochin and knew of its importance as a port. With no cannons or arms to protect the port, Parukutty and the Raja came up with an ingenious plan. Coconut trees were cut and these were placed around the harbour in such a manner that they appeared to be guns defending the shore. This was done so well that Lieutenant General Dixon, who was commanding the Southern army, appreciated the effort because he too had initially been taken aback and wondered how Cochin had acquired so many guns.[5]

The war was, to an extent, a godsend as it gave Raja Rama Varma XVI and Parukutty a chance to sweeten their relationship with the Viceroy with huge donations. Cochin contributed

Rs 1,426,880 towards war loans including stocks and bonds by the people of the state. The state also gave a donation of Rs 32,000 for war purposes and at the end of the war another Rs 100,000 was donated. In addition, there were many other cash donations such as a monthly contribution of Rs 4,000 for a period of four months; contribution for war expenses of Rs 100,000; a contribution of Rs 1,500 to the French Red Cross Fund; contribution for the banquet for Indian delegates of the Imperial War Conference of Rs 400; contribution to the Imperial Indian Relief Fund of Rs 20,000; contribution of Rs 16,100 to a day fund; and contribution to the Red Cross Fund, the Hospitalization Fund and others of Rs 712.[6]

When peace was declared on 13 November 1918, Raja Rama Varma XVI and Parukutty wanted everyone to know how ecstatic they were. Diwan Bhore was called and commanded to declare the day as a public holiday. Following that, on 17 November 1918, thanksgiving services took place at all places of public worship. This was to let the British know that everyone in Cochin was delighted with their victory. Two days after the peace treaty was signed with Germany on 28 June 1919, flags were flown, church bells rung and public holidays were declared. A public durbar was held at Ernakulam and the peace terms were read. Dharma kanji was given to the poor every day in Ernakulam and Trichur for a month.[7]

The British Government appreciated the efforts made by Cochin, and Raja Rama Varma XVI was made a Knight Commander of the Most Eminent Order of the Indian Empire—G.C.I.E. This was officially conferred on him at the banquet hall of the Government House in Madras by Lord Pentland, the Governor of Madras, on 24 March 1919.[8]

Rama Varma VI after being invested with the G.C.I.E.

The war had been a time of austerity and also a period when Parukutty had to focus entirely on Cochin. With the end of the war in sight and peace likely to follow shortly, Parukutty decided that the time had come to celebrate and what better way than with a thalikettu kalyanam for her two daughters. Her elder daughter Ratnam was fifteen and her younger daughter Vilasini was thirteen. The Raja fully involved himself in this ceremony. If fact, this was one of the reasons he cited to Diwan Bhore for delays in considering his various proposals.

Thalikettu kalyanam is a Nair custom which takes place once in ten to twelve years, when all the Nair girls between the ages of five and sixteen participate in a mock marriage ceremony. In this ceremony, a thali is tied round the neck of a girl by the so-called bridegroom. No cohabitation takes place, but the ceremony is followed by four days of feasting, at the end of which the so-called bridegroom leaves and has no further responsibility or obligation. This ceremony is an imperative for Nair girls to later enter into sambandhams. Parukutty wanted to make the thalikettu kalyanam a huge celebration. She invited all the eligible girls from the two branches of her Kuruppath tarwad in Trichur—the Vadakke Kuruppath and

Thalikettu Kalyanam of Ratnam and Vilasini

the Thekke Kuruppath.[9] Preparations began in February for the celebrations in May. A few days before the celebration, a huge pandal was erected at the east end of the Hill Palace. The main pillar was the trunk of a jackfruit tree. On the eve of the ceremony, rich silken carpets were placed on the floor. At the centre, there were several paras filled with rice, coconuts and areca nuts. Thousands of champak flowers covered the bamboo pillars and emanated a sweet fragrance.

On the morning of 8 May 1918, the girls who were to have the thalis tied were taken to the kolam for a bath in a procession to the accompaniment of music. After they had bathed, they were dressed in gorgeous kasavu mundus and wore their jewellery. They were then taken to a specially decorated room where a string was tied round their right wrists in a rite known as kaapu kettu or pratisara bandham. This signified a solemn resolve to go through with the ceremony.

At around 9 a.m., men with swords and shields arrived in a procession at the entrance of the Hill Palace. This included six enangars who were to participate in the ceremony. At the same time, men from the Hill Palace with swords and shields descended from the palace and met the procession. Then the enangars and those with them were escorted to the pandal with music from the uruttu chenda, the kuzhal, the elattalam and the pandivadyam. The procession went along a pathway of flowers strewn by a group of young women. At the entrance of the pandal, the enangars were met by the mothers or aunts of the girls who were to participate in the ceremony holding the ashtamangalam—the eight sacred articles. The six enangars had their feet washed by six young unmarried boys from the Kuruppath family. The enangars were then escorted to the centre of the pandal where there were six lighted lamps surrounded by paras of rice, banana fronds, coconuts and exotic fruits. After the enangars had been escorted into the pandal, Ratnam, Vilasini and four of their cousins were led to the centre by their maternal uncles. The enangars chosen for them tied the thali around their necks. After that, the other girls had their thalis tied. Thereafter, the girls along with the enangars were led to another pandal where an elaborate sadhya had been laid out for them. The thalikettu kalyanam was followed by four days of feasting and celebrations after which the enangars left.

It had been a huge festivity and all the leading Nairs had been invited. Over 10,000 persons were fed every day. The cost of the wedding was Rs 17,731 and an additional Rs 6,261 was spent on jewellery—an enormous sum.[10]

The Thampurattis were upset at the extravagance and the manner in which the thalikettu kalyanam had been conducted. They were appalled that a Nair ceremony of such a scale had taken place at the Hill Palace—a ceremony that they could not participate in. However, there was nothing that they could do as it pertained to the Raja's children and had the Raja's full approval. Parukutty, though aware of their anger, was unconcerned. More so as she remembered the many slights she had to bear when she first came to Thrippunithura.[11]

Shortly after that there was another joyous occasion that kept Parukutty very busy. Her eldest daughter Ratnam entered into a sambandham with Mr Ramunni Menon Palat, the son of Sir Chettur Sankaran Nair. Sir Sankaran Nair was at the time the only Indian member of the Viceroy's Executive Council. In view of his exalted position, many important personages attended from all parts of India, and Raja Rama Varma XVI and Parukutty entertained their guests with a lunch at the Durbar Hall in Ernakulam, and later at a garden party at the Hill Palace.

This alliance was also a very tactical move. Sir Sankaran, as a member of the Executive Council, ranked higher in precedence to the Governor of Madras, Rajas and Maharajas. He was also on excellent terms with the Secretary of State for India, Edwin Montagu. And he was recognized as the most powerful Indian at the time. The union gave Parukutty and Raja Rama Varma XVI an unassailable position.

14

For the People

One of the first acts Raja Rama Varma XVI and Parukutty upon assuming power of the Cochin state focused on was the expenditure of the kingdom. To address this, they appointed a committee of 12–15 officials and 7 non-officials to overhaul the system, identify weaknesses and to cut out wasteful expenditure. Parukutty chaired this committee. In the initial stages, she met the committee every week and discussed their deliberations in detail. Implementing the suggestions of the committee, Parukutty, in five years, reduced wasteful expenditure by 25 per cent.[1] In addition, she was able to route these savings for welfare measures, such as education, or for projects that brought in income, such as agriculture.

Education was for both Parukutty and Kunji Kiddavu a very significant matter. Cochin was recognized as the state that had the highest literacy rate in British India. Parukutty had not received much of a formal education. During her childhood, she had learnt Malayalam and music. Most of her learning had come from self-effort and from what her father and Kunji Kiddavu had imparted to her. Parukutty clearly regretted losing out on the benefits of a formal education and wanted to ensure that other girls did not miss out. Perhaps her emphasis on education came from the fact that her father had encouraged her in all her learning pursuits. He was the one who had realized that she should not be relegated only to household duties. Forward thinking and progressive in her views, she wanted girls to be as well educated as the boys. Incentives were given for the education of the girl child. More schools were opened. In the first four years of Raja Rama Varma XVI's reign, the number of students in Government-aided schools more than doubled, rising from 37,674 to 79,232.[2] Of these, 65.4 per cent were boys and 34.6 per cent were girls, who were studying in 1,883 aided and unaided schools. Scholarships and several incentives were also offered to those from economically challenged backgrounds. To encourage parents to send their children to school, free meals and a waiver of fees were offered. Several rural industrial schools were also set up to train students in the making of handicrafts and for training in specialized arts. An agricultural college was also opened. During Raja Rama Varma XVI's rule, the amount spent on education rose from Rs 375,520 to Rs 676,600, signifying the importance given to education.[3]

With regard to medical facilities, a five-year plan was drawn up—the intent being to open new hospitals, new dispensaries and offer better facilities. Special X-ray and ophthalmological departments were opened, new buildings were erected and it was ensured that nursing staff and doctors were adequately trained. A maternity hospital was opened in Trichur. Dispensaries were opened in towns such as Chittur. Sanitation was also looked into, and the roads and drainage systems were improved as these were prerequisites for healthy living.[4]

Having grown their wealth by buying farmland, Parukutty had a deep and abiding interest in agriculture. Recognizing agriculture as a huge source of income, she revamped the agricultural department. On her insistence, a central agricultural farm was created, and on this farm, experiments were initiated to develop crops that produced larger yields. Rural agricultural exhibitions were conducted to educate farmers on better methods of cultivation. To encourage cultivation, agricultural loans were provided to farmers.[5] Every effort was made to create a thriving economy.

A department of minor industries was started to deal with those industries that provided a living to a large number of artisans and handicraftsmen. The intent was to offer alternative means of livelihood to the labouring classes, to improve existing industries by popularizing new methods and introduce producers to newer markets. An industrial bureau was also started as a medium for the sale of local products.[6]

Apart from this, the salaries of all Government officials were increased substantially. In some cases they were doubled while in a few instances they were trebled. This was achieved by cutting down on wasteful expenditure, increasing taxes from new industries and through the growth in agricultural produce.

These initiatives spearheaded by Parukutty reinforced the faith that Raja Rama Varma XVI had in his consort's capabilities.

15

The History of a Harbour

Cochin emerged as a port on account of the geophysical changes that occurred as a consequence of the flooding of the Periyar river. This flood silted up the harbour of Cranganore,[1] the premier port at the time. Apart from this, a branch of the Periyar river that merged into the Vembanad Lake, the second largest freshwater lake in the world, opened wide its entrance from the sea to the lagoons. It also created a large piece of land—13 miles long and 3 miles broad. This new water passage provided safe anchorage and good shelter for ships. It came to be known as Kochazhi or the small harbour to distinguish it from the large older harbour at Cranganore. Eventually, Kochazhi was shortened to Cochin.[2]

On account of the safety it offered, merchant ships began to frequent the port from the beginning of the fifteenth century. The King of the Perumpaddappu Swaroopam, seeing the port's potential of procuring large customs duties that would accrue to him, shifted his residence from Mahodayapuram to Cochin in 1405, and thereafter, he came to be known as the Raja of Cochin. By 1440, the city of Cochin grew to about 5 miles in circumference around Mattancherry. Trading activities with the Chinese and Arabs also, gradually, grew over the years.

The earliest documented references to Cochin occur in the books written by the Chinese voyager Ma Huan during his visit to Cochin in the fifteenth century as part of the treasure fleet of Admiral Zheng He. There are also references to Cochin in accounts written by the Italian traveller Nicolò de' Conti, who visited Cochin in 1440. The port in its initial days attracted European merchants, predominantly Dutch and Portuguese, and later the British. The traditional port was near Mattancherry. This was the reason for the capital of Cochin and the palace of the Raja being at Mattancherry.

In 1869, with the opening of the Suez Canal, the distance between India and Britain was reduced by 4,500 miles. No longer did ships have to go around Africa to come to India. By the end of the 1800s, the Port of Cochin had grown, and cargo volumes placed pressure on the port's infrastructure.

Parukutty's focus was always on increasing the wealth and thus the prestige of Cochin. She realized that this could be accomplished by developing the Port of Cochin. Raja Rama Varma XVI's predecessor had made some efforts in this regard but had not been successful. By developing the port, revenues and customs duties could be increased substantially. Cochin was located at the western tip of peninsular India and all traffic to the east would need to pass via Cochin. Another important point was that there was no other deep harbour in British India between Bombay in the west and Calcutta in the east. This would also make the port of Cochin the premier port in south India and the port of choice for the export of spices, teak and other goods from south India. The First World War had already shown how important the port could be for movement of cargo and troops.

However, during the period when Bhore was the Diwan, even though the issue of developing the port was raised, the Government of Madras under Lord Pentland showed no particular interest. This was mainly because the project did not have the support of the Governor. The members of the Chamber of Commerce in Madras were connected with promoting harbours in other parts such as Tuticorin and did not think a harbour in Cochin was possible or essential. Several advised against it. These included Mr G. Robertson, who had designed the Madras harbour; Messrs Coode, Son and Mathews, who were the consultants for the Colombo harbour; and Mr Bell of Chittagong.[3] However, in 1918, on Parukutty's insistence, consulting engineers Sir John Wolfe Barry and Partners prepared the first comprehensive study of a harbour in Cochin. The report emphasized that the development should follow existing shorelines.[4]

Fortunately for Raja Rama Varma XVI and Parukutty, Lord Willingdon, an old India hand, having earlier been the Governor of Bombay, was appointed Governor of Madras on 10 April 1919 replacing Lord Pentland. The arrival of Lord Willingdon as the Governor of Madras changed the attitude of the Government at Madras. Parukutty rightly assessed that this change would be advantageous for them in securing British approval for the Cochin harbour project.

Within a month of his assuming charge, Lord Willingdon moved to Ooty, the summer capital of the Madras Presidency. Raja Rama Varma XVI and Parukutty too were holidaying at the same time at Springfield Palace in nearby Coonoor. Parukutty, sensing an opportunity, had the Raja's aide de camp Chondath Raman Mannadiar travel to Ooty, 15 miles away, to seek an appointment with Lord Willingdon.[5]

Lord Willingdon, a very social person, was more than happy to meet a ruler of one of the states that was part of his area of authority.

On the day of the meeting, Parukutty ensured that Kunji Kiddavu dressed regally as she wanted him to make an unforgettable impression on the Governor. The Raja was dressed in a flowing knee-length coat made of gold silk that had an intricate and delicate design woven into the cloth. This he wore over custom tailored dark trousers and a soft white linen shirt. On his head was placed his jewel-encrusted royal turban—the insignia of his kingship. Parukutty wore a brilliant white silk sari along with a simple gold chain. She did not want to draw any attention away from Raja Rama Varma XVI.

The night before, Gopalan Menon, the chauffeur, had supervised Venu and Achuthan, the footmen, as they cleaned and polished the beautiful Lanchester limousine that would be used for the visit. The deep-brown leather upholstery of the seats shone to perfection as did the large gold headlamps and the gleaming body of the black car.

After an early breakfast of fruits, idlis and freshly ground and brewed coffee, the royal couple prepared to leave for Ooty. It was a few minutes past nine when they drove out of the palace gates. As the 15 miles from Springfield Palace to Government House in Ooty would take them approximately an hour and a half, Parukutty and Kunji Kiddavu, after a quick recap of how they planned to approach the subject of the harbour with the Governor, settled back in their seats and quietly absorbed the tranquillity of the verdant Nilgiri Hills.

The Government House, built between 1878 and 1881 by the Duke of Buckingham, is on the western ridge of Dodabetta, the highest peak in the Nilgiris, and overlooks the sprawling botanical gardens. The estate occupies an area of 86.72 acres. The two-storeyed building built and furnished at a cost of about Rs 8 lakhs and built in the midst of ornamental gardens of 9 acres of land and a lawn of 3 acres, consists of over 50 rooms, including a large banqueting hall, ballroom, drawing room, several public reception rooms and offices.

On their arrival at the Government House, the royal couple was graciously met by Lord and Lady Willingdon at the entrance. Lord Willingdon was of medium height with a military bearing, having served for many years in the Sussex Artillery before entering the House of Commons. He was a sportsman, having captained the Eton cricket team, and had played for the University of Cambridge. His wife Marie, the daughter of Baron Brassey, was a very ambitious lady who wanted to do all that she could for her husband and their family. She was also very keen to know as much about India and its rulers as she could and was especially fascinated with their wealth.

Moving forward, Lord Willingdon extended a warm and welcoming handshake to the Raja. Parukutty was glad to observe that Lord Willingdon seemed impressed with Raja Rama Varma XVI's regal bearing. They were guided to a well-appointed drawing room. The room was large with seating set up for four groups. There were comfortable sink-in sofas, two three-seaters facing each other, with two single-seaters on either side. A heavy mahogany table, its surface polished to a mirror shine, was placed in the centre of each group of sofas. Lord Willingdon pointed to the seating section to the left of the doorway and gestured for Raja Rama Varma XVI to be seated. The Raja politely offered the ladies their seats while he chose a single seater for himself. Parukutty glanced around the room. All across the wood-panelled walls were giant-sized portraits of a succession of English sovereigns—Queen Victoria and King George V occupying prominent positions. She mentally made a note to commission a special portrait of Kunji Kiddavu on their return to the Hill Palace. The wall at the far end, instead of royal portraits, displayed a series of coats of arms. The high ceilings were bordered with heavily gilded designs, and in the centre was an ornate panel in glistening white. Once they were all comfortably seated on the soft, velvet upholstered sofas, the Governor thanked the Raja for taking the trouble to call on him. They exchanged pleasantries, while staff in white uniforms with gold and black cummerbunds and matching turbans silently entered with heavy silver salvers loaded with tea cakes, sandwiches and fresh scones with dollops of cream. Parukutty was delighted that her cup of steaming hot tea was made from local tea leaves—after all, there was nothing quite like a cup of Nilgiri tea with its delicious aroma and unmistakeable flavour. Once the tea and the small talk were over, Lady Willingdon asked Parukutty whether she would like a tour of the exquisite grounds. It was a lovely day. There was a cool breeze and a gentle nip in the air; yet the warmth of the late morning sun made it indeed a pleasant day for a walk. Parukutty readily agreed as this would give Kunji Kiddavu an opportunity to talk privately with Lord Willingdon about their plans for the Cochin harbour.

Raja Rama Varma seized the opportunity, while the ladies were away, to speak to his host at length on the harbour project. Lord Willingdon was an achiever. He wished to make a mark in Cochin, to contribute to its progress. Naturally, therefore, he was very interested in not only industrialization but in the development of ports and roadsteads.[6] He was aware that there had been discussions with the Madras Government and as he was keen to dispose of pending matters, he asked the Raja to have his men meet the Madras Government officials the very next day.

That evening, at the Springfield Palace, which was the Cochin Raja's residence in the Nilgiris, Parukutty called in the Sarvadhikariar Narayana Pisharody, the Diwan Mr Vijayaraghavacharya and the Chief Engineer Mr G.E. Browning, and impressed upon them the importance of the Cochin harbour project and charged them to ensure the support of the Madras Government. Mr Browning had closely worked on this project and was very excited. He promised Parukutty that they would secure Lord Willingdon's support.

The next day, Raja Rama Varma XVI, along with the Cochin contingent, met Lord Willingdon's team. In the meeting overseen by Lord Willingdon, they were able to arrive at an understanding. Raja Rama Varma XVI then invited Lord Willingdon to visit Cochin and see for himself what a magnificent harbour could be made there.

Parukutty during their visit had impressed on Lady Willingdon the beauty of Cochin. An excellent judge of character, she had noticed that Lady Willingdon had a penchant for the finer things in life. This could prove very advantageous to anyone who wished to persuade her or win her approval.

Lord Willingdon soon after his return to Madras transferred Robert Bristow, an Admiralty harbour engineer who was also qualified in architecture and surveying, to Cochin to look into the possibility of improving the harbour there.

Bristow was thirty-nine years old when he arrived in Cochin in April 1920. He had worked at the ports of Malta and Portsmouth as also the Suez Canal before he came to India. He was a bespectacled man prone to being fat, and was interested in music and rowing as opposed to the more popular English pursuits of hunting or playing polo. On his arrival at Madras,

Lord Willingdon had told him that Cochin was a marvellous place to have a harbour, and Lady Willingdon also mentioned that her husband was very keen on the harbour. This made him resolve that he would indeed make a good harbour in Cochin.[7] It was apparent from Lord and Lady Willingdon's enthusiasm that the royal couple had very clearly won them over.

Bristow observed,

> Cochin was in no two minds as to the effect of the completed harbour on the fortunes of the state. Cochin though physically in a backwater was one of the most literate states in India, and more so than any part of British India. Its Government, on the whole was progressive, stable and benevolent . . . It was not a rich state, and it believed that a port would help finances by bringing more trade to the state, possibly from new sources and by the creation of more industries in Cochin, which would be stimulated by the proximity of a first-class harbour and improved communications. Yet, Cochin State was not merely out to take. It was willing to rebuild the old railway, to contribute towards new ones, to advance the rest of the reclamation and to contribute its share towards the new harbour works. For a small state, not over-blessed with riches, Cochin ventured a good deal, and it is not surprising that its ruler resisted the cession of jurisdiction over an area which was prized so highly and formed so great an asset economically.[8]

The British Government wanted Travancore to be a working partner as Travancore was five times the size of Cochin and much wealthier. Additionally, Cochin was dependant on the hinterland of British India and Travancore for the commercial existence of the port. Travancore, on the other hand, was not inclined to support the project or help develop Cochin due to ancient rivalries. Therefore, they did not support the venture and Cochin paid for the entire development.

Lord and Lady Willingdon came to Cochin in October 1920. Lord Willingdon, after spending three days in the Cochin forests at Parambikulam, where he hunted, was met by Lady Willingdon, who had come by train to Chalakudy. At Chalakudy, Lord Willingdon embarked on the special train that had brought his wife from Madras and departed for Ernakulam, where he was welcomed by Raja Rama Varma XVI and the Elaya Raja at the station.

Parukutty and the Raja were intent on ensuring that the Willingdons had a favourable impression of Cochin. They wanted the Willingdons to see, apart from the backwaters and the harbour, the other historical sights of Cochin.

Later that day, shortly after tea, the Willingdons were escorted to the old Dutch Palace and shown the coronation and other state rooms and then were taken to the Jew town where they visited the old synagogue and met with leaders of the Jewish community. They were also shown scriptural rolls and other sacred objects of antiquity. The next morning, Lord Willingdon visited the harbour, and the Diwan and other officials showed him everything he needed to see. Lord Willingdon met Bristow and, after meeting with him, was convinced of the logic and benefits that a harbour would result in, and promised full support.

At noon, Raja Rama Varma along with the Diwan and other important personages made a state visit to Bolghatty Palace, where Lord and Lady Willingdon were staying. That evening, Lord and Lady Willingdon returned the Raja's visit and met him at the Durbar Hall, after which the Raja held a state banquet in honour of the distinguished visitors. In his speech while at Cochin, Lord Willingdon said that the Madras Government and Cochin were in complete agreement. He mentioned too that Robert Bristow, the harbour engineer, was doing a great job.[9] He also alluded to men and money given by Cochin for the Great War and that Cochin was a state the British Government could rely on.[10]

A state dinner

Just as Parukutty had assessed on her very first meeting, Lady Willingdon had very quickly gained a reputation of being avaricious. Her desire for acquisitions became such common knowledge that it was said that when rulers heard that the Willingdons were visiting them, they would bury their best jewels lest Lady Willingdon, on glancing at the valuables, commented on their beauty. Should she ever do so, the ruler was expected to immediately pack the said valuables and have them sent to her. It is rumoured that the Baroda royal family buried state jewels at the time of her visit. It was also said that she was always accompanied by a person with a bag with a very wide mouth. The bag used to be filled with pearl necklaces and other expensive baubles. The Willingdons were said to have furnished Rideau Hall, their official residence in Canada, with rare carpets, screens and objects of art that they had collected from India and China.[11] Mr Aravindaksha Menon, who was Raja Rama Varma XVI's younger son, was in charge of the preparations for the Willingdon's visit, and he mentioned that the preparations took a year. Wine and expensive liquor had to be imported. Furniture for the Bolghatty Palace, the guest house where the Willingdons stayed, had to be procured from France. Tongue-in-cheek, he wryly observed that if Lady Willingdon smiled and commented appreciatively on any item of furniture or some other object, it had to be packed up and sent to Madras.[12] The abdicated king in his autobiography says that the palace also bought old silver for Rs 30,000 from Lady Willingdon, suggesting too that this was an outrageous price.[13]

With Lord Willingdon's endorsement and the palace's support, work on the harbour gained momentum. Bristow became Chief Engineer of Cochin Kingdom's Port Department. From that point forward until the port's completion, he and his team were actively involved in making a greenfield port. He had an excellent rapport with the palace, and Parukutty asked the Diwan to help him in every way possible. In his frequent meetings at the Hill Palace, Bristow spoke of his belief that Cochin could become the safest harbour in India if the ships could enter the inner channel and kept Parukutty and the Raja abreast of the progress he was making.

Tea with Robert Bristow at the Hill Palace

Aravindaksha, Parukutty's son, who was now an engineer, was Bristow's main liaison with the Palace. Aravindaksha, being interested in all things structural, spent considerable time with Bristow, and he and his wife Malathy developed a close friendship with the Bristows.[14]

Bristow, after studying the harbour, was convinced that a port could not exist without deep water wharves with rail and road connections up to the wharf. He was assisted by a young harbour engineer F.G. Dickinson.

Aravindaksha Menon and wife Malathy Menon
at a garden party

The main obstacle in constructing the harbour was a massive rock-like sandbar that stood across the opening of the Cochin backwaters into the sea. Its density prevented the entry of all large ships—those requiring more than eight or nine feet of water. Those against the harbour project argued that it could not be removed. After some study, Bristow solved the issue by building granite groynes parallel to the shore that overlapped each other. These made possible automatic reclamation, and protected the shore from monsoon seas. With full backing from the palace, Bristow had the plans submitted to the Madras Government, and these were approved. A dredger was constructed, and between 1926 and 1928, the dredged material was used to create a new island of 3.2 square kilometres, which was named Willingdon Island in recognition of Lord Willingdon's support. It had been artificially created with the mud sledged out for the harbour construction from the Vembanad Lake.

Aravindaksha had by then become the Chief Engineer of the state. He helped Bristow in the movement of men and machinery in the construction of the harbour. After the initial difficulties were resolved, work progressed smoothly.

In 1932, the Maritime Board of British India declared the Port of Cochin as a major port and it was opened to all vessels up to 30 feet draught.

16

Inner Circle

Parukutty and Raja Rama Varma XVI realized that it was important that they have a Diwan whom they could trust and control, and who was entirely loyal to them. Though Mr Bhore, the abdicated Raja's Diwan, had a good rapport with the abdicated Raja, his first and foremost unquestioning loyalty was to his British superiors. On account of this, Raja Rama Varma XV had many a time faced absolute frustration at not being able to exercise his authority as the ruling prince. Making it even more difficult for him was the fact that the British Resident and the Diwan were often in cahoots as they were either British or deputed from the Madras Government. The abdicated Raja had observed, 'The attitude of the British Resident in my court gradually became more and more formal, and I failed to get that degree of sympathy and consideration as I used to get . . . The Residents were disposed to be more critical than helpful.'[1] The Diwan too tended at times to act without consulting the Raja.

The position of the Diwan was crucial. He acted as the liaison between the Raja and the British Resident and was able to exert influence through the Resident on the Government of Madras. The Resident was always a Britisher and was responsible for both Travancore and Cochin. However, as Travancore was five times the size of Cochin and far richer, he spent most of his time there. The royal couple knew that a British Diwan, especially one from the Madras service would have amicable relations with both the Madras Government and the British Resident. Therefore, it would not be very easy to influence him. Additionally, his loyalty would be to the British Government. He would in essence be not only the eyes and ears of the Government within Cochin but also its instrument. This is reinforced by the fact that in a conversation with Raja Rama Varma XVI, the Resident, Mr Forbes, advised him that as the Diwan was a member of the Indian Civil Service, it would be safer for the Raja to accept all the proposals and advice that the Diwan offered.[2]

Parukutty and Raja Rama Varma XVI did not wish to suffer the same difficulties with the Diwan as their predecessor. Hence, when the time came for Bhore to depart in early 1919, Parukutty and the Raja did not ask for an extension of his term. They had already assessed that Bhore was unyielding[3] and would cramp their authority and freedom to rule, which would result in several confrontations.

Parukutty and Raja Rama Varma XVI were clear that they wanted a Diwan of Indian origin as opposed to an Englishman. Apart from being unable to fully understand Indians and hence being hard to convince on projects relevant to the state, an English Diwan would be very expensive. Additionally, they knew and feared that English Diwans would be more on the side of the Government at Madras than that of Cochin's.

It was at this stage that the Government of Madras proposed that Sir Thiruvalayangudi Vijayaraghavacharya, an

Indian civil servant and administrator, be appointed the next Diwan. Vijayaraghavacharya was a slim, hawk-eyed, intense individual. A hard worker, he was a generous person of whom it was said that even cheats in the garb of beggars benefitted from his largesse.[4] He had worked in the Government of Madras as Secretary to the Board of Revenue and as Director of Industries. The Raja could not gainsay the Government, even though the appointment of the Diwan was his prerogative. The royal couple met with Vijayaraghavacharya and was pleased with his outlook and interests. They were happy that he was an Indian. Vijayaraghavacharya's focus was on developing industries in Cochin and he was keen to work with the palace on reforms. Thus, Sir Vijayaraghavacharya succeeded Bhore as Diwan.

By this time, the Raja had severe diabetes. As there was no proper treatment at the time, he spent long hours in bed or at an Ayurvedic treatment centre in Ollur, near Trichur. Parukutty knew she had to safeguard their position. She wanted no one to know that the Raja was seriously ill as this would be seized as an opportunity by his detractors to depose him. Among them were many princes who disliked her because they felt that she had been instrumental in reducing their allowances. If they knew the Raja was incapacitated in any way or ailing, they would petition the Government to remove him. In order to keep the Raja's ill health a secret, she ensured that all the rumours about his health were completely quashed. She also made sure that Raja Rama Varma XVI, whenever he was well, visited different parts of the state and made appearances at functions.

Parukutty, to safeguard her position, had, over the years cleverly guarded herself against detractors by surrounding herself with persons who were either family or intensely loyal to her. The conduit of information between the palace and the Diwan and the Resident was the Sarvadhikariakar. She had made sure that this position was held by Narayanan Pisharody, who was completely loyal to her. When the incumbent Chief Engineer retired, she had her son Aravindaksha Menon appointed to that position. Even though Aravindaksha was fully qualified having trained in the United States, her detractors were quick to allege nepotism. But this did not deter Parukutty.

At this time, there was also a vacancy in the Medical Services—that of the Civil Surgeon at Trichur. As opposed to promoting the senior-most assistant surgeon, Parukutty had a Dr Mannathazhath, who was the son of her cousin Mr V.K. Kochunni Menon, appointed to the post. However, when the time came to confirm him, the Chief Medical Officer Dr Coombes refused to pass him as medically fit for public service. Parukutty had this ignored and Dr Mannathazhath was confirmed. Though the matter was not of his concern, the abdicated Raja, once again voiced his protest. His protest was ignored, and this time, he was advised not to pursue this with the Government as it was an internal matter.[5]

17

Fires to Fight

The World War had taken its toll on Cochin. In early 1919, on account of the war, food had become scarce and expensive. Parukutty felt that their subjects, who had endured so much in the four years, had to be cared for. Her thought was that 'life should be made worth living not for the favoured few but for the mass of the people'.[1] Parukutty suggested the import of rice from Burma. This was done and distributed to the poor in towns and villages, well below the market rate. Maximum selling prices of local paddy and rice were also fixed to ensure there was no opportunistic pricing. Government depots were opened for the sale of rice to the poor. At Trichur, the Government opened a trial poor house to give kanji to the destitute. Fifty lakh rupees were spent in this manner.[2] Relief works were opened to give employment to the unemployed.

Parukutty realized that food scarcity could be an issue in the future too. Rice was the staple food of the state. The state produced about 10.5 million paras, while the annual consumption was 16.8 million paras. Meeting this deficit partially by procuring rice from other states and by importing rice from Burma was not the answer. A permanent solution had to be found. Parukutty discussed the food situation with the Raja. They decided to meet the new Diwan Vijayaraghavacharya, and together they concluded that the best way to solve this would be by bringing wasteland under cultivation. Reclamation of land from the backwaters was permitted. In addition, it was agreed that better methods of cultivation must be introduced to improve yields and that new sources of irrigation had to be constructed.[3] The cost of an acre of land was reduced from Rs 25 to Rs 13. Land was provided to the landless in the form of perpetual lease.[4]

Unfortunately, more misfortune befell the state as shortly afterwards, in Mattanchery, plague, cholera and influenza broke out. Medical aid was rushed to treat those diseased. Apart from this, Parukutty impressed upon Diwan Vijayaraghavacharya that to control this outbreak, it was important that apart from the patients, their families were also looked after well. Arrangements were made through the hospital to ensure that patients and their families were fed. Initiatives were also started to improve the housing of the poor and their water supply. Culverts were built to improve the drainage of the land.[5]

Parukutty's efforts were recognized by the British Government, especially the work she had done to alleviate grain shortage, to curb the plague and the initiatives she had taken in education and agriculture. She was presented with the Kaisar-i-Hind[6] medal by the King Emperor George V, and was, thereafter, addressed as Lady Rama Varma. She was also, in her own right, given the entitlement of a 17 Gun Salute—the first Indian lady to be, thus, honoured.

However, matters within the state were heading towards a sharp downturn. The spirit of nationalism and the non-cooperation movement had taken root in Cochin State. The secretary of the Congress party in Trichur was a cousin of Parukutty, Kurur Neelakantan Nambudiripad. On 16 February 1921, a meeting was held in Trichur to commend the bravery of Congress and Khilafat[7] members arrested in Calicut. Hearing of this, a group of Christians who supported the British disrupted the meeting and burnt chairs and benches.[8] Though the disruptors were not penalized, Neelakantan, along with another Congressman, N. Narayana Menon, was arrested by the Cochin Government under the orders of the Diwan and sentenced to six months imprisonment. This had occurred without Parukutty's knowledge or consent. This was the first political arrest in Cochin State. This arrest was surprising as those arrested had not held any demonstration but only conducted meetings by inviting leaders from other states.[9] The arrest began to cause discontent among the people.

Adding fuel to fire was the growing agrarian discontent against landlordism. The discontent exploded when the Congress leader C. Rajagopalachari visited Trichur and at a meeting he presided on 20 February 1921, congratulated those agitating and explained how important non-cooperation was. While the meeting was on, several supporters of the British Government created further trouble by pelting stones and disrupting the meeting. This disturbance created a tense atmosphere.

The Christians, who were viewed as supporters of the British, decided that there should be no meetings such as those conducted by the Congress. The Nairs and the Muslims disagreed. The result was that the Christians with reinforcements of members of their community from other parts of the state attacked the Hindus in Trichur.

Then, on 26 February, four Muslims from Ernad near Calicut were arrested and sentenced to six months imprisonment for refusing to abstain from attending political meetings and delivering speeches. This resulted in a large number of Muslims armed with knives and sticks gathering at a mosque in Calicut. The gathering was finally dispersed after a two-hour confrontation with the district magistrate and the police.

In this tense situation, on 27 February, the Christian and Ezhava communities took out a loyalty procession in Trichur with music, condemning non-cooperation and carrying a picture of the King Emperor. The Ezhavas stopped the music as ordered by the police on approaching a mosque but the Christians continued the procession to the mosque with music. This upset the Muslims and resulted in communal violence.[10] The marchers burnt four Muslim houses and shops, while the police remained mute spectators to the carnage. By 5.30 p.m. the procession reached a hospital and to an audience made up of prominent citizens, a lawyer gave a speech on the importance of devotion to the British.

Following this, the Muslims and Hindus banded as a group against the Christians.

The next day, people converged at the central maidan, Thekkinkad, where the situation was tense. To disperse them, the police started firing blanks at the crowd. The people responded by pelting the police with stones. A few prominent Hindus were able to stop this by asking the people to disperse.

However, the Christians felt compelled to show their allegiance to a foreign ruler—the British. They attacked homes and shops and destroyed bank records. They threw firecrackers filled with glass pieces and nails. Fearing for their safety, people began to flee from Trichur. About 1,500 women and children fled to other parts of the state.

In this tense situation, the Hindus came up with a plan. They sought help from the Muslims from Malabar. On receiving the plea for help, thousands of Muslims from Malabar, incensed at the arrest of Khilafat members, arrived in Trichur.[11]

On hearing this, Diwan Vijayaraghavacharya and the Resident arrived in Trichur as did the 75 armed British reserve police under the command of DSP Sawyer sent by the Madras Government.[12] By then, 1,800 Muslims took a procession that went around the town chanting 'Allahu Akbar'. At this tense time, the Resident and the Diwan held a meeting and with great effort were able to pacify the crowd. The Muslims from Malabar left the city after taking out a victory procession.

It was widely held that the Diwan supported the Christians against the Nairs. It was alleged by newspapers such as the *Malayalam Manorama* that the communal rivalries and the riots were a result of the policy of the Cochin State. The Diwan was blamed for supporting the Christians against the Nairs. *Kerala Chandrika* reported 'Not one or two or even 100 Vijayaraghavacharyras will be able to repress the non-cooperation . . . Which will only bounce up, the more they have pressed down.'[13]

The manner in which the riot had been handled stirred popular sentiment against the Government in Cochin. Parukutty, who was a Nair, was upset that Vijayaraghavacharya supported the Christians against the Nairs. The handling of the riot had been in accordance with the Diwan's and Resident's orders. The Raja had been bypassed completely in this matter.

Parukutty also saw the imprisoning of her cousin Neelakanta Nambudiripad as the work of the Diwan. This further strengthened her resolve that she should have as the Diwan someone who was not an outsider, but one she could trust, and who would be loyal to Cochin. She was now keen to have the Diwan replaced.

In order to make amends, a central relief committee was formed. Mobilization for public subscription for relief was also taken up. In Trichur, a relief camp was set up. At its peak, there were 8,452 persons in the camp, and they were provided with food and accommodation. In total, the Government spent Rs 17,995 for relief aid. Prohibitory orders were withdrawn. The state slowly limped back to normalcy.[14]

It had been a turbulent year for Cochin. Perhaps the only glimmer of joy for the royal couple was that the King Emperor through the Viceroy, Lord Chelmsford, in the New Year's Honours List of 1921—in recognition of the support of Cochin during the Great War and the reforms that were introduced along with its increased revenue—elevated Raja Rama Varma, through a sanad, to being a Maharaja. He, thus, became the first hereditary Maharaja of Cochin State. The ceremony commemorating this was held on 7 June 1921 and at this ceremony the Resident, Mr. Burkitt, handed him the sanad.[15]

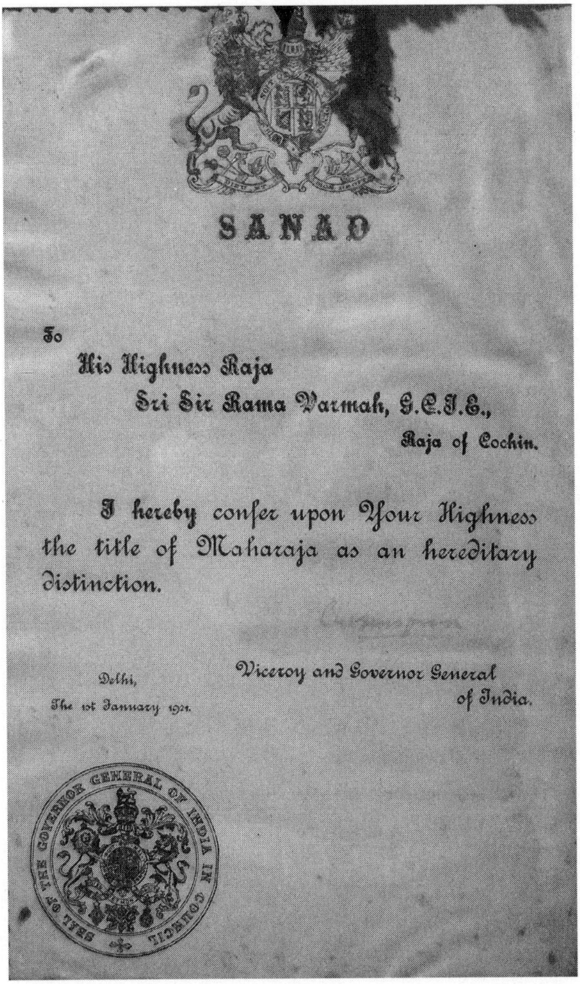
SANAD

To

His Highness Raja

Sri Sir Rama Varmah, G.C.I.E.,

Raja of Cochin.

I hereby confer upon Your Highness the title of Maharaja as an hereditary distinction.

Viceroy and Governor General of India.

Delhi,
The 1st January 1921.

SEAL OF THE GOVERNOR GENERAL OF INDIA IN COUNCIL

Sanad from the Viceroy making Raja Rama Varma XVI the Maharaja

Diwan Vijayaraghavacharya's term ended in 1922. However, towards the end, it was felt that as the Diwan, he had really achieved nothing in three years and his relationship with the Palace was not very good. Upon his departure no farewell party was thrown for him at the Hill Palace, as was customary.

Diwan Vijayaraghavacharya was succeeded by P. Narayana Menon.

Narayana Menon had worked in the Madras Government. He was a lawyer and born in Ernakulam in Cochin State. The Madras Government had no objection to his appointment. Parukutty believed that as he was from Cochin State, he would be loyal to the state and easier to convince and control. Through him, Parukutty intended to manage the executive branch of the Government.

18

Contingency Plans

The Maharaja's health was deteriorating. Parukutty was concerned for his mortality. She had from her childhood been acquisitive by nature. Perhaps, this desire to hoard and acquire as much wealth as possible could be traced back to the days when as a motherless child she associated the coins her father gifted her on his sporadic visits to her tarwad with security and affection. The young child had kept her stash safely as it held the promise of her father's return. As she grew, her understanding of money and financial matters grew too, but old habits die hard, and Parukutty till the day she died remained tight-fisted. Money represented to her filial love and security, and she could not bear to part with even a single pice.

She knew that should Kunji Kiddavu die, his personal property would be merged, as per custom, with the Palli-Ara Muthalpidi. True to her nature, Parukutty had no intention of allowing their personal wealth to vest with the ruler who succeeded Kunji Kiddavu.

Maharaja Rama Varma XVI's death would also entail Parukutty having to leave the Hill Palace, which would, thereafter, be occupied by the new Raja. Parukutty realistically assessed her position. She knew that on Kunji Kiddavu's demise, she would be destitute and forced to rely on the next ruler's largesse for her livelihood and that of her children. She was well aware of the fate of the widowed consorts of other rulers. She had no intention of being dependant on anyone. Parukutty was also aware that she was not particularly liked by the other members of the royal family—the Thampurans and the Thampurattis—and therefore, did not wish to remain in Thrippunithura after the Maharaja's demise.

She firmly believed that all the personal assets that Kunji Kiddavu and she had accumulated over the years should go only to their own flesh and blood, their children and, thereafter, to their children's children. Much of this wealth had been acquired before Kunji Kiddavu had ascended the musnad. She saw no reason for their personal wealth to be absorbed into the royal coffers of the Palli-Ara Muthalpidi estate. A proud woman, she was also very sure that she did not want to be beholden to either the successor to the throne or the Government. The previous Raja, Raja Rama Varma XV, was dependent on a pension from the Government. The palace that he resided in was built by the Government, and being the property of the Government,[1] would revert to the state on his demise. Parukutty was also aware of several cases of the partners of Rajas being in penury and on begging for assistance being granted a pittance, varying from Rs 60 to Rs 100 a month.[2] Parukutty was very clear that she would not allow this to be her fate.

She saw her task as twofold—to secure the assets that she and Kunji Kiddavu had jointly accumulated and to ensure that she had a house and enough wealth to live comfortably.

As she had been totally involved in propping up the state's economy and increasing its revenues, she knew that there was a lot of Government land that was not tilled or in any way developed. She proposed to the Diwan that she would take some of these lands over and develop them. Her proposal was that she would either buy these lands or take them on lease from the state. Apart from enriching the state's coffers, this would also result in regular income through taxes. The Diwan put this to the Revenue Secretary, who, after studying the proposal, agreed that this would be a welcome move and help the finances of the state. As a result, several thousand acres were either sold or leased to Parukutty. She then, through her own resources, developed them.[3] In this manner, she acquired property in her own name.

As she did not wish to continue residing in the royal town of Thrippunithura after Kunji Kiddavu passed away, she purchased four adjoining properties in Trichur near her old tarwad of Padinjare Shrambi, which jointly amounted to nearly seven acres of land. The central property had been the house of an earlier diwan of Cochin State, Sankunny Menon. This property had a one-storey building comprising several rooms on the ground floor and on the first floor; there was a large hall with a bedroom and a study with an adjoining long and wide veranda.[4] On the next property, she built herself a large single-storey ettukettu in the traditional style. In the front, as one entered, was a large hall, which was approximately 10,000 square feet in size. This hall was to be both an audience room and a retiring room, and was furnished with chairs and beds. It was divided into three distinct areas. At the entrance was an area for visitors awaiting an audience with Parukutty. This was segregated from the rest of the room by a small ledge about three feet high. The other side of the ledge was divided into two areas. On the left were couches and chairs. This was the area where Parukutty met visitors. To the right was a bed that was suspended from the ceiling with poles at the end of which were rings, permitting the bed to swing. There were also a few beds on which slept close relatives who were staying with her. To the right of the hall was a bathroom with a sunken bath and an open area leading to the lavatory. On the left of the hall was a large prayer room. In this room, there were three-feet-high clay idols of several gods and goddesses. In the prayer room, taking pride of place, was a pair of padukas that belonged to Parukutty's father. Quintessentially Parukutty was the steel vault at a far end of the prayer room. A long, very wide corridor ran the length of the hall, the prayer room and the dining room. The hall and the prayer room faced a courtyard or nadumittam. On the opposite side was the dining hall. The dining hall led to a spacious pantry and then to an open courtyard, to the right of which was an enormous kitchen. The kitchen had a storeroom in which all the food provisions were kept. To the left of the courtyard were the servants' quarters. This house was named Ratna Vilas, after her two daughters, Ratnam and Vilasini.

On the third property was a large house that had belonged to the ancient Komattil tarwad. This was also a massive house which she retained for her daughters. It was occasionally used as her guest house.

The fourth property comprised several small bungalows. These she used as residences for her managers, and also as the offices required to manage her vast holdings.

In this manner, Parukutty secured for herself residences that she owned that she could always move into should the Maharaja pass away. She would now not be dependent on either the Government or the Thampurans for a roof over her head.

As Parukutty had left her ancestral tarwad to reside with Kunji Kiddavu in Thrippunithura, she had no claim under marumakkatayam on her ancestral property or the right under that system to return to her tarwad.[5] This she felt was unfair to women.

Marumakkatayam is a matrilineal system followed by the Nairs of Kerala, whereby the family traced its descent from a common ancestress, and inheritance devolved through females. All members of the family resided together and were known as members of a tarwad. The Nairs also did not have monogamous marriages but sambandhams, which were consensual relationships.

Sambandham was a custom that permitted a man and a woman to cohabit and recognized a partnership between them. Men and women could both have several partners, and they could break away from them at will. As paternity sometimes was uncertain, women had property rights and the children inherited from their mothers and not their fathers. Fathers had almost no responsibility in bringing up their offspring—this devolving on the maternal uncles of the children. The Nambudiri brahmins encouraged this system as apart from the eldest among them, the others were not permitted to marry. They, therefore, had sambandham with Nair women, with the added advantage of not being responsible for the welfare and upkeep of any children who may have been born out of the relationship.

Although property and assets descended through females, the control of all the assets was in the hands of the eldest male member of the family—the Karnavan. He controlled these as though he was the sole owner. The Karnavan was supreme in the management of the tarwad properties and the other members—the Anandiravans—had no right to compel the Karnavan to give them a share of the property or even a decent education, however rich the tarwad was.[6]

With the advent of the British in Malabar, Cochin and Travancore, changes started appearing in the system.

Earlier, Nair men either stayed in their family tarwads or at the king's palace or their chief's residence as soldiers. With the disbanding of armies after the British established their supremacy, many joined the British service in varying capacities or took to the legal and other professions.

The introduction of schools and structured education also resulted in a huge change. Apart from Christians, Nairs were among the first to take advantage of Western education. They were thus exposed to Western concepts. Many attended colleges in Madras and began working in either cities like Madras or in provincial towns. The younger Nairs often took Government jobs. As they were in receipt of regular salaries, they were no longer dependent on the munificence of the Karnavans. This affected, in no small measure, the traditional Nair tarwad as it necessitated the youngsters leaving the ancestral houses to pursue their jobs in cities and other towns. As they were either salaried employees or professionals earning an income and not dependent on Karnavans for expenses, they did not contribute to the common fund, the argument being that as their earnings were through their own efforts and not from the tarwad properties or investments,[7] they were not obliged to contribute to the tarwad's expenses. These Nairs, as opposed to offering their income to the common tarwad fund, began to spend it on their wives and children. This changed the fundamental basis on which the tarwad system was based. These educated Nairs also elected to follow the Western practice of monogamy and began to live-in with their wives and children. They were against the traditional sambandham system. They argued that their earnings and their assets should devolve on their wives and children. One of the reasons for this breaking away was that some Karnavans abused their authority and as opposed to ensuring that all members of the family were treated equally, tended to pass on common property to their own wives and children. This prompted more and more young Nair men to seek an English education in order to better their job opportunities. They opted to work away from their ancestral homes, often because their fortunes were limited in the traditional household.

In order to prevent them from acquiring the necessary qualifications for jobs in the city, the Karnavans sometimes placed impediments. One of the methods they resorted to was by refusing to pay for the education. This caused further resentment. In these cases, often if the father was well-to-do, financial aid would be sought from the father. Thus, slowly patriliny gained ascendancy over matriliny. Friction between members of the tarwad grew. Soon, there were instances where educated Nair youths began to file petitions against their Karnavans for their share of the tarwad property.

The first legal change was initiated by Mr (later Sir) Chettur Sankaran Nair who brought this matter up in the Madras Legislative Council, resulting in the Malabar Marriage Commission being set up in 1891 to investigate the matrilineal system, and to recommend whether laws should be passed regarding the traditional method of marriage, family organization and inheritance. This council's submissions resulted in the Malabar Marriage Act, which was passed in 1896. This Act allowed those practising marumakkatayam to register a sambandham as a marriage. It was a liberal rather than restrictive law. Whether or not a relationship was registered was entirely the decision of the people involved in that relationship. Imbibing the demand of the educated minority, the Act made the husband or the father the legal guardian of the wife and the children, and the wife and the children were entitled to be maintained by the husband or the father, while retaining at the same time their right of maintenance from the tarwad too. The wife also had the right of maintenance, the right to half the property of the Nair husband if he died intestate and the right of alimony in the case of divorce for unjust reasons.

After the passing of this law, Nairs in Travancore and Cochin too began agitating for a change, especially as several of them had been educated in Madras and served in the Government. Many Nairs had even travelled to England and qualified as barristers, engineers, doctors and educationalists.

Consequently, in 1912, the Travancore Nair Regulation of 1912 was passed, which granted half of a person's self-acquired property to his wife and children and the other half to his sister's children. It, however, did not permit partition of tarwad property.

As these legislations in Malabar and Travancore involved property and financial matters, Parukutty had naturally been studying the changes taking place in these states. She was aware too that within Cochin State there was a growing demand for legislation, especially on account of the autocratic tyranny of Karnavans, who were known to favour their progeny at the cost of the tarwad.

Parukutty was a wealthy woman in her own right—a rarity in those times. She was also in no way dependent on her tarwad. Though she had no need or desire for her share of the wealth from her tarwad, she was not about to have her personal wealth absorbed into the tarwad either. Under the laws of that time, it was possible for a member of her tarwad to demand that after her demise, her personal wealth be merged into the tarwad. Parukutty was adamant that her personal wealth be left only to her own children and not to the tarwad. She was not about to allow the wealth that she and Kunji Kiddavu had accumulated through their own efforts to be given away either to the tarwad or the royal estates. What they had earned belonged solely to them, and it would be given to only those they chose to give it to. It was because of this that she wished for legislation similar to those passed in Malabar and Travancore to be enacted in Cochin too.

Very early on in Raja Rama Varma's reign, Parukutty had suggested to him that they invite Mr T.K. Krishna Menon, a lawyer and a member of a prominent Nair family, to the Hill Palace to discuss the drafting of a bill similar to that passed in Travancore and Malabar. Menon met Raja Rama Varma XVI and Parukutty at the palace on 1 April 1916.[8] The discussions were lengthy, and the Maharaja and Parukutty made in-depth observations about the intricacies of such legislation. The Travancore and Madras legislations were analysed and studied in detail. This was followed by another meeting in which T.K. Krishna Menon discussed the provisions that could be incorporated in the bill. A point that emerged during their discussions was that apart from Karnavans, the main opposition to the bill would be from the Nambudiri brahmins,[9] as they were till then able to enter into relationships with no responsibilities regarding the maintenance of the women or the children that resulted from the union.[10] Parukutty, known to be dogged and adamant, firmly impressed upon Menon that this should not be seen as an impediment.

Accordingly, a committee was formed to draft the bill on Nair marriages. Thereafter, Nair men and women were asked their opinions on the recommendations that had been drafted. Parukutty, who was extremely keen that this legislative reform be passed, kept in close touch with the committee in order to keep abreast of their proceedings. The committee met in different parts of the State—Trichur, Kunnamkulam, Vadakkancherry, Pazhayannur, Cranganore, Irinjalakuda, Chalakudi, Chittur and Nenmara. The details of the meetings of the committee were sent to the places well in advance, and Nair men and women were invited to give their views. Non-Nairs were also asked for their thoughts.[11] Parukutty travelled to both Trichur and Chittur when meetings were held there. Her personal involvement ensured that T.K. Krishna Menon kept her abreast of all the proceedings. This also resulted in her thoughts and suggestions on the matter being taken into consideration and incorporated. This was indeed very characteristic of Parukutty in that once she had decided upon a matter, she would pursue it relentlessly until it was completed to her satisfaction. This quickly earned her the reputation of being stubborn, aggressive and very domineering.

Finally, a bill was drafted and submitted to Raja Rama Varma XVI. In the initial draft, the concerns of the Nambudiris were addressed and no mention was made of their responsibilities towards their children. Parukutty was not in agreement and said so vociferously. The Raja concurred with her opinion and asked T.K. Krishna Menon, 'Why do you halt halfway?' T.K. Krishna Menon went back to redraft the bill.

Despite Parukutty's best efforts, the process of discussing and drafting the regulation was time consuming and slow, and took four years to finalize.

The Cochin Nair Regulation was passed only in 1920—Regulation XIII of 1095[12]—and it limited the powers of the Karnavan and legalized customary marriages. It declared that the wife and children were entitled to maintenance by the husband or the father.[13] It also made all husbands including non-Nair husbands—much to the angst of Nambudiris—responsible for the maintenance of their Nair wives and children. The regulation also made the Karnavan bound to account for his management to the Anandravans, and to give them separate maintenance based on the means of the tarwad and even a share of the tarwad property.[14]

This was the first social legislation in Cochin. This revolutionary Act brought about the complete disruption of marumakkatayam as an institution and freed the members of the joint family from the shackles of autocratic Karnavans. It cut short the rights and control of the Karnavan in the tarwad property. The wife and children of a husband or a father became the legal heirs of his property.[15] The Act also provided that when a non-Nair husband of a Nair female died, half of his property would devolve on the Nair wife, her children and descendants of predeceased daughters and the other half would go to his heirs, if any. The Act also gave rights to widows/children of Nair husbands/fathers. Polygamy was made illegal by this Act bringing about a complete disruption of the marumakkatayam system. Each and every member of the joint family was given the right to the tarwad property—in short, the right to seek a partition of the family property.[16] The responsibility of protecting the wife and children under the regulation fell on the husband, and this was effective for both the Nairs and the Nambudiris.[17]

The new legislation sounded the death knell of the joint family tarwad in Cochin State. This Act ensured too that Parukutty's properties would remain with her, and after her time, would pass onto her children and their children. By this legislation, she had safeguarded her personal assets from being absorbed into the tarwad and had instituted an important social reform.

Ironically, two decades later, her brother, and thereafter, her eldest and favourite son attempted to use Regulation XIII of 1095[18] that Parukutty had introduced in 1920 against her and demanded a partition of the family property on the grounds that it was tarwad property, and as members of the tarwad, they had rights to it. Parukutty went on to fight these cases in court and proved that these properties were not inherited, and hence, did not belong to the tarwad. They were bought from her personal earnings, and she had a right to dispose of them as she thought fit. She did win the case but it broke her heart. Parukutty had won the legal battle, but she had proverbially lost the war. Her brother, whom she had loved so dearly from the moment he was born, severed all relations with her. Later, her favourite son too chose to break away from the family and live apart.

These cases were fought several years after the Maharaja's demise. Yet, so great was the esteem Parukutty was held in that the cases were not fought in the law courts but at her home in Ratna Vilas. The judge heard the cases and the plaintiffs presented their arguments at Ratna Vilas. Parukutty was never required to leave the comfort of her home.

19

Vox Populi

The Cochin Rajas had long realized that it would not be possible for them to look after every aspect of the lives of their subjects and that they should empower the people too. In this, Cochin was a step ahead of the rest of British India as it had the highest literacy rate and the people were capable of being effective in managing affairs.

Raja Rama Varma XVI, as was noted by T.K. Krishna Menon, was a constitutional monarch,[1] and he and Parukutty were determined that power should be passed onto their subjects.

In 1914, just before Kunji Kiddavu ascended the musnad, the Cochin Village Panchayat Regulation was passed. Under this regulation, a limited number of panchayats were established in each of the five talukas of the State. These comprised four persons nominated by the Government from the leading families in the village and the fifth was the parvathiakaran—the village officer.[2] The Diwan Peishkar[3] controlled the panchayats with the help of the tahsildars. The panchayats were entrusted with the responsibility of improving public lanes and canals, cleaning and repair of public wells and tanks, maintenance and repair of minor irrigation works, maintenance of avenues and water tanks, rural sanitation, conservancy and prevention of epidemics and formation of cooperative societies.

Parukutty took special interest in the workings of the panchayat as she wanted to ensure that the villages were managed well. Since everything was being done satisfactorily, in 1917, six of the panchayats were given judicial powers and authorized to form courts and adjudicate petty cases in their domain.

It was found that the panchayats were also taking an active interest in public matters and were an effective channel in representing the concern of their people to the Government. As a consequence of the representations made, the Government took steps in promoting education, public health and sanitation. During the First World War, several panchayats managed rice depots and conducted relief work.

Seeing their effectiveness, more panchayats were established. As panchayats grew in capability, additional responsibilities were given to them. These included constructing roads and bridges, improving sanitation, etc.[4]

Panchayats were, however, restricted to the rural areas. With regard to towns, prior to 1909, there were no municipal or local boards in the State. The Public Works Department looked after the arrangements regarding sanitation and cleanliness of the towns. There were committees of officials and non-officials who supervised the sanitation in the more important towns such as Mattancherry, Ernakulam and Trichur.

Between 1909 and 1911, town councils or municipal councils[5] were formed in Trichur, Ernakulam and Mattancherry.[6] The intent was to introduce municipal administration in towns, and to look after and oversee conservation and sanitation improvement. The councils consisted of a president and a number of councillors—not less than six but not more than twelve in number. One third of the councillors were elected and the others were either nominated by the Government or elected by the councillors themselves. The president was either nominated by the Government or elected by the councillors.[7]

The town councils were made responsible for the construction, repair and maintenance of roads, watering of public streets and places, street lighting, regulating and controlling offensive and dangerous trades, registering births and deaths, housing and maintaining destitute orphans and the crippled, providing accommodation for the sick, constructing and maintaining public gardens, parks, libraries, museums, dharmsalas and rest houses, planting and maintaining avenue trees, providing markets and slaughter houses, arranging for sweeping and cleaning streets and constructing public lavatories.

As these involved expenditures, the councils were empowered to raise funds by levying taxes. They were also permitted to levy tolls on vehicles.[8]

Those elected and appointed to the councils were responsible and did their work diligently. This was monitored by the Diwan and the Palace. Parukutty and Maharaja Rama Varma during their frequent visits to Ernakulam, Trichur and Mattancherry were glad to see the improvements being made. As they wanted citizens to take on more responsibility, in 1921, local self-governance was further strengthened by Regulation XI of 1096.[9] The strength of the council was increased to a minimum of 15 members and there was no maximum. At least two-thirds had to be elected, the remaining one-third being nominated by the Government. The chairman of the council was to be elected by the councillors. Payment of taxes was made the basis of being elected to the council. There was, unlike other States, no gender disqualification and each of the councils had women councillors.[10]

The stage was now set to further empower the citizens of Cochin State, and Parukutty wanted them to take on more responsibilities and, thus, more power. Her intent was to create a legislative body in Cochin—an institution that did not exist anywhere else in India. Until then, all regulations emanated from the ruler with the blessings of the British.

Prior to the British ascendancy, Cochin had no written laws apart from the Dharma Sastras. Additionally, there were no courts to administer the laws. The Raja, as the fount of justice, as in other States, dispensed justice either directly or through panchayats that he constituted or through kariakars, who were in charge of the administration of taluks. With the advent of the British, the British Resident Colonel Munro established regular courts.[11]

After that the Government wanted to bring the general laws in line with that of British India, and consequently, several of the laws in British India were introduced in the form of regulations in Cochin.[12]

As the Rajas of Cochin were keen on reform, between 1893 and 1903 a Law Committee was formed consisting of a president and seven members. They were to draft laws as directed by the Diwan. This was not particularly effective, and so, after this committee was disbanded, the Diwan would, whenever it was felt necessary to legislate on a matter, require the Government advocate, law officer or anyone else he thought fit to prepare and submit a bill for consideration. The Diwan, after making whatever corrections or changes he thought were required, would then publish the bill in the Gazette for public criticism after which the bill would be submitted to the Government of Madras. On receiving the assent of the Government, it would then be passed to the Raja and with his approval it would become law and be called a regulation. In addition, the Raja, with the approval of the Madras Government, made proclamations and these too had the force of law.[13]

Later, another committee was created with two officials and two non-officials in 1916. This committee was later increased to 10 members in 1921.[14]

Soon after Raja Rama Varma XVI ascended the musnad, he and Parukutty decided that a group of prominent subjects should be formed to draft the rules for a Mahajana Sabha—a Council of the People. These subjects were to be from all over Cochin State.

Parukutty initiated the Mahajana Sabha asking T.K. Krishna Menon, the lawyer who had helped her with the Nair Regulation, to meet her and the Raja at the Hill Palace. Krishna Menon answered the summons promptly. On his arrival, he spent several hours with Parukutty. She briefed him on what was expected of him and the manner in which the rules should be drafted. She then took him to meet the Raja and apprised him of their discussion. The Raja was in full agreement and asked him to draft rules which could, thereafter, be discussed and refined.[15]

The first set of rules was drafted by 24 February 1916. This was brought to the Hill Palace. Parukutty went through the rules, made her comments on them and recommended some additions, and then told him to discuss the rules with some prominent citizens of the state for their views.

Shortly after that, on 22 March, T.K. Menon arranged for a group of eminent persons to meet—C. Achutha Menon, V.K. Krishna Menon, Varadarajan Iyer, D. Iyer and the Paliath Valia Achan. Menon told them of his meeting at the Palace and the draft rules that had been discussed and the brief that he had been given. This group again met on 15 April 1916 at the Banerji Memorial Club in Trichur to discuss the formation of the Mahajana Sabha and its constitution. During these discussions, it was agreed that every taluk, every community and every interest group must be considered and that the people should take a livelier interest in the development of the State. It was also agreed that the primary objective should be for a council for Cochin.

The committee met at Ernakulam, Trichur and Chittur and finally, a memorandum of needed reforms was submitted to the Palace on 17 July 1919.[16]

On 5 February 1923, the Government appointed a central controlling body at Ernakulam and district councils at Trichur and Chittur. The Palace gave premises for the council and it was decided that the Maharaja would be the patron.[17]

The council was inaugurated in April 1925 under the Cochin Legislative Council Regulation of 1923, which established a 45-member legislature in Cochin comprising 30 elected and 15 nominated members. The Diwan was the ex-officio president. Franchise, however, was limited, dependent on several factors including property ownership and allied qualifications. Besides general constituencies, there were also special constituencies created to represent specific classes such as those of landlords and planters.

The rules and regulations were similar to that in British Provincial Councils as were the powers but with one exception—that the president and deputy president were nominated by the Government as in other states in the Madras Presidency as opposed to being elected by council members as in British India.[18]

On Parukutty's insistence, Cochin became the first to nominate a lady to the council—the counsellor being Thottekad Madhavi Amma. This was possible because of the high literacy among women in Cochin. She was also the first woman to be a member of the legislature in India.

Maharaja Rama Varma XVI formally declared the Legislative Council open at the Durbar Hall at the Hill Palace. On this momentous occasion he said, 'As I have repeatedly announced on previous occasions, it has been my earnest desire to associate my people in an increasing measure with the Government of the State, and I feel happy that this desire has this day been fulfilled.'[19]

As it was expected to help the Government, the council was allowed to introduce bills, obtain information from the Government by asking questions, move resolutions and discuss and vote on the budget demands before the budget was passed. The council was also permitted to seek an adjournment of the House if it had some serious concern that required the Government's attention for immediate action.[20]

The first council president was Diwan T.S. Narayana Iyer. Shortly after, it began functioning. In 1926, two select committees were formed to examine issues placed before the council prior to their being passed as laws.

The council met at the Legislative Council building in Ernakulam that was offered by the Palace for its functioning.

Such measures initiated by the Maharaja and Parukutty won them the support of the people of Cochin State. Their focus on the welfare of the people and their constant endeavour to give them more responsibility was well appreciated by their subjects. The significant support of her subjects had even Parukutty's fiercest opponents tread carefully.

20

Wedding Bells

After the First World War, there was a weakening in the manner the States were governed by the British. After much debate, in 1923, it was decided that the British Resident be replaced by an Agent to the Governor General who would report directly to the Central Government in New Delhi and no longer to the Governor at Madras. As there were several of these Agents around India reporting, from various parts of the country, to the Governor General, the Central Government, inundated with reports, spent less time on Cochin's affairs as it was one of the smaller States. I.N. Menon, the abdicated Raja's son says, 'The Cochin durbar fully realising its opportunity, never failed to keep these new Agents to the Governor General in good humour.'[1] He adds that the Cochin durbar looked after them and kept them so happy that they were ornamental.[2]

The first Agent was Charles William Edgeton Cotton, a product of Eton College and Oxford. He had worked in Madras Presidency as an Assistant Collector, a Magistrate and as Collector of Customs and Director of Industries. Then, in 1920,

Agent to the Governor General
William Edgeton Cotton

Image courtesy: Manu Pillai

he was appointed the British Resident in Travancore and Cochin after the departure of H.H. Burkitt. In 1923, he was redesignated as Agent to the Governor General. He was a bachelor and quickly earned a reputation of being a dashing playboy. His exploits were so legendary that it was said, 'There is no bed in Cochin without Cotton.'[3] He was also very fond of alcohol. As he was a happy-go-lucky person, he did not get too involved in what was happening in the administration and let the Diwan do whatever he wanted, so long as British paramountcy was not threatened. This suited Parukutty very well.

However, the British Government came to be concerned about his ways and told him that should he wish to continue in this position, he must marry. Fortunately, soon after, on a holiday to Ceylon, he was introduced to Violet Mainwaring, daughter of Sir Philip Tatton Mainwaring, in Colombo, where Sir Mainwaring was posted. Cotton proposed to her soon after and it was initially planned that they would get married in London. However, as Cotton was the Agent to the Governor General, it was decided that a wedding in Trivandrum would be much grander, and they opted for this. The wedding preparations began in September. Unfortunately, Queen Alexandra, the mother of George V, passed away in November and a period of mourning was declared. Consequently, the

Image courtesy: Manu Pillai

Parukutty with Agent to the Governor
General Cotton

wedding on 12 December 1925 in Trivandrum was a subdued affair. There was no guard of honour apart from a few soldiers from the Nair Brigade.[4] Aravindaksha, Parukutty's second son, went as Cochin's representative. Prior to attending the wedding, he was sent to Madras to purchase a gold tea set from P'ORR and Sons. This magnificent set cost Rs 3,000.[5] This was debited to the Government of Cochin.[6] Additionally, when Aravindaksha Menon's travel allowance was also debited to the State, a furore was raised by the Legislative Council. It was protested that as this was a personal gift by the Maharaja and not the State, the expenses should not be borne by the State. In order to quell the uproar and fearing that Cotton might now refuse the gift, its cost was borne by Parukutty.[7]

Parukutty too was keen that all her children marry. Ratnam, her elder daughter, was married to R.M. Palat, son of Sir Chettur Sankaran Nair. Vilasini, her younger daughter, married Prince Rama Varma Thampuran of the Cochin royal family. He was also Maharaja Rama Varma's direct nephew as he was his sister Kunjikkavu Thampuran's son. Her elder son, V.K. Raman Menon, had married a girl from Travancore, Madhavi, who was exquisitely beautiful. Sadly, their wedded bliss was short-lived as Madhavi succumbed to tuberculosis within a year and a half of their wedding.

Her younger son Aravindaksha had just returned from the United States, where he had worked at General Motors. Parukutty was keen that he too be wed. It was decided that he would marry Malathy, the daughter of a well-known contractor V.K. Narayana Menon. Menon was a cousin of Parukutty. Astrologers were consulted, horoscopes matched and it was decided that the nuptials would take place at Trichur in May 1924. At that time, the Maharaja's health was on the decline. As per custom, Thampurans did not attend the sambandhams of their children. Hence, there was no fear of any questions being raised or of any suspicion being aroused regarding the Maharaja's absence from the celebrations.

Two days prior to the wedding, Parukutty and her four children boarded the Diwan's train to travel to Trichur where the wedding was to be held. Parukutty was happy to have this opportunity to meet all her relatives. Being controlling by nature, she made it a point to oversee all the preparations for the wedding, even though making the arrangements for the sambandham was entirely the bride's family's prerogative. The ceremony was to be at Pandyala—the residence of her cousin, the bride's father. The house was conveniently located in the centre of town and very close to the famous Vadakkunathan Temple. Parukutty, an extremely religious woman, naturally visited the temple as did many of the out-of-town guests and relatives.

On the day of the ceremony, as they were leaving the Trichur Palace for the wedding venue, a messenger approached Parukutty. He had been sent by the Sarvadhikariakar Narayana Pisharody. The moment she saw the messenger, her heart sank. Intuitively, she felt that something was very wrong. With some trepidation, Parukutty tore open the envelope ripping the royal seal. Her worst fear had come true. Kunji Kiddavu had suffered a diabetic stroke and was in a very critical condition. All of a sudden, her mind was flooded with memories of her very first meeting with Kunji Kiddavu. It had been here at Trichur at the Elaya Raja's palace. It was there that he had made her parade up and down the veranda so that he could get a better look at her. When after their sambandham he told her of this, she had feigned indignation and retorted that she would never have acquiesced to such an absurd request had she not been so young and naïve. They ended up laughing heartily about that incident. Now, Kunji Kiddavu was very sick and she was far away, feeling helpless and alone.

Pulling herself together, she glanced up from the note that the messenger had brought and showing absolutely no emotion she said, 'It is almost time for the muhurtham. Let us proceed quickly.' Parukutty was first and foremost the consort of the Maharaja of Cochin. Her son, the prince, was about to be married. This was not the time for a display of emotions. Besides, it was important that no one be made aware of the Maharaja's condition. Her duty, as the consort of the Maharaja, lay in being present at her son's sambadham until the ceremony was completed. The sambandham had to go exactly as planned.

Parukutty and her children proceeded to the bride's house. The sambandham ceremony was simple and over in minutes. Aravindaksha tied the thali around Malathy's neck. Malathy, as opposed to receiving golden gifts as befitting the daughter-in-law of a reigning Maharaja, received a simple pendent on a black thread which Aravindaksha tied around her neck.[8] The couple exchanged garlands, the pretty bride rising on tiptoe to garland Aravindaksha. Parukutty remained at Pandyala for just 15 minutes after the ceremony. After blessing the young couple, she sped off to the railway station citing affairs of the State. She left her son Raman and her daughters Ratnam and Vilasini at Trichur to partake in the wedding festivities, including the grand sadhya that had been laid out. Her abrupt departure was not questioned as Parukutty was known to be brusque. She boarded the Diwan's train and left for Cochin. Raman, Ratnam and Vilasini stayed for two hours at the bride's home, and then returned to the Trichur Palace. The Diwan's railway coach returned to Trichur the next day to take Raman, Ratnam, Vilasini, Aravindaksha and Malathy to the Hill Palace.[9]

On her return to the Hill Palace, Parukutty discovered that as a consequence of the stroke the Maharaja was in a coma. With some ministration, he slowly recovered the next day, but his speech was impaired. In addition, he had difficulty in walking. Parukutty knew she could not afford for anyone to know of his condition as that would encourage her enemies to petition the British authorities to oust the Maharaja from the musnad. Therefore, Parukutty made sure that no one other than a tightly knit inner circle met the Maharaja. In fact, even Malathy, Parukutty's new daughter-in-law said that she met her father-in-law only a few times during the eight years she stayed at the Hill Palace: One of these meetings was during Vishu, the Malayalee new year. The Maharaja gave her a gold coin and asked her a few questions.[10] Even her meetings with Parukutty were few and far between—on some important occasions and on festivals such as Onam and Vishu.

Despite her rather cold and indifferent behaviour with most people, Parukutty was very fond of children, especially her grandchildren—Sankaran, the son of her elder daughter Ratnam, and Malyni, the daughter of Aravindaksha. These children had unfettered access to all parts of thc Hill Palace. In addition, her brother's son Gopi lived at the Hill Palace as did his father. Another child who spent considerable time at the Hill Palace was her cousin's son Balan. Balan became world-renowned later in life as Swami Chinmayananda. These children were always up to some mischief. It was customary for a bugler to sound his instrument below the Maharaja's window every morning to awaken the Maharaja. Very often, when no one was around, the children would, armed with drums and flutes, go where the bugler would stand and make a cacophony of sound, jolting the Maharaja rather abruptly from a deep slumber. The children would then run away and hide. Parukutty was aware of their antics, but she had a soft corner for them and would either let it pass or admonish them only mildly. This encouraged them and often they would run helter-skelter through the palace halls, yelling and shouting much to the chagrin of the guards and other officials who wanted decorum in the palace.

Grandchildren Sankaran and Malyni at the Hill Palace

Though he was very ill, the Maharaja, at this stage was not totally incapacitated. He did cut down on his royal obligations and would only, when absolutely necessary, preside over important occasions. He also began to take a back seat to Parukutty in matters of the State. However, he continued to pursue his passion of Ayurvedic medicine, and would treat persons bitten by snakes or suffering other ailments, whenever he could.

On account of his difficulty in walking, the Maharaja was forced to use a wheelchair to move around. In order that he could travel comfortably, a motor car, an open topped Delage, was purchased. The car was customized so that the Maharaja's wheelchair could be easily wheeled in. Being an open-topped vehicle, it served Parukutty's purpose of ensuring that Maharaja Rama Varma XVI was clearly visible to his subjects. This, she knew, would allay any doubts and rumours of him being incapacitated. Hence, every evening, Maharaja Rama Varma would be driven from the Hill Palace to Thrippunithura and back. On occasion, they would venture up to Ernakulam. For these trips, he would wear his turban and his royal golden robes. Parukutty would accompany him. When she was unable to ride with the Maharaja, one of his daughters would go along with their grandson, Sankaran, who would also be dressed in royal robes just like the monarch.[11] This became a regular practice and was intended to show the public that Maharaja Rama Varma XVI was in good health and in full control of his faculties.[12]

Maharaja Rama Varma being driven in the evening to meet his people

As the Maharaja's health was steadily deteriorating, and Parukutty did not wish this to be disclosed, she felt that she now needed to get control of both the royal estates. Accordingly, in 1925, Parukutty had the Valiamma Thampuran estate merged with the Pali-Ara Muthalpidi estate, and formed the Valiamma Thampuran Kovilakam Trust through a proclamation. She entrusted the trust to a manager who reported to Sarvadhikariakar Narayana Pisharody.[13] By doing this, she gained control of both the estates.[14]

It was also in 1925 that Diwan Narayana Menon's three-year tenure was coming to an end. It had, for the most part, been largely uneventful. It was during his tenure that work on constituting the Legislative Council had begun, but came to fruition only shortly after his departure. Towards the end of his term, Parukutty began to feel that he was rather ineffectual. She wanted to have him replaced. Being a rather shrewd man, he was aware of this. He realized that as he had fallen out of favour with Parukutty, he was unlikely to be granted an extension. Throwing caution to the winds, he wrote a letter in November 1924 to the Agent to the Governor General, 'Keeping me on for another year does not commend itself to the consort and she wants to let me go at the end of my term and put in Narayana Iyer instead . . . On account of the condition of His Highness' health, the administrative machinery has I fear gone out of order.'[15] In this letter, he was quite clearly hinting that Parukutty was in complete charge of the Palace as the Maharaja was ill. In short, he was revealing that she was the de facto ruler.

After receiving Diwan Narayana Menon's letter, Cotton, on 6 December 1924, wrote to the Maharaja stating, 'Having regard to the state of your Highness' health, you may perhaps wish to avail yourself for [a] further term of Mr Narayana Menon's experience, and the fact that he is so doughty a champion of the Durbar's interest in the problems connected with the Cochin harbour scheme will make him difficult to replace until they are settled.'[16]

Parukutty, in order to safeguard her position, needed a Diwan who was as completely loyal to her as was the Sarvadhikariakar, Narayana Pisharody. Diwan Narayana Menon, though a local man, had been in the Madras Government and was in constant communication with the Government. She wanted a local person with no Madras contacts because she did not wish the Madras Government to be informed of all that occurred in Cochin.

Hence, Parukutty was not agreeable to extending Diwan Narayana Menon's term. A confidential letter from the Maharaja on 24 December 1924 to Mr Cotton clearly mirrored Parukutty's stance, 'I propose to appoint Rao Bahadur Mr T.S. Narayana Iyer, my present Chief Judge to succeed Mr Narayana Menon. I am glad to say that I am rapidly improving in my general health and there is less difficulty in walking.'[17]

Narayana Iyer was a lawyer and had been elevated as a judge at the relatively young age of 27. He was the Chief Judge of Cochin State. He was not experienced as an administrator and Parukutty saw in him someone who could be moulded to do her bidding.[18]

On 5 February 1925, Cotton wrote to Patterson, the officiating Secretary of the Government of India, Political Department.

> Mr Narayana Iyer is not a flyer and has no recent administrative experience. But his reputation is good, and if the selection is restricted to the officials in State Service, he is certainly the best man available. Narayana Menon was too steadfast a guardian of the State finances . . . no longer acceptable to the Maharaja's consort who is the de facto ruler

> of the State. It is to be presumed that she has hopes that Mr Narayana Iyer will prove more accommodating. The Maharaja is too old and too feeble to take any real active interest in the administration and the Diwan has to be constantly on his guard to prevent undue interference on the part of the consort, whose ruling passion is the acquisition of wealth for her already wealthy family.[19]

However, Parukutty was a fighter. She was not going to let her control be thwarted or Maharaja Rama Varma XVI be removed from the musnad. She ensured that Narayan Iyer succeeded Narayana Menon as Diwan.

21

Rumblings of Revolt

Narayana Iyer was appointed Diwan in 1925 after Narayanan Menon's term ended.

In the first fifteen years of Maharaja Rama Varma XVI reign much had been achieved.

When the Maharaja had ascended the musnad in December 1914, the state's revenue was Rs 46 lakhs with a surplus of Rs 12 lakhs. At the same time, there were also large loans that he had inherited as a consequence of the projects undertaken by his predecessor. It was also a very difficult period as the First World War had just started resulting in a dislocation of commercial activity. Additionally, there was the real fear that the British might annex Cochin and make it a part of Madras Presidency.[1] Creditably, in five years, Rama Varma XVI had repaid all the loans. By 1928, the State's revenue had risen to Rs 86 lakhs and the surplus to over Rs 70 lakhs. This had been accomplished in spite of liberal expenditure on education, agriculture and the development of industries. Salaries of Government officers had also been tripled.[2]

The agriculture department was reorganized several times. Agricultural farms were opened to test and develop better crops that yielded more. Agricultural loans were given to farmers in need. Interest on agricultural loans was reduced from 6.25 per cent to 3 per cent. Several irrigation schemes were undertaken. Improvements were made in the method of cultivation. By 1928, there were 5,985 acres under coffee and 13,878 acres under rubber plantation.[3]

The cooperative department was reorganized. There were 200 cooperatives and these were of enormous help to agriculturists and tradesmen.

Shortly after the Maharaja ascended the musnad, in 1915, the Tenancy Act of 1090 (1915) was passed. This was to grant fixity of tenure to those who took lands before 1885 on rent and to provide compensation to tenants for improvements effected by them.[4]

With regard to industry too, several industrial and technical schools had been opened. Facilities were also extended for industrialization after the First World War and companies such as Tata Oil Mills were established in Cochin. Loans were also granted to joint stock companies and industrial concerns such as Sitaram Spinning and Weaving Mills.[5]

Soon after the Maharaja's accession, a central bank was established. Its profits grew to Rs 11,367 in 1929 from Rs 68 in 1918.[6]

Apart from this, the Cochin Harbour Project had been taken up in earnest. The mud dredged to make a deep harbour had been utilized to develop the Willingdon Island. In 1928, the harbour was opened and shortly afterwards was declared a major port.[7]

The railways were extended and work was done on improving it.[8]

Parukutty had also focussed on education and by 1928, Cochin was the most literate State in British India. The allotment for education during this period was raised from Rs 5 lakhs to Rs 14 lakhs by 1928, and the total expenditure of the State for education rose from Rs 44 lakhs to Rs 67 lakhs.[9] The total spend on education was 18.7 per cent of the budget—Mysore and Travancore only spent 13.5 per cent and 17.5 per cent, respectively.[10] The amount in 1915 had been just 10..3 per cent.[11] The number of schools during this period rose from 295 to 715. Of these, 38 were high schools, out of which 11 were for girls.[12] There were also 950 schools imparting primary education. Primary education in vernacular was free and the number of children taught rose from 45,141 to 136,818. Several technical and industrial schools were opened. Children of depressed classes did not need to pay any fees. Muslims, Ezhava and other backward classes were required to pay only half the fees.[13] Scholarships were given to girls. A minimum qualification was prescribed for teachers. Baden Powell, the founder of the worldwide scout movement visited Cochin and inaugurated the Cochin chapter of boy scouts and girl guides.[14]

At the time of Maharaja Rama Varma's accession, there was only one second-grade college. By 1928, there were three first-grade colleges, of which one was for women. These were affiliated to the Madras University. In addition, primary education was made free in all schools. Private schools were given Government grants. To encourage the economically challenged communities to send their children to school, free meals, clothes and books were provided. The Provident Fund for teachers in Government-aided schools was started in 1918.[15]

Breaking away from tradition, Maharaja Rama Varma XVI had sent his sons abroad for higher studies. His nephews were also permitted to travel abroad for further studies. This was the first-time that the princes had been abroad for their continued education.

Parukutty Neithyaramma at the Hill Palace

Parukutty was keen on the upliftment of the depressed classes. These were those that lagged behind in wealth and education such as Kanakkans, Kudumbis, Arayans, Pulayans, Thattans and Velluvans. She improved the condition of the depressed and backward classes by setting an example. She established a depressed class development society, and this was managed by Aravindaksha and Vilasini, her son and daughter, who were assisted by a few of their friends.[16] Additionally, fields adjacent to the palace were opened to all classes of workmen. The Maharaja gave audiences to visitors of every class and community, so they could air their grievances.

In 1922, Parukutty arranged for a proclamation to be made allowing equal access to scheduled castes to temple roads and public places.[17] In this, Cochin was well ahead of its neighbours such as Travancore. Temples, at this stage, were not opened to the scheduled castes because of the unbending attitude of the Thampurans and the Nambudiris. Parukutty was, however, instrumental in the opening of the gates of the Royal City of Thrippunithura to commoners,[18] who hitherto were not even permitted entry into the royal city.

A club named the Lotus Club that accepted both Indians and Europeans of both sexes irrespective of their caste and creed, as members was opened during this time.[19]

Apart from agriculture, industry and education, Parukutty and the Maharaja were very keen on the well-being of their subjects. Several hospitals and dispensaries had been opened during their reign, and the number of persons treated had nearly tripled. A maternity hospital had been established. Additionally, X-ray machines were installed and medical buildings were constructed in Trichur and Ernakulam.[20] Medical aid and sanitation had also been focussed on and improved. Medical relief was given to those who could not afford it. Given the Maharaja's interest in Ayurveda, it was but natural that the practise of Ayurveda gained an impetus during his reign.

Parukutty was extremely keen on the progress of women. She felt that women, like herself, should come out of the shadows of their spouses and families. Women, she was certain, could make huge contributions to society, if they were permitted to do so.

In this connection, shortly after the Great War, she called in lawyer T.K. Krishna Menon, and asked him to arrange for a ladies association to be formed. The idea was for the ladies to acquaint themselves with all the happenings within the State, so that they could involve themselves, in the same way as men, in the recommendation of reforms. After speaking with Parukutty, Krishna Menon approached four prominent and progressive men—Ambady Sankara Menon, Justice Pallathil Narayana Menon, P.S. Narayana Iyer and Marayil Krishna Menon. They held a meeting in one of the rooms in the Ernakulam Public Library. The meeting resulted in the founding of Stree Samajam or Ernakulam Women's Association. After its formation, Krishna Menon informed Parukutty. To add weight to the idea of a women's association, Parukutty herself told Diwan Vijayaraghavacharya that she was fully supportive of the samajam and requested that a building should be made available to house the newly formed association. It was decided that Parukutty would be the founder. Parukutty invited V.K. Lakshmi Kutty Amma to be the Stree Samajam's president.[21] The Stree Samajam was started in March 1918.[22]

In 1920, the Poornathraseeya Temple went up in flames at 2 a.m. and the wooden structure of the temple, one of the gopurams and the thatched elephant sheds burnt down. Fortunately, and miraculously, the idol was saved. As the Maharaja was ailing at the time, Parukutty took charge of restoring the temple. Parukutty was very clear that the famous temple had to be rebuilt in the traditional way. She called several architects and conferred with them, and eventually chose Eachara Warrier. He redesigned the temple and built it in concrete, cleverly covering the structure with copper plates, wooden panels and granite tiles to recreate the traditional style. The side walls of the sanctum sanctorum were also covered with brass sheets inscribed with figures of gods and goddesses. While the roof was covered with copper sheets, the entrance to the sanctum sanctorum was covered with gold sheets.[23] It was uncanny that the temple she had once turned away from due to the slights of the Thampurattis was the very temple she had been called upon to restore to its original glory. Grateful for this opportunity to make amends, Parukutty whole-heartedly supported the restoration.

To preserve the history of Cochin, undertake the publication of manuscripts of historical importance and carry out research in Kerala's history, Parukutty established the Rama Varma Research Institute in 1925. The state appointed an archaeologist to oversee its work.[24]

Despite all the work accomplished during Maharaja Rama Varma XVI's reign and despite the fact that it was common knowledge that much of the expansion, improvement and introductions were Parukutty's initiatives, the Thampurans disliked her. The Thampurans resented her for the power she wielded. They were constantly petitioning the Government at Madras, their grouse being that with Maharaja Rama Varma XVI ill, the state was being run by Parukutty, Diwan Narayana Iyer being her tool. Of Narayan Iyer, T.K. Krishna Menon writes, 'He had no hint of any extraordinary gifts. His conspicuous gift was negative. It was his silence. Events always played the trump card for him. His luck was a legend, and he was loyal to the last breath of his life.'[25]

It was during Narayana Iyer's tenure that the rumblings among the junior male Thampurans peaked into a revolt. They resented that Parukutty and her children were living comfortably at the Hill Palace while they had restricted allowances. The base of their resentment was that they abhorred the fact that the state was being managed by a woman. Parukutty had not just infiltrated a hitherto male bastion; she had taken over the reins. This hurt their incredibly fragile egos. They felt humiliated that a woman, and a Nair woman at that, was managing the country.

Even though the Thampurans were envious and did not like her, Parukutty, as the consort of the Maharaja, ensured that the Thampurans and Thampurattis did not go wanting. New palaces were built to accommodate the ever-growing family. She introduced an allowance for the widows of the Thampurans, who until then had been left destitute,[26] following the death of their sambandhis. Parukutty ensured that the Thampurattis had adequate rice and other necessities, and that the children were well cared for.[27] With this and other reforms benefitting women, the Thampurattis gradually reconciled to Parukutty, especially because there was a visible improvement in the economy and in their own lives. But not so the Thampurans. Here was a woman breaking traditions, casting aside age-old norms, setting an example that other women would be quick to emulate. Parukutty travelled with her husband. Until then, when the ruler travelled, his consort stayed at home. Parukutty was by her husband's side during important discussions on matters of the state, instead of being concerned with household matters and looking after the children. Her opinion was sought by the Maharaja. She instructed state staff. She was changing the comfortable and familiar world of the Thampurans into something that they clearly opposed.

After some procrastination, five Thampurans[28] decided it was time to voice their indignation and outrage. They sent a message to Lt. Colonel C.G. Crosthwaite, Agent to the Governor General, on 10 October 1928, four days after the state had celebrated Maharaja Rama Varma's seventieth birthday, seeking a meeting with him at the Bolghatty Palace to have what they said was an informal talk on family affairs.[29]

Intrigued, Crosthwaite thought this over and agreed to meet them when he was next in Cochin.

The meeting took place in Cochin in February 1929. As Crosthwaite did not want it to appear as though he was siding with the dissidents, he invited Diwan Narayana Iyer for this meeting.

When Narayana Iyer received the invitation, he went directly to the Hill Palace and informed Parukutty. Parukutty with her ears to the ground and totally clued into what was happening in her state had been expecting some kind of a revolt from the Thampurans. She was aware of the petty jealousies and envy she had aroused. As was her custom, she informed Kunji Kiddavu of the impending meeting. Together, they decided that the Diwan should attend the meeting to know what transpired. This would enable them to ascertain the nature of the complaints the dissidents presented to the Agent to the Governor General. Parukutty knew that being forewarned was to be forearmed.

On the appointed day, Diwan Narayana Iyer arrived at the Bolghatty Palace just after 4 p.m. Shortly afterwards, Lt. Colonel Crosthwaite came in dressed formally in a white suit. He was of medium height, with brown hair, a receding hairline, a wide forehead, and a bushy moustache. The Diwan apologized for his early arrival mentioning that he would like to discuss a few state matters before the arrival of the Thampurans.

At around 5.30 p.m., the dissident Thampurans arrived by boat. On arrival, they were seated at the formal reception room. Lt. Colonel Crosthwaite and Narayana Iyer joined them shortly after they were seated.

The Thampurans were taken aback on seeing the Diwan. They immediately realized that whatever transpired in the meeting would be reported back to Parukutty. They looked at each other with much concern. Kerala Varma—eighth Thampuran—and the fifteenth Thampuran exchanged glances. However, as they had taken the plunge, there was no going back. They decided to stay the course.

After exchanging pleasantries, Crosthwaite asked the Thampurans what their concerns were. The eighth Thampuran mentioned that they had some family matters which they wished to bring to his attention and seek his advice. Crosthwaite replied formally that the request was unusual as the Government did not normally get involved in family affairs. However, as they had requested this meeting, he would hear their concerns.

The eighth Thampuran began by saying that they felt that the management of the palace funds, on account of the increase in number of Thampurans, should be entrusted to a committee of Thampurans. Their reason for this was that there were rumours that the fund was not being managed properly. They claimed that the surplus of the funds was being transferred to a miscellaneous account, which was contrary to the original intention. The Diwan immediately took umbrage to this, asking whether they felt that the Maharaja was mismanaging the money. The Thampurans were taken aback by the Diwan's retort and were a little nonplussed as they did not want to be seen as finding fault with the Maharaja. Crosthwaite stepped in and advised the Diwan to desist and let the Thampurans air their grievances.[30]

Their next concern was regarding the Amma Raja estate that had been taken over by the state with the approval of the Government of India during the time Mr Cotton was Agent to the Governor General. The seventeenth prince quickly interjected that they had no objection to this but that, in their opinion, the estate should be managed by the Senior Rani. He even stated that the prestige and prerogative of the Senior Rani was affected when the management was taken over by the Government. The prince contended that the princesses were reluctant to petition the Government regarding their difficulties. On the other hand, if it vested with the Senior Rani or a council of Thampurans, they would have no difficulty in voicing their concerns or grievances. The Diwan again dismissed this by stating that the appointment of a committee would be out of place, and that such a management would lead to difficulties.[31]

The unvoiced reason behind this complaint was that they felt that the funds managed by the state were under the direct supervision of Parukutty, and that these were being used for the benefit of Parukutty and her children.[32] Diwan Narayana Iyer dismissed this because under marumakkatayam law the Maharaja as the Karnavan could do what he wanted with the income.[33] Additionally, it was the Senior Rani who had asked the Maharaja to manage the Amma Raja estate.[34]

The seventeenth Thampuran then spoke about the Palli-Ara Muthalpidi. He admitted that these were crown lands and the Maharaja as the Karnavan could do what he wished with the income as long as the corpus was not touched. He said that he was simply emphasizing that the corpus should not be touched and that he was not bringing up anything else.[35] The Thampurans added that when the Maharaja was 'in full mental vigor, everything went on in an eminently satisfactory manner; that His Highness the Maharaja was the kindest of masters and that he was very much interested in the members of the Ruling family . . . His Highness by reason of old age and ill health was not able to judge for himself; that he was being influenced by others and that what was really taking place was not His Highness's judgment, but the judgment of others.' The Thampurans went on to the extent of saying that, 'His Highness was just like a child.'[36]

Another complaint was that the Residential Palace where junior Thampurans were educated had been under the control of a senior Thampuran. After the last Thampuran had resigned, the Residential Palace began to be administered by the state. The Thampurans asserted that no one else other than a senior Thampuran would be able to exercise the required control over the junior Thampurans. As an example, they mentioned that a junior Thampuran had been turned out of the Residential Palace for misbehaving. The Diwan pointed out that the palace had been under the wardenship of a senior Thampuran—the eighth prince—but that he had resigned and as a consequence, others not connected with the royal family had to be appointed. The eighth prince remonstrated that he had resigned because he resided in Ernakulam and had to entertain other members of the royal family when they visited. As his was an honorary position, this had resulted in him being 'out of pocket'. He added that when he submitted his expenses for reimbursement, he had been asked to submit his private accounts for scrutiny and to submit himself for an examination by officers appointed by the durbar. He sanctimoniously asserted that no self-respecting member of the ruling family should agree to this, especially as the position was honorary.[37]

The next concern raised by the Thampurans was that the princesses and princes were not given adequate conveyances to travel to Ernakulam for their education or other purposes. The two buses available for them were insufficient as they were also used for other purposes, and hence, were not always available. They were indirectly indicating that they should be allowed access to the Maharaja's vehicles. The Diwan immediately dismissed this by stating that they could not claim any conveyance from the Maharaja's garages.[38]

The Thampurans mentioned that Cochin House in Madras had been purchased for the residence of those Thampurans who were there to study. They stated that Rule 6 (vi) of the rules framed for the education of the young Thampurans in 1912 expressly stated that the Thampurans studying in Madras should reside in the residential quarters built for them in Tullochs Garden—Cochin House. However, they were not being permitted to stay there and had to rent accommodation. The Thampurans did have a point in this objection but the Diwan emphasized to them that it was the prerogative of the Maharaja as to who stays at the house.[39]

The Thampurans asserted that as members of the royal family they had to maintain a certain level of distinction and standard of living, but due to the small allowances given to them, they did not have the means to do so. It became apparent that the crux of the Thampurans' issues was money. They wanted access to more funds. During the abdicated Raja's reign, the estates had been mismanaged and were incurring losses. The reduction in their allowances had been made on account of being in excess of their requirements. The decrease in allowances was the primary cause of their ire. They were particularly upset that Parukutty, her children and their relatives, who were not members of the ruling family, were living better than they were and felt it was at their expense. They reiterated that if the Maharaja was well, they would have had no issue; but he was ill and that the country was being ruled by others in his name.[40] The Diwan disagreed and said the Maharaja was well aware of all matters.[41]

The sixth Thampuran then stated that there was no authority other than the Political Officer, meaning the Agent to the Governor General, who could interfere and set matters right when there was a real grievance. The others iterated that the need for intervention by Crosthwaite was indeed imperative.[42]

There was nothing Crosthwaite could do as these complaints were domestic matters and such complaints occur in all families. Additionally, this was a delicate matter and as it did not affect British interests, he was not inclined to act on it. He, therefore, with customary British courtesy told the Thampurans that he would look into these matters, knowing that he had no intention of doing so.

Though the Thampurans disliked Parukutty, they, out of fear and respect, never failed to address her as 'Parukutty Amma'. This was in spite of the customary practice of the Thampurans addressing Nairs by their name, as they viewed Nairs as inferior to them and classified them as Sudras. In fact, during Maharaja Rama Varma XVI's reign in Thrippunithura, even the Maharaja himself was referred to as the Neithyaramma's Thampuran—the consort's king. Such was the power Parukutty wielded and so immense was her aura.

Therefore, when the Diwan came and told her of what had transpired, she tossed aside the complaints of the Thampurans with indifference and scorn. However, she knew it to be a warning too and realized that this was the first of many assaults. She, therefore, began to take steps to guard herself.

It so happened that there was an English doctor from London visiting Cochin. The doctor was requested to meet and examine the Maharaja. The reason given by the wily British was that the doctor could meet and understand from the Maharaja the nature of his illness and ascertain and aid his recovery to full health. As Parukutty could not refuse this incursion, she acquiesced. The doctor came to the Hill Palace to examine the Maharaja.

Parukutty's grandson Sankaran Palat stated what transpired. Parukutty sent word that the doctor should visit the Maharaja in the evening. When the doctor arrived, he was taken to a room that was dark. It was explained that bright light hurt the Maharaja's eyes. Maharaja Rama Varma XVI was at the far side of the room and behind him was a screen. The doctor sat a little away from him. Though the visit was to ascertain the nature of the Maharaja's illness, Parukutty ensured there was no physical examination. Instead, the doctor was asked to speak with the Maharaja to determine his condition. Having no other option, the doctor asked him several questions, which were answered. Parukutty, in order to ensure that the Maharaja's impaired speech following his stroke was not misunderstood or misrepresented as a mental frailty, had a person sit behind the screen and respond to all the questions. The doctor was satisfied. As the room was dark, the doctor did not realize that it was not the Maharaja answering the questions.[43]

Following the examination, the English doctor pronounced that the Maharaja was an old man who tires easily but there was nothing wrong otherwise with him.[44]

The British after this episode wrote, 'Well that is that. We tried. We lost. Give up.'[45]

22

City Fit for a Consort

Parukutty knew that should Kunji Kiddavu pass away, she would be evicted from the Hill Palace. She had already made provisions for her residence when she built her Trichur residence—Ratna Vilas. She now decided that she would also work on improving the city of Trichur, which she had chosen as her place of residence. She decided to make Trichur the best city in the state.

During the abdicated Raja's period of rule, the Central Jail at Ernakulam had been transferred to a park in Viyyur,[1] near Trichur, to a location that had once housed the Trichur Zoo. That zoo had been closed in 1912 and the animals had been sent to Madras. Parukutty sold a thousand acres in Viyyur that she personally owned to the state for Re 1. Of these, 200 acres next to the Central Jail were utilized to extend the jail grounds. She wanted to use the remaining 800 acres to create a township—Rama Varma Puram—in honour of Maharaja Rama Varma XVI.[2] The intent was to create a university town similar to Oxford and to move the main colleges such as the Maharaja's College in Ernakulam to these premises. She also wanted to establish an engineering college, a veterinary college, an agricultural college and a medical college there.

The local jail in Trichur was in the heart of the town, alongside the Vadakunnathan Temple. The jail had been established there because, in the old days, before the British system of courts had been established, the Raja and the chief priest of the temple used to dispense justice outside the temple. Parukutty felt that it was inappropriate to have prisoners incarcerated outside a temple. As the Central Jail at Viyyur was now in spacious grounds, she relocated all the prisoners from Trichur Jail to the new jail premises at Viyyur and Trichur Jail was dismantled.

In May 1914, seven months before Kunji Kiddavu ascended the musnad, Raja Rama Varma XV had shifted the state museum from Ernakulam to Trichur. This was on account of the humid climate of Ernakulam being unsuitable for the storage and display of the exhibits. Once Kunji Kiddavu ascended the musnad, Parukutty began to take a special interest in the museum and the treasures being exhibited there. Around the same time, it was also decided that the zoo in the Krishna Vilas Palace at Ernakulam be shifted to Trichur, and that the animals be housed in a zoo next to the museum.[3] Accordingly, suitable buildings were built alongside the museum. Initially, the zoo housed just two pairs of sambar deer, five pairs of spotted deer, three pairs of wild boars, three rabbits and two pairs of Malabar giant jungle squirrels. As time went on, Parukutty had several snakes, a bear and other animals added, including a panther that was presented by Avanapparambu Nambudiripad.[4] Later a hyena and a lion from Bordeaux Zoo were obtained in exchange for a black panther.[5]

Parukutty had been told that Pataliputra, the capital of Chandragupta Maurya, was built around a mount 10 metres high. On the crest of this mount was a temple. The temple was on a sloping field of around 70 acres. Beyond this was the town with its shops and other establishments. Parukutty decided that she would model the city of Trichur along the same lines. Trichur was already blessed with an impressive temple on a slope. She created a maidan of 65 acres around the temple and built a circular road around it.[6] She, then, had the road concreted. To do this, she engaged a British company. Prior to the concreting of the road, she had culverts dug around it. Then concrete pipes were laid below the road up to the fields. Pipes that would feed rainwater to the culverts were also placed strategically in the maidan. By doing this, Parukutty ensured that the road would not, even in the heaviest monsoon, get flooded. The contract with the British firm also stipulated that they had to maintain the road for the next fifty years, failing which no other person in Cochin State would contract them for any work. Additionally, it was stipulated that only 70 per cent of the contracted amount would be paid on completion and the balance would be paid on assessing how well the contracting firm maintained and repaired the road.[7]

In addition, to ensure Trichur should not be starved of water, she had a large reservoir, the Peringavu kolam, built. The reservoir was 9.5 metres deep. The sides were secured with hardstone. A foot below the water level, permeable stones were placed. Steps leading to the water were built. Pumps were fitted to draw water, which was made available to the residents of Trichur through pipes. Trichur residents, thus, became the first in the state to get piped water in their homes. In other cities such as Ernakulam this facility was not available for another twenty years.[8]

Parukutty conceptualized a dam being built at Peechi, 12 miles away from Trichur. It was to supply water from there for the town and to harness the waterpower to give the city electricity. This, unfortunately, did not materialize during Maharaja Rama Varma XVI's lifetime; but later the Kerala Government, studying her plans and seeing the breadth of her vision, built a dam at Peechi and it is from there that even today the electricity needs of Trichur are met.

Parukutty had several impressive buildings built, including the town hall.[9] She had the roads widened and avenues of trees were planted. She transformed Trichur into a well-planned, modern city.

Her work was so highly appreciated that Ravi Achan, the son of a former Elaya Raja, says that several years after Maharaja Rama Varma XVI's demise, when he visited a home in Trichur, he saw a larger-than-life portrait of a woman placed prominently in the main room. When he enquired who the lady was on the assumption that it was an ancestor, he was told that it was a picture of Parukutty Neithyaramma. He then asked how she was related to the family. The people informed him that she was not related to them but that she was from Trichur. Such was the reverence with which she was held by the people of Trichur.[10]

More recently, Dr Alexander Jacob, Director General of Police, named the park at the Trichur Round as Parukutty Neithyaramma Children's Park. It is apparent that the people and the city of Trichur have still not forgotten her.

23

Fighting Fire with Fire

Parukutty was a formidable woman. As opposed to meekly awaiting what might happen next, she prepared herself to withstand the combined onslaught of the Thampurans and the British.

Kurur Nilakantan Nambudiripad, Parukutty's cousin, a prominent nationalist was elected President of the Congress Party in Cochin in 1925 for 12 years. Parukutty decided that she would ally with the freedom struggle. This was a masterstroke as the British had realized, in the explosive period after the Jallianwala Bagh massacre and the Punjab atrocities, that they should be more careful in their handling of Indians. More so as the famous O'Dwyer v Nair case fought at the court of the Kings Bench in London broadcast to the world the tyranny of the British in India.[1] There was a wave of resentment and anger against the British and a strident call for freedom. Parukutty, unlike other Indian princes who chose to be subservient to the British in order to protect their thrones, became a nationalist. The British were thrown out of gear by Parukutty's strategy. Should they now consider deposing Maharaja Rama Varma

XVI, it would appear as though they were casting aside a ruler because he advocated independence from the British for his country. Such a person would instantly be seen as a martyr, further inflaming the nationalists.

Parukutty Neithyaramma

As she was busy with affairs of the state, Parukutty encouraged her younger daughter, V.K. Vilasini Amma to write to Mahatma Gandhi.[2] She did, and Mahatma Gandhi, delighted to have such a supporter, kept in correspondence with her. Parukutty, in this manner, got her family involved in the freedom struggle.

Mahatma Gandhi came to Kerala in March 1925. The purpose of his visit was to stop caste discrimination and untouchability. He had a satyagraha at Vaikom in Travancore with the intent of opening the temple there to all Hindus. After that he came to Ernakulam by boat from Alleppey in Travancore and addressed the municipality. During this visit on 26 March 1925 while speaking to a women's organization he mentioned that in Cochin the royal family was wearing khadi and also spun yarn.[3] This was most upsetting to the British. An intelligence report sent to Delhi stated, 'The Hill Palace is the centre of nationalist activity and charkhas have been introduced to assist the weaving of khadi.'[4]

Gandhi visited Cochin again on 13 October 1927. During this visit, he was treated as a state guest and was offered the state guest house, Krishna Vilasam Palace, to reside in. Shortly after his arrival, Parukutty made a very bold move. She had earlier sent word to Mahatma Gandhi that she was keen to meet with him. Gandhi had offered to visit the Maharaja and her at the Hill Palace. Parukutty did not want Gandhi to know how ill the Maharaja was. She felt that if Gandhi became aware of his illness, the news would spread across India. Therefore, she put it to him that as Gandhi would be tired after gruelling tours, that she would visit him. Gandhi was most pleased and agreed.

Along with Diwan Narayana Iyer, Parukutty, wearing a white khadi sari that she had spun and bereft of any jewellery, called on Gandhi. Mahatma Gandhi had heard that Parukutty was a very autocratic and power-hungry woman who ruled the state with an iron hand and tolerated no opposition. This slightly plump lady in a plain khadi sari was entirely different from what he had imagined. On meeting the Mahatma, this powerful woman, in the north Indian custom, bowed down and touched his feet. Moved beyond words, Gandhi blessed her and gestured for her to sit next to him. She spent the next two hours with him. Parukutty told the Mahatma how much she believed in his cause and regaled him about all that was being done in her state.[5] She presented him with cheques and cash as a gesture of her commitment to independence. At this juncture, her cousin Kurur Nilakantan Nambudiripad, who was also present, endorsed all that Parukutty had said. Gandhi was both impressed and pleasantly surprised with Parukutty. Unlike in Travancore, here was a lady in power who was not only sympathetic but actually supportive of the national movement. Parukutty spared no efforts in winning Gandhi's approval. When she heard Gandhi's travel plans, she generously offered him the use of a state vehicle and chauffeur and had her younger son Aravindaksha accompany him while in the state.[6]

In his speech on 13 October 1927 in Ernakulam, Gandhi announced, 'On behalf of the Durbar, I received this morning a cheque of Rs. 500 from the Diwan Sahib and I also received through the consort of his Highness the Maharaja notes valued at Rs. 300 on behalf of the Maharaja's daughter Shrimati Vilasini Devi. What is more I have also received a parcel containing fairly well spun yarn by her sister Shrimati Ratnam, a portion of which was spun by the Consort of the Maharaja herself. Evidently this fact that khadi is favored by the Maharaja house is responsible for the favorable atmosphere that I see in Ernakulam. I thank the Maharaja for extending to me hospitality of the State, as also the gift he has sent me [*sic*].'[7]

At Ernakulam the next day, Gandhi stayed at Jadavji Keshavji's Rice Mill and addressed Gujaratis. When he went to Trichur he was again put up at the state guest house, Rama Nilayam, near the Trichur Palace. He held public meetings in the grounds and visited schools such as the Vivekodayam school.[8] He was escorted all through this trip by Aravindaksha and had a state vehicle to convey him.[9]

Later, when Jawaharlal Nehru, Kamala Nehru and their daughter Indira came to Trichur at the end of May 1931[10] on their way back from Ceylon, they rested at Mr V.K. Narayana Menon's house Pandyala[11]—Mr Narayana Menon being Aravindaksha's father-in-law and a cousin of Parukutty. Many years later, the elder daughter of Narayana Menon, Saraswathy, married Dr Sri Ranjan, the Vice Chancellor of Allahabad University and a family friend of Pandit Nehru. She recalled that soon after their wedding, they had invited Pandit Nehru to their home in Allahabad for dinner and when the Pandit came to know who her father was, he remembered Narayana Menon and his wife's gracious hospitality.[12]

By endorsing the freedom movement and establishing close contacts with the powerful Indians of the time, Parukutty had astutely made sure that it would be increasingly difficult to depose either the Maharaja or her.

24

The Opposition Unite

The resentment of the Thampurans continued as they felt that their complaints to Crosthwaite had not been addressed in any way. They resented the fact that the state was being ruled effectively by Parukutty and they continued to voice their grievances to the British. In the meantime, C.G. Crosthwaite was succeeded by A.N.L. Cater on 4 December 1929 as Agent to the Governor General.

Taking advantage of the change of guard, soon after Cater took over, the Thampurans voiced their complaints again. In a letter to Cater they wrote that they 'felt compelled to complain as they knew that things which were done in His Highness's name were done by others and that, so far as they knew the Maharaja had practically ceased to function, and that his powers and authority were being usurped by others . . . they prayed to be freed from a rule by people other than the legitimate Ruler'.[1]

This time round the Thampurans had collected much more ammunition for their attack against Parukutty. They had palace insiders work surreptitiously to provide them information, facts and figures. Then, in support of the assertions that amounts were being siphoned off by Parukutty, the Thampurans submitted a list of questionable expenditure that they had by stealth secured from one of the palace accountants. This list showed that in 1918, Rs 17,731 had been spent on the thalikettu kalyanam of the Maharaja's daughters and that Rs 6,261 had been spent on the making of ornaments. Then in the following year, Rs 10,500 had been taken as pocket money that had not been accounted for and Rs 4,290 had been spent on the wedding of the Maharaja's eldest daughter. They claimed that in 1920, Rs 30,000 had been spent in the construction of a house for Parukutty and her children. In following years, large amounts ranging from Rs 25,000 to Rs 30,000 were taken from the Palli-Ara Muthalpidi estate and were either used in the making of ornaments or as pocket money, ostensibly for the Maharaja.[2]

They claimed that two forests, Vellinkulangara and Mattathur, extending over 500 acres and assigned by the state to the Palli-Ara Muthalpidi, were leased to Parukutty at a rent of Rs 800. Parukutty sold trees valued at Rs 17,000 to a cousin of hers, V.K. Ammunny Menon, who in turn sold them to a Paul Lewis at a profit of Rs 4,000. The consort paid the Palli-Ara Muthalpidi just Rs 4,000.[3]

The Thampurans stated that income from the Palli-Ara Muthalpidi estate was for the benefit of the male Thampurans, and previous Rajas had never drawn on these estates. Rather, the Raja's personal properties were merged with this fund. In this case, since the illness of the Maharaja, large sums had been withdrawn from these estates. The compound adjoining the first prince's palace was the private property of the Maharaja. As opposed to merging this with the Palli-Ara Muthalpidi on becoming the king, as was the custom, the Maharaja had gifted it to Parukutty. She sold it to Palli-Ara Muthalpidi for Rs 13,000. Thereby, a property that should have by right belonged to the Palli-Ara Muthalpidi had to be purchased by it.

They also claimed that in addition to the amounts that they had enumerated, much more money had been taken. They maintained that lands leased to the Sarvadhikariakar's wife and other managers' wives were a cover for the consort. Further, the lands belonging to the Amma Raja had been sold to Parukutty. However, they could not provide proof for these claims.

They were also upset that scant courtesy was being given to members of the royal family by the Sarvadhikariakar. As an example, they mentioned that when the Viceroy Lord Irwin was to visit Cochin in December 1929, the Elaya Raja had requested Diwan Narayana Iyer, that in view of the small allowance that he received, the formal clothes he planned to purchase be paid for by the state. This request was conveyed by the Diwan to the Sarvadhikariakar to be placed before the Maharaja. The Elaya Raja was advised that as this was contrary to precedent, the request could not be entertained. The Elaya Raja, not being one to give up so quickly, wrote to the Diwan that the Maharaja had verbally agreed that the dresses should be paid for by the durbar. Diwan Narayana Iyer forwarded this letter too to the Sarvadhikariakar on 8 September 1929. On 23 October 1929, a letter was received from the Sarvadhikariakar stating that the Maharaja was 'greatly surprised to receive the misleading statement . . . that His Highness sanctioned the Elaya Raja's request with pleasure

Lord Irwin, Viceroy of India

* https://creativecommons.org/licenses/by-sa/3.0/nl/deed.en>, via Wikimedia Commons

when it was verbally made to His Highness in the course of a personal interview. His Highness has only to inform you the statement is not true and His Highness could hardly believe that His Highness, the Elaya Raja, would have permitted such a statement to be made in an official letter to the Diwan of the state . . .. His Highness is afraid that personal interviews are sought to be taken undue advantage of so as to embarrass the Diwan and to place His Highness in a rather awkward and delicate position.'[4]

The Thampurans wanted an enquiry into several transactions. Their submission was that in the normal course, they could have filed a suit. However, they were precluded from doing so as their Karnavan was also the ruler. Therefore, they felt that if the Government considered it expedient to permit a mentally defective ruler to retain his powers, then it was for the Government to devise some way of protecting them from being robbed.[5]

No matter how forceful the barrage of complaints, Parukutty was by no means easy to contend with. With regard to the allegation that Parukutty had built her residence from the palace funds, Parukutty, to clear her name, promptly presented detailed financials to account for how she had acquired the property and built her residence.[6] These could not be refuted.

With Diwan Narayana Iyer's term coming to at an end in 1930 and her enemies closing in on her, Parukutty needed someone who would be totally trustworthy and would not break under pressure. She had already successfully installed her second son-in-law Rama Varma Thampuran, who had married her younger daughter Vilasini, as the Diwan's private secretary, ensuring that there would be an ally in the Diwan's office irrespective of who the Diwan was. She was sure that he would keep her informed of all that transpired at the Diwan's office.

Her choice of successor to Diwan Narayana Iyer was her son-in-law Ramunni Menon Palat, the son of Sir Chettur Sankaran Nair. Palat was married to Parukutty's elder daughter, Ratnam. Mr Palat was a lawyer, a large landholder in Malabar and a politician. He had been the president of Palghat District Board and, thus, familiar with administration. He represented the West Coast Landholder's Constituency in the Madras Legislature. All things considered, Parukutty felt Ramunni would make an excellent choice as Diwan.

Ramunni Menon Palat (son-in-law), whom Parukutty wished to make Diwan

The British, however, were clear that they would not have an Indian as Diwan. Their stand was that Cochin had had two local men in succession as Diwan and that both had been subject to palace influences, particularly Diwan Narayana Iyer. The British took this seriously and concluded that no local man could possibly hope to stand up against palace influences.[7]

Cochin State did formally propose the name of Ramunni Menon Palat as the Diwan. However, the Government at Madras turned it down and appointed C.G. Herbert as the Diwan in 1930.[8]

C. G. Herbert, Diwan of Cochin

As Parukutty had aligned herself with the national

movement, it had become increasingly difficult for the British to remove the Maharaja from his position without causing a national outrage.[9] Adding to this was the fact that the people of Cochin liked, respected and were loyal to the Maharaja. They were happy that the economy was doing so well and that their lives had improved considerably during Maharaja Rama Varma XVI's reign. The British had ascertained that the citizens of the state would be 'gravely disturbed and indignant if any public affront were offered to the ruler such as enforced abdication, an upset to the established order of succession or any overt enforced delegation of authority.'[10]

The British knew they must tread carefully. Therefore, the policy they adopted was one of tactful intervention. The British wanted the Maharaja to follow the advice of advisors they appointed. Herbert, being fiercely loyal to Britain, was just the man they were looking for. Accordingly, he was briefed thoroughly even before he arrived in Cochin.[11]

The reason why the British were paying more attention to the internal affairs of Cochin and entertaining the complaints of the Thampurans was because of the growing economic importance of the port of Cochin. It was located on the direct sea route to Australia and the Far East, and was also an important place to embark and disembark for the whole of south India.

Herbert was a thin-lipped severe man with deep-set brooding eyes and strong likes and dislikes. A disciplinarian who lived by the rules, he did not particularly like native states and believed the whole of India should be governed directly by the British. He felt that the ruling princes were an effete group of wastrels, and the earlier they were disposed of, the better.

Herbert was in the Madras service and prior to actually arriving in Cochin, he was briefed thoroughly on the situation in the state, especially with regard to the Maharaja's health and the influence of Parukutty.[12] He, thus, came with biased notions—against the Maharaja and Parukutty. He was bent on reducing palace influences and he made great efforts to achieve this.[13] According to the Agent to Governor General Pritchard, 'Herbert was self-opinionated and heedless of the Maharaja's opinions and wishes, and eventually lost all favour with the Maharaja.'[14]

Herbert being an imperialist was appalled by Parukutty's nationalist leanings. He was determined to not only reduce her influence but remove her from power. And he was horrified of her support of Gandhi. The thrust of Herbert's fortnightly intelligence reports in the National Archives was that Parukutty was corrupt and as such influenced the whole administration and was a most dangerous threat to British interests in India. One of the reports said, 'The Hill Palace is the centre of nationalist activity and "çharkhas" have been introduced to assist the weaving of Khadi and that Parukutty's daughters are spinning khadi.'[15] Herbert said, 'Depose the Maharaja if we are not to lose Cochin to the clutches of the nationalists.'[16]

Mr Herbert finding the Thampurans as an ally in his attempt to depose the Maharaja was prompt in his support for them. In his comments on the matter of the curt reply of the Sarvadhikariakar to the Elaya Raja on his request for an allowance for formal clothes he states, 'Considering that this is a communication written by the Sarvadhikariakar about His Highness, the Maharaja's heir apparent, its tone could barely be more impertinent. There is not the least likelihood that the Elaya Raja would have stated that His Highness had verbally sanctioned his request if in fact His Highness had not done so. The incident is an illuminating example of the way in which the Sarvadhikariakar exploits His Highness' present condition and his own in the palace.'[17]

Maharaja Rama Varma XVI was well aware of the fact that Herbert had come with a bias against him.[18] Parukutty disliked Herbert on sight and was intent on thwarting him at all costs and at all times. She had the Maharaja overrule him at every opportunity with the intent of frustrating him to the extent that he would either buckle down and toe the line or leave Cochin. Herbert began to quite rightly believe that his recommendations were negated not because of any reason but to just frustrate him.[19]

Herbert confirms this in a note a year after he had assumed office, wherein he states that since assuming office, he has encountered serious difficulties.[20] Herbert was convinced that the cause of the difficulties was because the Maharaja was old and in bad health, and that on account of this, the state was being administered by Parukutty and the Sarvadhikariakar in the Maharaja's name. The problem he faced, as a consequence, was that under Cochin's constitution many matters could only be transacted under the orders of the Maharaja or with his concurrence. Herbert felt that the orders passed in the Maharaja's name were being done by others, namely Parukutty and the Sarvadhikariakar, who had taken over Maharaja Rama Varma XVI's place in the administration.[21]

Herbert thought long and hard on how he could break Parukutty and the Sarvadhikariakar's control over the administration. Finally, he concluded that the best way would be to break what he felt was an unholy alliance, and that was to remove Narayana Pisharody and appoint one of his own persons as the Sarvadhikariakar. This, he felt, would certainly clip Parukutty's wings. An opportunity presented itself when Ramalinga Ayyar, the Commissioner of Devaswoms,[22] reached the age of retirement. Herbert thought that he could move Narayana Pisharody into the position of Commissioner of Devaswoms. Thereafter, in the vacated position of the Sarvadhikariakar, he could place a confidante of his, Subramania Iyer, a lawyer.

Accordingly, Herbert wrote a letter to Maharaja Rama Varma XVI on 10 August 1931 stating that he proposed to appoint Narayana Pisharody as Commissioner of Devaswoms and suggested the name of N.S. Subramania Iyer to succeed Pisharody as the Sarvadhikariakar.[23] The Maharaja responded with his objection the very next day stating that Pisharody had been his Sarvadhikariakar for over thirteen years and had his complete trust and he wanted no change.[24]

On receiving this missive, Herbert wrote on 13 August that he would then have no alternative other than to extend the period of Ramalinga Ayyar.[25] Ayyar's term was extended by a further month.[26]

Though thwarted, Herbert was not about to give up. He made another attempt with Maharaja Rama Varma XVI on 10 September 1931.[27] The Maharaja was immovable and replied stating that he was unable to alter his decision and that he would like Narayana Pisharody to continue in his service.[28]

Herbert was nothing if not relentless and he wrote once again to the Maharaja. And yet again he received on 16 September 1931, the same response from the sovereign that he did not wish to have Pisharody transferred as the Commissioner of Devaswoms.[29]

Replying to the Maharaja on the very same day, Herbert wrote, 'It is in the circumstances impossible for me to properly offer to your Highness any other suggestion than these which I have already offered. Were I to do so I should be guilty of tendering to your Highness' advice which I did not believe to be made in accordance with the interests of the state. Should your Highness be unable to agree to the arrangements I have suggested, it appears to me, after active consideration, that the best course would be for me, with your Highness' concurrence, to explain to the Agent to the Governor General the situation which has arisen and request him to move the Government of India to withdraw my services.'[30]

Herbert's aggressive intent led Maharaja Rama Varma XVI, on 18 September 1931, to forward to the Agent of the Governor General, Lt. Colonel H.R.N. Pritchard, who had succeeded Cater, copies of the letters exchanged between Herbert and himself. He then went onto explain, 'I am sure you know that the post of Sarvadhikariakar is one of great personal trust and confidence and that person occupying it should be one whom I can allow free access to me and on whom I can safely rely. The person should be competent, trustworthy, honest and absolutely faithful to me in all matters including my domestic and private affairs. The present Sarvadhikariakar has been serving me as such for the last nearly fourteen years, almost the whole period of my administration and has been giving me entire satisfaction. I feel it is impossible for me at this stage of my life and health to go on without having by my side such an experienced and reliable man. I am unable to stand the strain of initiating another to the various duties. I am sorry we have to have this correspondence. I am sorry that the Diwan cannot suggest anyone else for Devaswom Commissioner.'[31]

In the meantime, Herbert had prepared a detailed note to Pritchard adding the complaints of the Thampurans to further strengthen his case.

Pritchard consulted the Government in Madras and it was agreed that this impasse could not be allowed to exist. Therefore, in early October Pritchard came to Cochin and sought a meeting with the Maharaja.

On arrival in Cochin, Pritchard met Herbert to ascertain from him Maharaja Rama Varma's mental condition and his ability to administer the state.[32] Herbert told him very categorically his views and his reasoning for wanting to replace the Sarvadhikariakar. Herbert also told him that the proposal to shift the Sarvadhikariakar would be met with stiff resistance as that would result in the total extinction of Parukutty's influence in state affairs. He advised that action must be taken to overcome her resistance.

On 12 October 1931 Pritchard met the Maharaja along with his Indian assistant. He then wrote a note to the Government of India wherein he built a case that Maharaja Rama Varma XVI was in his dotage. About this meeting, Pritchard stated that he had begun his conversation by commenting that the weather was warm, which apparently the sovereign did not understand. Pritchard then says that he mentioned that the rains the night before were heavy and enquired whether the Maharaja had heard the rain. Apparently, the Maharaja had not heard the rain. After these pleasantries, Pritchard told Maharaja Rama Varma XVI that the purpose of his visit was to understand the king's objections to the transfer of Narayana Pisharody, his Sarvadhikariakar, as Devaswom Commissioner. As the Maharaja did not answer him, this was repeated thrice and Pritchard even had his assistant translate this in Malayalam. The Maharaja then answered that he had objections. When asked what his objection was, the Maharaja said that Narayana Pisharody had been with him for a long time and that if a new person was appointed, it would take time to teach him. When Pritchard then took out a letter, the Maharaja wondered whether it was Herbert's and whether he had complained. Pritchard said that it was not Herbert's letter but the Maharaja's to him. The Maharaja then asked Pritchard whether he would insist on Narayana Pisharody's transfer, to which Pritchard replied that he would not at that time. He remarked that 'It was his solitary flash of intelligence throughout the interview'.[33] He also adds, 'It seems to me to be apparent that the Maharaja had been apprised beforehand of the nature of my visit being in connection with the Sarvadhikariakar and that he had been tutored; that he was mentally incapable of following the line of thought laid for him, and that it required a considerable effort on his part to appreciate at all that he was expected to discuss a matter pertaining to himself, Herbert and the Sarvadhikariakar . . . I carried away a strong impression that he would not suffer any disturbance of mind if the Sarvadhikariakar was transferred. I was certainly not able to detect that the prospect of parting company with the Sarvadhikariakar had evoked any mental distress or excitement.'[34]

Parukutty, after the exchange, felt that it was important to inform Pritchard that the manner in which he acted was incorrect. Therefore, taking the offensive, a letter was written purportedly by Maharaja Rama Varma XVI stating that he was sorry that Pritchard had thought fit to cross-examine him regarding his Sarvadhikariakar. He was unhappy and dejected as to how he could continue if the veracity of his letters was doubted.[35] In other words, the Maharaja was questioning as to how an Agent to the Governor General could doubt and interrogate a ruling prince. Pritchard had no other alternative but to backtrack and reply that he had not intended to cross-examine His Highness.[36]

On 18 October 1931, the Maharaja wrote to Pritchard that he had received his letter of 14 October and his assurances that it was not his intention to cross-examine the Maharaja. He candidly stated that he had felt uncomfortable regarding the nature of questions put to him.[37] Pritchard passed this letter onto Herbert. Herbert then wrote that the Maharaja may agree to delegate his powers of managing the family estates of the

Palli-Ara Muthalpadi and Amma Raja estates to his nephew and son-in-law Rama Varma Thampuran, who was also Herbert's secretary. He felt that this may not improve matters but would appear to be a more practical solution.[38]

However, no action was taken.

Herbert had by now reached the end of his tether and felt both impotent and frustrated. In order to force action, he wrote a letter on 24 December 1931 and enclosed with it, a note.

In the communication he stated, 'Certain serious difficulties have arisen in the administration of the state of Cochin. These difficulties had their ostensible origin in differences of opinion which occurred nominally between His Highness the Maharaja and myself as Diwan on certain administrative matters. In fact, however they are fundamental and raise the whole question of the present method of the administration of the state and the part His Highness takes in it. It has been evident to me since I took over as Diwan rather more than a year ago that His Highness owing to his age and ill health is incapable of taking any personal part in the administration. Under the constitution however many of the affairs of the state can only be transacted under the orders of the Maharaja or with his concurrence, and in spite of the present Maharaja's incapacity orders continue to issue in his name. Obviously, therefore these orders are passed on his behalf by others who have taken His Highness's place in the administration.' He then says that this in itself would not cause harm, if complete trust could be reposed on those who acted in the Maharaja's name. But in his opinion that was not so, as the administration was being handled by Parukutty and the Sarvadhikariakar, who were focused on their own well-being.[39] In his note, he mentioned that any proposal that would eliminate or change the Sarvadhikariakar would be resisted by Parukutty and the Sarvadhikariakar, as it would 'involve the total extinction of their influence in state affairs'. He felt action, therefore, would be needed to be taken to overcome this resistance. Whether Herbert's strong diatribe was to enable British influence and control in the governance of Cochin or for the welfare of the Thampurans and the people of Cochin is unclear. However, it might have well been due to the former reason, especially when one considers the clever manipulations of the British in gaining control in several other parts of India. It certainly did not reflect the opinions of the subjects of the state, who seemed quite content with the administration.

Herbert says that though it would be possible to appoint a Regency Council to carry on the administration, 'It has no advantage which is not possessed by the appointment of the Elaya Raja as regent.'[40]

He sums up the note by stating that intervention could be in two forms. The first would be by transferring the Sarvadhikariakar with a request to the Maharaja to not interfere in the administration in future. The other alternative would be to appoint the Elaya Raja as Regent. He adds, 'It would also be possible not to intervene at all but to let matters continue as they are till the Maharaja's death or until the situation becomes so bad that the intervention of the Government of India became inevitable.' He concluded by saying that if this last course was adopted, it would be better to let Parukutty and the Sarvadhikariakar choose their own Diwan to avoid friction in the administration. He added that his own continuance in the state seemed futile as any recommendation that he made would be overruled by Parukutty, not on its merits but because of personal reasons.[41] He ends it by saying 'One thing is clear. The time has now come when a definite decision has to be taken whether on the one hand to allow the consort and the Sarvadhikariakar to continue their interference in the affairs of the state; or, on the other to limit, if not terminate, that interference altogether.'

Herbert had literally, by this letter, given Pritchard a final ultimatum—do something. If not, there is no point in having a British Diwan, and hence, he should be relieved of his position as Diwan.

25

Checkmate

Pritchard, Agent to the Governor General, received Herbert's letter shortly before the new year, and he called Herbert to Trivandrum to discuss his concerns and to ascertain the extent of the Maharaja's inability to administer. Seeing how dogged Herbert was regarding a change being implemented or else being permitted to resign from service, Pritchard decided to put his weight behind Herbert.

Pritchard on 3 January 1932 wrote to Sir Charles Watson, who was the Political Secretary to the Government of India.

In this letter he mentioned at length the details of his meeting with Maharaja Rama Varma XVI on 12 October 1931 regarding the transfer of the Sarvadhikariakar. He recounted the difficulties he had in communicating with the ruler. In order to further establish his viewpoint regarding the Maharaja's mental incapacity, he wrote of another occasion when the ruler displayed mental deficiencies. The occasion was the presentation to the Maharaja of an official letter—a kharitas—from the Government of India to the Maharaja to inform him that Lord Willingdon was taking over as Viceroy from Lord Irwin. The kharitas is normally presented at a durbar. Pritchard states that he had, after his meeting in October 1931with the Maharaja, 'wondered how he would go through a durbar'. Pritchard mentions that it was these doubts that prompted him to write to His Highness enquiring, if he did not 'feel well enough to hold a durbar', that the kharitas could be presented by Pritchard himself at a call. The reply that he received was to the effect that the Maharaja would prefer to have the kharitas presented at the customary durbar. Pritchard in his letter commented, 'I did not anticipate that the Maharaja would be quite as irresponsible as he showed himself to be, and as far as I can judge, it would appear that his mental defectiveness is more profound than it was a year ago.'[1] Pritchard goes on to give a detailed account of the Maharaja's behaviour at the durbar held in connection with the presentation of the kharitas informing him of Lord Willingdon assuming charge as Viceroy from Lord Irwin. Pritchard writes, 'As I shook hands with him, he broke into a guffaw of inane laughter, which I must confess was somewhat disconcerting. I tried to enter into the usual brief conversation, but His Highness remained completely dumb until I asked whether he found the climate cooler in Thrippunithura than in Ernakulam. I must mention that we were then sitting in his palace in Thrippunithura. His Highness turned to me and said, "Where is Thrippunithura?" Then, during the Viceregal salute His Highness created some embarrassment by repeatedly calling out, "What is the firing for" . . . He didn't know what to do with my garland and finally his hands had to be raised over my head by the Diwan. When my wife received hers, His Highness again emitted a peal of laughter saying in a loud voice "Lady Sahiba". It was altogether an extremely undignified durbar.'

To press home the point of the Maharaja's incapacity, Pritchard informs that the Thampurans are in agreement with Herbert that Parukutty and the Sarvadhikariakar have eliminated the Maharaja from the administration and are looting the Palli-Ara Muthalpidi properties. He adds that Herbert had requested that 'a definite decision be taken as to whether on the one hand to allow the consort and the Sarvadhikariakar to continue their interferences or on the other hand to limit, if not to terminate it'.

Pritchard reaffirms Herbert's statement that there is 'not the slightest doubt that these two people have abrogated to themselves the role of ruler, and it is, I consider now essential for the Government of India to make the decision to which Herbert refers'.

Pritchard continues, 'It is impossible to allow the present situation to drift, and I consider that the interference of the consort and the Sarvadhikariakar must be terminated once and for all, and not limited. Otherwise, it is quite certain that the trouble will only be temporarily scotched, and that a recurrence of it will either entail the action which is, in my opinion, immediately called for, or Herbert's resignation of his office.'

He then adds that it would be a calamity if Herbert severs his connection with the state. He praises Herbert and says that should he leave, it would be nigh impossible to find another suitable British ICS officer to assume charge.

He then listed Herbert's suggestions, which were to insist on the Sarvadhikariakar's transfer, to request the Maharaja to not interfere in the administration and to appoint the Elaya Raja as Regent, giving him the management of the Palli-Ara Muthalpidi estate.

Pritchard opined that he did not consider the transfer of the Sarvadhikariakar would go far enough, as the consort would still be there and she might only temporarily stop issuing orders in the Maharaja's name. If she was debarred, there would no longer be anyone to pass on papers to the Maharaja. He also did not agree with Herbert's proposal that a warning to the Maharaja to not interfere with the administration would work as 'the Maharaja is an absolute cipher who has been totally eliminated'. He stated that if a letter of that nature was sent to the Maharaja, Parukutty would leak the contents to the people of Cochin and would undoubtedly, getting their support, have them protest that Maharaja Rama Varma XVI is 'by no means so deficient in intellect that he should be deprived of his powers'.

The suggestion Pritchard made was that the Government should prove beyond all reasonable doubt that the ruler was 'incompetent to attend to any affairs of the state'. The first step, therefore, would be to authorize the examination of the Maharaja by a European mental expert. He recommended that Dr Somervell of the South Travancore Medical Mission should be associated with the expert. The reason he recommended this particular doctor was on account of the fame and respect he enjoyed in 'these parts' and hence, felt it would be politic to have Dr Somervell endorse the findings of the expert.

He concluded that should such steps be taken and then the Maharaja relieved of his powers, it would not create a stir despite the consort's supporters' assertions of the Maharaja's mental competence to continue to administer his state.

With regard to Maharaja Rama Varma XVI's successor, Pritchard describes the heir apparent, Elaya Raja, as 'a wizened old man of about seventy who possesses a most unimpressive presence and who is very far removed from being the stamp of a man one would like to select'. He then added that should the Maharaja die the next day, the Government would have to recognize the Elaya Raja as the Maharaja. Therefore, if he was appointed regent with immediate effect, the experience he would gain in the transaction of state business would stand him in good stead. Pritchard then added the clincher that he hoped that, should the Elaya Raja be appointed regent, 'in view of his inexperience, he will prefer to rely on the unbiased advice tendered by Herbert, rather than allow himself to be swayed by the opinions of time-servers',[2] thereby clearly indicating that the reason he was supporting the Thampurans in ousting the Maharaja was that the British were unable to control Cochin as they wished to with Maharaja Rama Varma XVI and Parukutty at its helm.

On receiving Pritchard's detailed letter, the Political Agent Sir Charles Watson took it to the newly arrived Viceroy Lord Willingdon, who when he had been Governor of Madras had visited Cochin and supported the harbour project. Willingdon was fond of the Maharaja and had had a memorable experience in Cochin. However, Watson was insistent as Pritchard had made his position and his plan of action very clear. Watson did not want any problems to arise by not following the recommendation of the men in situ—Pritchard and Herbert.

Willingdon accepted, with some reticence, the recommendation of Pritchard. Consequently, Watson sent Pritchard a telegram on 29 January 1932 that read, 'His Excellency the Viceroy directs that you should arrange to have His Highness, the Maharaja of Cochin examined at once by a European mental expert with a view to ascertaining his mental condition and capacity to rule. Doctor Somervell should if possible be associated with the mental expert in this examination.'

On the very next day, a delighted Pritchard informed Herbert that Maharaja Rama Varma XVI was to be examined by a European mental expert along with Dr Somervell.[3] Wasting no time at all, on the same day Pritchard also sent a letter to the Government in Madras saying that the Viceroy had decided that the Maharaja of Cochin should be examined by a European mental expert with a view of ascertaining his mental condition and capacity to rule and asked whether they had an expert who could examine him.[4] On 2 February 1932, Somervell of Travancore Medical Mission confirmed to Pritchard that he would be willing to assist in the examination of the Maharaja. On 4 February 1932, the Madras Government replied to Pritchard stating that they had no European expert who could examine the Maharaja.[5]

As a consequence, on 9 February 1932, Pritchard sent a letter to C.W.A. Turner, Secretary to the Government of Bombay, Political Department. In that, he told him that the Viceroy had directed that Maharaja Rama Varma XVI be examined by a European expert with a view to ascertaining his mental condition and capacity to rule. He also advised that the Viceroy had directed that Dr Somervell of the South Travancore Medical Mission should be associated with the medical expert in this examination. As the Madras Government had no medical officer with the required qualifications, Pritchard enquired whether the Government of Bombay had anyone. He confirmed that the costs would be borne by Cochin.[6] Mr Turner confirmed on 22 February 1932 that E.C.A. Smith, Superintendent of the Central Mental Hospital, would be deputed. It was agreed then that Dr Smith would examine the Maharaja and that the expenses would be borne by Cochin State.[7]

As the Maharaja was in Madras, it was arranged that the examination would take place in Madras.

On 27 February 1932, Pritchard wrote a letter referring to the earlier letter of 22 February 1932 thanking the Bombay Government for deputing Major E.C.A. Smith to examine the Maharaja. However, as the Maharaja was apparently ill at the time, he said that he would advise them as to when Major Smith would be required. On 16 March 1932, Pritchard was advised that the charge proposed by Bombay for Major Smith's deputation would be Rs 300 per day for the period of his absence from Bombay plus travelling expenses.

On 25 March 1932, His Highness Sir Sri Rama Varma G.C.I.E., Maharaja of Cochin, died at 7.45 a.m. at Cochin House, Madras.

He was never subjected to any mental examination.

Mr T.K. Krishna Menon in his book *The Days That Were* writes that he met the Maharaja shortly before he left for Madras and that he was perfectly lucid and that there was no mental impairment. He says, 'It was said of him that he was in the worst state of health and unconscious even before he went to Madras for expert medical help. When certain interested parties were guardedly circulating this rumour in the state, I had reasons to see His Highness whom I found to be keenly alive to the affairs of the country, and who on one or two occasions even adversely criticised the answers given by the Government to the supplementary questions asked in the Council.'[8]

Parukutty too held that the Maharaja was in control of all his faculties while agreeing that he was very ill with diabetes.

The Thampurans had their personal reasons to oust Maharaja Rama Varma XVI from the throne. The British, eyeing the potential of Cochin harbour, wanted a docile ruler they could manipulate. Hence, they too wished to unseat him. Was insanity, therefore, the sinister solution the English came up with to remove an efficient and benevolent ruler from his throne?

Maharaja Rama Varma XVI foiled all his detractors and ruled for the full length of his reign and until his demise in 1932.

26

Afterword

Since the day that Kunji Kiddavu had ascended the throne, it had been Parukutty's endeavour to allow no one to snatch away his rightful position from him. She had made sure that at every stage of his rule, she outwitted his opponents and protected his crown. Maharaja Rama Varma XVI ruled till his death and Parukutty made sure that no one dethroned her Maharaja.

On Kunji Kiddavu's demise, Parukutty knew that she would have no further role in Cochin. She had prepared for this day. She did not wish to remain in Cochin in her diminished role. Nor did she wish to watch her many disparagers revel in her fall from power.

She applied to the Government for a passport for herself and her eldest grandson Sankaran. Sankaran was then just eleven years old. The Government was only too happy to grant it to her as they did not want her now to be working with nationalists, especially as she had a powerful following in Cochin.

Parukutty took Sankaran with her to Switzerland and enrolled him in the Institut Le Rosey near Lausanne. This move did raise several eyebrows as Parukutty had never been abroad and had no knowledge of French. It was also very unusual for a lady of her position to be travelling alone without a male escort. She stayed in Lausanne for two years, after which she went to England and enrolled Sankaran in a prep school in Bickley in Kent and then at Charterhouse, a renowned public school.

Parukutty loved cars and when in England, while visiting the Bentley showroom off Piccadilly, she saw a beautiful car. It had been custom-built for a raja who had apparently lost interest in it. The car was a very spacious one. The passenger area had been designed like a small room and accommodated a pull-out bed, a writing table and two chairs. Parukutty immediately purchased it and had it shipped back to her house in Trichur.

During her stay in Switzerland, she visited Paris and Belgium several times and had furniture, chandeliers and Belgian glass shipped back to India. A person who loved gadgets, she even had a wringing machine—to wring water from clothes after they had been washed—shipped back.

Back in India, Parukutty had no desire to spend the rest of her days in splendid isolation as the abdicated Raja had done. She bought two tea estates between Coonoor and Kotagiri, near the Cochin State Palace at Springfield. These were named RV, for Rama Varma, and Garswood. She also bought several houses in Coonoor—Homedale, The Grange and Range View—and began spending the bulk of her time in the beautiful Nilgiris.

Despite no longer being the consort of the Maharaja, her prestige and influence did not diminish. When co-author Raghu Palat's parents, Parukutty's grandson Sankaran[1] and her granddaughter Malyni,[2] married on 7 September 1946, every important person in the state including the incumbent Maharaja, the Diwan and all the important state officials attended the wedding at her home Ratna Vilas in Trichur.

In fact, it was almost a state holiday. Such was her power and eminence, and this remained undimished throughout her life.

Her son Aravindaksha, after his retirement as Chief Engineer of Cochin State, built a tea factory at Homedale and stayed with his mother along with his family. Parukutty's grandson Sankaran and his wife Malyni, who was also Aravindaksha's daughter, stayed half a mile away in the eight-bedroom sprawling bungalow, The Grange.

Parukutty with grandson Sankaran Palat and co-author Raghu Palat

While Parukutty spent the summer months in the exquisitely scenic blue hills of the Nilgiris, she would, as winter approached, venture down to the plains. Every year just before the icy frost set in, Parukutty would be driven in her Bentley to Ratna Vilas at Trichur. While there, her younger daughter Vilasini would keep her company. Trichur was Parukutty's hometown, and while in Trichur, she would meet all her cousins and well-wishers. Every day she would have a stream of visitors who came to meet her, and Parukutty enjoyed meeting them and kept an open house. Whereas in Coonoor she lived a semi-retired, quiet life, at Trichur she got a taste of life as it had once been. The city had several reminders of her past—the Parmekkavu and Vadakunnathan Temples, the Trichur round, the Thekkinkadu, and the statue of her beloved husband Maharaja Rama Varma XVI at the bus stand outside the Municipal Office. It always brought back happy memories, and she would often sit in Ratna Vilas's enormous drawing room with her great-grandson and reminisce about those 'good old days'.

Not one to let life pass her by, Parukutty remained active all through her life. She continued to take a keen interest in agriculture, an interest that had been inculcated in her by the late Maharaja, who had been passionately interested in agriculture. She would spend her mornings in her gardens, admiring the colourful blooms and instructing gardeners on what should be pruned or planted. At Trichur, she had had planted a profusion of pepper, cashew, sapota and mango trees, and in Coonoor, an abundance of peaches, pears and plum trees.

On 25 February 1963, at the age of eighty-eight, Parukutty died very peacefully at her home in Coonoor with her family right there beside her. In accordance with her wishes, she was cremated at the RV tea estate in the Nilgiris. Her son Aravindaksha and her daughter-in-law Malathy were by her side along with her grandson Sankaran Palat when she breathed her last.

Bibliography

BOOKS AND ARTICLES

Ananthanarayanan, G.H. *Shree Chottanikkara Devi Temple*. Mumbai, Bharatiya Vidya Bhavan, 2001.

Biju, M.R. *Politics of Democracy and Decentralisation in India: A Case Study of Kerala*. Delhi, Atlantic Publishers and Distributors, 1997.

Bristow, Sir Robert. *Cochin Saga—A History of Foreign Government and Business Adventures in Kerala, South India, by Arabs, Romans, Venetians, Dutch and British Together with the Personal Narrative of the Last Adventurer and Epilogue*. London, Cassel and Company, 1959.

Cochin Administration Report. 'Diwan Mr. Bhore's Administration under the Present Maharaja—His Highness the Maharaja's Installation. 1915.

Dalal C.B. *Gandhi 1915–1948: A Detailed Chronology*. Gandhi Peace Foundation, 1960.

Fawcett, F. *Nayars of Malabar*. Madras Asian Educational Services, 1990.

Gandhi, Mahatma. *Collected Works of Mahatma Gandhi*. Delhi, Ministry of Information and Broadcasting, Publications Division, 1958–1995.

Gangadharan, T.K. *Evolution of Kerala History and Culture*. Calicut, Calicut University Central Cooperative Stores Ltd, 2012.

'Hill Palace Thrippunithura'. Thiruvananthapuram, Publication Unit, Department of Archaelogy, Government of Kerala, 2004.

Iyer, L.K. Ananthakrishna. *The Cochin Tribes and Castes*, Volume I and II. Madras, Higginbotham and Company, 1909 and 1912.

Jacob, Dr Alexander. 'Central Prison Viyyur. Remarks on Visiting Central Prison on November 2, 2009'.

Jacob, Dr Alexander. *Trichur News*. 4 April 2020.

Jaykrishna. 'The Thrissur Riot of 1921'. *Varnam*. 19 September 2020.

Jeffrey Robin. *The Decline of Nayar Dominance, Society and Politics in Travancore 1847–1908*. New Delhi, Vikas Publishing House, 1976.

Keen, Caroline. *The Power behind the Throne—Relations between the British and the Indian States 1870 to 1909*. London, School of Oriental and African Studies, University of London, 2003.

'Kingdom of Cochin'. Wikiwand. Last accessed 3 January 2021.

Koji, Kawashima. *Missionaries, the Hindu State and British Paramountcy in Travancore and Cochin, 1858–1936*. London, School of Oriental and African Studies, University of London, 1994.

Lakshmi, Raghunandan. *At the Turn of the Tide—The Life and Times of Maharani Sethu Lakshmi Bayi*. Bangalore, Maharani Sethu Lakshmi Bayi Memorial Charitable Trust, 1995.

Manmadhan, Ullattil, Maddy's Rambling. 'The King's Railway'. https://maddy06.blogspot.com, 28 November 2009. Last accessed 15 March 2021.

Menon, C. Achyuta. *The Cochin State Manual*. Ernakulam, Cochin Government Press, 1911.

Menon, C. Kunji Rama. *Kochi Valliya Thampuran Thirumanasu*. Trichur, Mangalodayam Co Ltd, 1918.

Menon, I.N. *The Rajarshi of Cochin, Autobiography and Biography of Maharaja Sir Sri Rama Varma*. Trivandrum, Kerala State Archives Department, 2010.

Menon, T.K. Krishna, *Progress of Cochin*. Ernakulam, Cochin Government Press, 1932.

Menon, T.K. Krishna *The Days That Were (Memoirs)*. Ernakulam, Industrial School Press, 1949.

Menon, A. Sreedhara. *A Survey of Kerala History*. Chennai, S. Viswanathan (Printers and Publishers) Pvt. Ltd, 2003.

Menon, A. Sreedhara. *Cultural Heritage of Kerala*. Madras, S. Viswanathan (Printers and Publishers Pvt. Ltd, 1996.

Navrang India. 'Parukutty Nethyar Amma: A Maverick Consort of Cochin Ruler'. 18 April 2020. Available at http://navrangindia.blogspot.com. Last accessed 15 November 2020.

Nehru, Jawaharlal. *Jawaharlal Nehru—An Autobiography*. New Delhi, Jawaharlal Nehru Memorial Fund, 1982.

Paanchajanyaa, *Hindu Post*. 'Rajarshi of Kochi—A Misunderstood Dharmika'. 11 December 2016.

Padmanabhan, N. *Formation of Kerala Society and Culture*. Calicut, Calicut University, 2011.

Palat, Raghu. 'Nair'. Mumbai, Cortlandt Rand Consultancy Private Ltd, 2010.

Pillai, Manu S. 'The Asset Case of Kochi's Royal Amma'. *Live Mint*, 17 February 2017.

Pillai, Manu S. 'The Crown without a Head'. Live Mint, 30 June 2018.

Pillai, Manu S. *The Ivory Throne*. Noida, HarperCollins Publishers India, 2015.

Pillai, Manu S. 'The Paliath Achans: A Cochin Family That was Once Richer Than the Maharajas'. *The Hindu*, 21 September 2019.

Priyadarshini, S. *The Hindu*. 'A Century in Service'. 7 February 2019.

Ramachandran, K.S. 'Hamlet in Monsoon—Rajarshi Rama Varma: The Untold Story'. 16 January 2015. Available at http://hamletram.blogspot.com, last accessed 19 June 2021.

Rejikumar, J. (ed.). 'Archives Treasury'. Trivandrum, Kerala State Archives Department, 2010.

'Report on the Administration of Cochin'. For various years from 1906–1907 to 1922–1923. Ernakulam, Cochin Government.

Ruling Princes and Chiefs of India: A Brief Historical Record of the Leading Princes and Chiefs in India together with a Description of Their Territories and Methods of Administration. Lahore, Pakistan, Sang-E-Meet Publications, reprinted 2005.

Shodganga. 'Architecture and Town Planning in Kochi'. Available at https://shodhganga.inflibnet.ac.in. Last accessed 23 May 2021.

Shodganga. 'Education and Literary Developments in Kochi'. Available at https://shodhganga.inflibnet.ac.in. Last accessed 23 May 2021.

Shodganga. 'Land Reform Legislation'. Available at https://shodhganga.inflibnet.ac.in. Last accessed 23 May 2021.

Shodganga. 'Nair Matriliny: An Overview'. Available at https://shodhganga.inflibnet.ac.in. Last accessed 28 January 2020.

Shodganga. 'National Antecedents'. Available at https://shodhganga.inflibnet.ac.in. Last accessed 23 May 2021.

Shodganga. 'Native Cochin and the Hinterland'. Available at https://shodhganga.inflibnet.ac.in. Last accessed 15 January 2020.

Shodganga. 'Re-Framing Marriage and Family of Nairs'. Available at https://shodhganga.inflibnet.ac.in. Last accessed 23 May 2021.

Simon, Salian C. *State and Society in Kerala*. Calicut, Calicut University, 2013.

Sriram, V. *The Hindu*. 'Madras' Pushy First Lady'. 23 October 2012.

Thayamkeril, J. Joseph. 'Sambandham'. Available at www.needofthehourbyjosephythayamkeril.blogspot.in. 25 December 2015.

Varma, R. Devan with Churchill David and Reusser Marc. *Journal on the Cochin State Forest Tramway*. Cochin Railway Fan Club, 2005. Available at https://wiki.fibis.org/w/Cochin_State_Forest_Tramway.

Varma, Dr Rama. 'History of the Cochin Royal Family'. Available at https://www.cochinroyalhistory.org. Last accessed 10 June 2021.

Varmha, Ram. `Sreemathy Parukutty Nethyaramma—The First Lady of Vadakke Kuruppath'. 2013.

Viswanathan, Sarita, Shodganga. 'Formation of Kochi Rajya P. Rajamandalam'. 25 September 2014. Available at https://shodhganga.inflibnet.ac.in. Last accessed 5 December 2021.

Letter and Reports

29 March 1916: Letter from the Raja of Cochin to the abdicated Raja on meeting Lord Bishop of Mylapore in connection with his son being in Germany.

13 April 1916: Letter from the Raja of Cochin to the abdicated Raja relating to his son V.K. Raman Menon arriving safely in Switzerland from Germany.

10 October 1928: Letter from 5 Thampurans to Lt. Col Crosthwaite seeking a meeting to discuss family matters.

21 June 1930: Letter from Agent to Governor General Cater to the Diwan to look into the complaint of the Thampurans.

19 November 1930: Letter from the Thampurans of Cochin state.

10 August 1931: Letter from the Diwan C.G. Herbert to the Maharaja relating to transfer of Sarvadhikariakar on retirement of Ramalinga Ayyar.

11 August 1931: Reply from the Maharaja to Diwan Herbert objecting to the transfer.

13 August 1931: Letter from the Diwan C.G. Herbert to the Maharaja asking him to reconsider the transfer of Sarvadhikariakar.

13 August 1931: Reply from the Maharaja to Diwan Herbert objecting once more to the transfer.

15 August 1931: Letter from the Diwan C.G. Herbert to the Maharaja extending the period of Ramalinga Ayyar.

29 August 1931: Report to Madras State Agency on the complaint of Junior Tampurans about the administration of Palace Funds and proceeding of meeting.

10 September 1931: Letter from the Diwan C.G. Herbert to the Maharaja once more on the transfer of Sarvadhikariakar.

13 September 1931: Reply from the Maharaja to Diwan Herbert objecting once more to the transfer and asking Diwan to find someone else as Devaswom Commissioner.

16 September 1931: Letter from the Diwan C.G. Herbert to the Maharaja once more on the transfer of the Sarvadhikariakar stating that since they could not agree, the best course

would be to request the Agent to the Governor General to withdraw Herbert's services.
16 September 1931: Reply from the Maharaja to Diwan Herbert extending the period of Ramalinga Ayyar for a fortnight.
18 September 1931: Letter from the Maharaja to Lt. Col Pritchard, Agent to the Governor General on transfer of Sarvadhikariakar. He says that the Sarvadhikariakar cannot be replaced and asks for help to avoid further correspondence in matter.
25 September 1931: Letter from Diwan Herbert to Lt. Col Pritchard that the previous diwan had been a tool of the Neithyaramma.
12 October 1931: Report on interview of Lt. Col Pritchard with Maharaja.
12 October 1931: Letter from Maharaja to Lt. Col Pritchard that he was dismayed at the tone of the meeting.
14 October 1931: Letter from Pritchard to the Maharaja that there was no cross-examination.
14 October 1931: Letter from Lt. Col Pritchard to Diwan Herbert.
18 October 1931: Letter from Maharaja to Lt. Col Pritchard on meeting with note from Pritchard on October 24, 1931, suggesting delegation of powers to the Maharaja's son in law Rama Varma regarding the management of properties.
24 October 1931: Letter from Pritchard.
31 October 1931: Letter from Lt. Col Pritchard to Diwan Herbert.
November 1931: Note written by Diwan Herbert regarding differences of opinion with the Maharaja and his recommendations.
24 December 1931: Letter from Diwan Herbert to Lt. Col Pritchard on the state of the Maharaja and his stand.

3 January 1932: Letter from Pritchard to Sir Charles Watson Political Secretary to the Government of India on the state of affairs in Cochin and the Maharaja's condition.

29 January 1932: Telegram from the Viceroy commanding that the Mahraja be examined by a European doctor with regard to fitness to rule.

30 January 1932: Letter from Lt. Col Pritchard to Dr Somevell to assist European doctor in examination of the Maharaja.

3 January 1932: Letter from Lt. Col Pritchard to Diwan Herbert on Viceroy's orders.

3 January 1932: Letter from Lt. Col Pritchard to Govt. of Madras enquiring whether there was a European doctor to examine the Maharaja.

2 February 1932: Letter from Dr Somervell agreeing to be present at the examination of the Maharajah.

4 February 1932: Letter from the Political Dept, Madras, stating there are no European specialists to examine the Maharaja.

4 February 1932: Letter from Lt. Col Pritchard to Sir Charles Watson that the Maharaja was ill.

9 February 1932: letter from Lt. Col Pritchard to W.A. Turner Secretary to Government of Bombay, Political Department, asking whether there is a European Doctor to examine the Maharaja.

22 February 1932: Letter from W.A. Turner to Lt. Col Pritchard that Dr E.C.A. Smith was available to examine the Maharaja.

27 February 1932: Letter from Lt. Col Pritchard to Mr W.A. Turner thanking him and confirming that E.C.A. Smith would be required.

15 March 1932: Letter from Lt. Col Pritchard to W.A. Turner informing him that the Maharaja had died.

VIDEOS

Cochin Royal Family Symposium 2003, Part 4 by Ravi Achan. Available at https://www.cochinroyalhistory.org. Last accessed 10 June 2021.

Cochin Royal Family Symposium 2003, Part 2 by Dr Kocha Varma. Available at https://www.cochinroyalhistory.org. Last accessed 10 June 2021.

Cochin Royal Family Symposium 2002–2005. Available at https://www.cochinroyalhistory.org. Last accessed 10 June 2021.

Dr Alexander Jacob IPS—Charithram Enniloode Safari TV on Parukutty Neithyaramma. Available at https://www.youtube.com/watch?v=ovA9Lgljba4&t=38s. Last accessed 2 April 2021.

Interviews and Correspondence with

Malathy A. Menon, daughter-in-law of Parukutty Neithyaramma
P.K. Satish, Cochin Royal Family foundation
Parukutty Neithyaramma
Prasanna Varma
Rama Varma, founder of Cochinroyalhistory.org
Raman A. Menon, grandson of Parukutty Neithyaramma
Ratnam Amma Palatt, daughter of Parukutty Neithyaramma
Sankaran Palat, grandson of Parukutty Neithyaramma
Usha Chettur Varma
V. Aravindaksha Menon, son of Parukutty Neithyaramma
Varada Menon, granddaughter of Parukutty Neithyaramma
Vikram Menon, great-grandson of Parukutty Neithyaramma

Glossary

Achan: Father

Adiparashakti: Supreme Goddess

Amma Raja estate: The income of this estate was used for the expenses and upkeep of the princesses of the Cochin Royal family

Amma Raja or Amma Thampuran: Senior-most princess of the Cochin royal family

Amma: Mother; a term of respect when addressing Nair ladies

Amme: Mother; often used to address a Goddess

Aranjanam: Girdle-like ornament tied round the waist of infants; a gold waist band

Ariyittu vazhchacha: Ceremony to be performed prior to the coronation of a new sovereign; it consists of pouring raw rice by a Nambudiri Brahmin over the head of the person to be installed as sovereign as a propitious congregation for long life and prosperity

Ashtamangalam: Eight auspicious ingredients which are raw rice, a circular bell metal plate with a handle called the Val Kannadi, a grandham or sacred writing, a newly washed cloth, a gold fanam or coin, two halves of a coconut with two wicks burning in them, a small round wooden or iron box containing an eye salve and a wooden box containing vermilion to place a circular red mark on the forehead. These eight articles were placed on a silver tray

Bhagavathy: Goddess or Devi
Changalavatta: A kind of lamp
Chechi: Elder sister
Chira: Public bathing pond
Deepastambham: Brass lamps set up one layer above another
Deepayeshtis: Torch-like lights
Devi: Goddess
Diwan: Chief executive of the state
Diwan Peishkar: Civil servant of the rank equivalent to a district collector
Edakka: Hour-shaped drum
Ettukettu: Eight halls with two central courtyards
Ela: Banana leaf
Elattalam: Brass cymbals
Elaya Thampuran, Elaya Raja: Heir apparent
Enangars: Persons from other Nair families with whom the family had sambandham
Ezhava: Lower caste, mainly farmers and agricultural workers
Gawli: Lizard
Gawli Shastra: Lizard astrology
Gopuram: The monumental tower at the entrance of South Indian temples
Homappura: Puja room
Iddiyappam: This is also known as noolappam; it is rice flour pressed into noodles which are pressed into a flat disc shape and steamed. In Sri Lanka, they are known as string hoppers.
Idli: Rice pancake
Illam : The house of a Nambudiri
Ilathalam: Metallic musical instrument which resembles a miniature pair of cymbals
Iruvathetta: 28th day ceremony; a Nair child is normally named on this day
Jadhagam: Horoscope
Jaggery: A type of solid dark sugar made in India from sugar cane and the sap of date palm trees
Kai vilakku: Handheld lamp
Kanji: Rice porridge

Kariakars: Officers responsible for administration of a village
Kariastan: Manager
Karnavan: Eldest male member of a Nair tarwad
Kasavu: Gold thread Kasavu mundu is cloth lined with gold thread
Kayneetam: Token of blessing, usually money, given by an elder to the younger members of the family for good fortune
Kharitas: Official letter usually presented at a durbar
Kindi: Brass vessel with a spout
Kochangadi: Area in west Cochin famous for an ancient mosque
Kolam: Pond for bathing
Kombu: C-shaped wind instrument made of brass
Kottakakam: The area around the Poornathrayeesa Temple and the Amma Raja Palace
Kovilakam: Palace
Kuttuvilakku: A kind of lamp
Kuzhal: A double reed wind instrument
Madapally: Royal kitchen
Maddalam: Drum made of the wood of the jackfruit tree
Mana: The house of a Nambudirpad
Marumakkatayam: The matrilineal system followed by Nairs in Kerala. They traced their descent to a common ancestress
Muhurtham: The most auspicious time to conduct a wedding
Mundu: Garment worn round the waist covering the legs and extending up to the ankles, worn by both men and women
Muri: May refer to cloth or room depending on the context
Musnad: Throne
Nada: Entrance
Nadumittam: Central courtyard
Nalukettu: Four halls with a central courtyard
Namaskaram: Salutation
Nambudiri: Kerala Brahmin
Navratna: Ring or necklace pendant with nine gems
Neithyaramma, neithyar: The consort of the Cochin Raja/Maharaja
Nendrapazham: Large bananas which are native to Kerala
Nettipattams: Solid gold head adornments placed on the head and trunk of elephants
Nuzzar: Offering given to indicate fealty

Nyaya: It is primarily concerned with epistemology and logic, and secondarily with ontology; it deals with the sources of knowledge, viz., perception, inference, comparison and testimony, and conditions of their validity, as well as the nature of the world, souls and God

Olakkuda: Palmyra leaf umbrella

Oottupura: Dining room

Onam: Harvest festival

Padinjare: Western

Padmasana: Cross-legged

Padukas: Single-pronged wooden sandals

Palaga: Low stool

Palli Sanku: Royal conch

Palli-Ara Muthalpidi: The income of the estate used for the expenses and upkeep of the princes of the Cochin royal family

Pallu: The part that hangs down the left shoulder of the upper garment worn by women

Pandal: A covering or tent-like structure held up by bamboos and covered with palm leaves

Pandivadhyam: Orchestra of five instruments

Pandivadyam: Reed pipe

Pappadum: Thin crisp flatbread

Para of rice: Eight kilograms of rice

Para: A vessel that measures rice

Parvathiakaran: the village officer

Patti: Dog

Payasam: Dessert

Pela: Period of mourning of 14 days, during which time family members are not expected to go to temples

Pice: Small coins—currency of the time

Poomukham: Entrance hall

Pooyam: One of the 27 stars in the Malayalam calendar, which appear every month

Pradishnam: Circumlocutions

Prasad: Sacrament given by temples, usually a mixture of jaggery, banana and ghee

Prashanam: Rolling of shells to find out the future and destiny

Puja muri: Prayer room
Puja: Prayer
Pulayi: Aborigine or tribal
Puthen: Coins
Puttu: Dish of coarsely ground rice and coconut shavings steamed in bamboo or a cylindrical vessel
Rakshas: Demon
Sadhya: Feast (usually with 28 accompaniments)
Sahasranamam: Prayer where the 1,000 names of a deity are recited in praise
Sambandham: It is a mode of marriage among Nairs. It denotes a cohabitation relationship between a man and a woman. As both polyandry and polygamy existed, a woman could have multiple relationships with many men and a man could similarly be in non-monogamous relationships with many women
Sambandhi: The persons in a sambandham relationship. Though both men and women could have relationships with many others, by the late nineteenth century, they tended to be with just one partner
Sanad: Letter having the force of an edict; a proclamation
Sarvadhikariakar: Personal secretary of the ruler
Sirkar: Government
Sreemoolastanam: Original seat of the deity
Stanam: Position
Stotra: Hymn
Sudra: Low caste
Swaroopam: Ancient name of the Rajas of Cochin
Tarwad: Nair matrilineal joint family
Thachu or Vaastu Shastra: Ancient science that helps one to get the natural benefits freely offered by the five basic elements of the universe in which we all live
Thali: Gold pendant shaped like a leaf worn by married Malayalee Nair women
Thalikettu Kalyanam: Mock marriage ceremony in the Nair community
Thampuran: Prince
Thampuratti: Princess; the father of Thampurattis, like Thampurans, were Nambudiris or Nambudiripads while their mothers were Thampurattis

Thimila: Hourglass-shaped percussion instrument
Triveni Sangam: The confluence of the holy rivers of Ganga, Yamuna and the mythical Saraswathy
Upanayanam cum Samavarthanam: Graduation
Uruttu chenda: Round drums
Vadakkunathan temple: Temple dedicated to Lord Shiva in Trichur
Valia Thampuran: Raja or Maharaja; the eldest prince
Valiya sadhya: Feast with over 60 accompaniments
Vallam: Country boat covered with palm leaves
Vassal state: Tributary paying an annual tribute for protection
Vedanta: Vedanta reflects ideas that emerged from the speculations and philosophies contained in the Upanishads, specifically, knowledge and liberation
Velichhappad: A medium who would mediate between a Devi and the devotee
Vilakku: Kerala bell metal lamp
Villakkar: Peon
Vishu: The Malayalee New Year
Vyakarana: Grammar and linguistic analysis in Sanskrit
Yakshi: Vampire

Acknowledgements

This book would not have been possible without the help and guidance we received from so many people.

We begin by thanking the protagonist of this book, Parukutty Neithyaramma. She regaled us with stories of her glorious past and tumultuous life. Little did we think then that we would one day pen her story. It is her narrations and the close and frequent interactions with her that have made it possible for us to bring her alive in our book.

We must thank too the Late Aravindaksha Menon, Parukutty Neithyaramma's second son. He was the Chief Engineer of the State of Cochin, and also the person she entrusted important matters to. He built the magnificent town hall in Trichur, renovated the Durbar Hall in Ernakulam and built numerous buildings and roads in the state. He entertained us with stories of Viceroys and Diwans, palace intrigues and of meetings held behind closed doors. A treasure trove of information, he vividly remembered the time he accompanied Mahatma Gandhi to Trichur and his mother's involvement in the independence struggle.

Malathy Menon, Aravindaksha Menon's wife, was a quiet and retiring woman. She had lived in the Hill Palace from the time of her wedding till Maharaja Rama Varma XVI passed away and was able to give us the impressions of an outsider who became a part of the family. It was at her father's house in Trichur that Pandit Nehru rested on his way to Ceylon.

The late Ratnam Amma Palatt, Parukutty Neithyaramma's eldest daughter, lived at the Hill Palace for many years from the time of Maharaja Rama Varma XVI's accession. She told us stories of the life at the palace and of the Neithyaramma's involvement in the nationalist movement. She also often spoke of her father, the Maharaja.

Sankaran Palat, Parukutty Neithyaramma's eldest grandson, shared many stories with us of his days at the Hill Palace—his antics as a child living there, the drives he went on with the Maharaja and his interractions with Parukutty Neithyaramma. The Neithyaramma took him with her to Switzerland after the Maharaja's demise. He told us of his experience with her and how well she managed, in spite of being a single lady in a strange land.

We are grateful too for incidents and stories narrated to us by Varada Menon and Raman Menon, who are grandchildren of Parukutty Neithyaramma.

Dr Vikram Menon, a great-grandson of Parukutty Neithyaramma, did his research for his doctorate at Oxford on royalty in south India. He was a great help to us. He shared his information unstintingly, and was always available if one had a query.

Dr Kocha Varma and his wife Usha deserve special thanks. Dr Varma has done extensive research on the Cochin royal family—his family. He has travelled to Portugal, the Netherlands, Scotland and London. He spent days and weeks at museums and libraries to source original documents and letters relating to the Cochin royal family. He has encapsulated this on the website www.cochinroyalhistory.org, which contains a wealth of information. His symposiums on the Cochin royal family were of great help in our research. His wife, Usha—herself a granddaughter of a Maharaja of Cochin—too shared her memories. They were always available to answer questions and clarify matters for us.

We must thank Mr P.K. Satish of the Cochin Royal Family Foundation. He sourced for us several interesting documents even without our asking, and was happy to answer questions that we had on the Cochin royal family.

We thank Prasanna Varma, also of the Cochin royal family, for her help. She was a mine of information on the customs of the time. It was with her help that we could capture the essence and ambience of the time more clearly.

Vineetha Sanjay, the great-granddaughter of a prince of Cochin, Rama Varma Appan Thampuran, was a blessing. She translated cheerfully a book that we had received written in Malayalam commemorating the sixtieth birthday of Maharaja Rama Varma XVI—a book that gave us a detailed glimpse of the first five years of his reign.

We would also like to acknowledge and thank Mr Ravi Achan, the son of a former Elaya Maharaja of Cochin, for the information he so willingly shared with us. It helped us understand the period during which Parukutty Neithyaramma ruled the state.

Our wonderful literary agent Kanishka Gupta was honestly a godsend. From the very start he encouraged, motivated and supported us. His enthusiasm for this book was very heartening and infectious.

Our first interaction with Manasi Subramanium, Executive Editor and Head of Literary Rights at Penguin Random

House, can only be described as extremely positive. The energy she brought into our conversation and her unbridled interest in our book delighted us. Thank you, Manasi, for your continued support.

We would like to thank Shubhi Surana, Editor at Penguin Random House for her suggestions. These were invaluable. It was such a pleasure working with her.

We would never have completed this book without the help and motivation provided by our immediate family. Our elder daughter, Divya, and our son-in-law, Aditya Hitkari, were instrumental in deciding the manner the book presents the life of Parukutty Neithyaramma. We have incorporated so many of their suggestions into our writing. Our daughter Nikhila contributed with creative ideas. Her husband, Vivan Bhathena, painstakingly restored the photographs of that time—the early 1900s—which we have included in the book.

This is a story that had to be told. Parukutty Neithyaramma had the courage to live life on her own terms. This was at a time when women had very few rights and were barely heard. Parukutty ruled. She stood by her convictions, uprooted age-old customs and left her indelible mark on Cochin. This is the story of a woman who would not let any man or custom stand in her way.

Notes

Preface

1. Until 1 January, the rulers of Cochin were Rajas. On 1 January 1921, Raja Rama Varma XVI was, through a sanad issued by the Viceroy, made Maharaja. This being a hereditary title, all later rulers were addressed as Maharaja.

Chapter 1: Divine Intervention

1. Ananthanarayanan, G.H. *Shree Chottanikkara Devi Temple*. Bombay: Bharatiya Vidya Bhavan, 2001, p. 17.
2. Ibid., p. 18.
3. Ibid., p. 18.

Chapter 2: Inhaling the Future

1. Nambudiripads were the highest level of Brahmins.
2. An incarnation of the goddess Durga. The Parmekkavu Temple was the family temple of the Vadakke Kuruppath family. Legend has it that one of the ancestors would go to pray to the devi

(Durga) at Thirumandhamkunnu Temple in Angadipuram, Perinthalmanna. He grew old and during his last visit was extremely depressed and wondered how he would pray to the devi. He returned to Trichur and on his way home put his umbrella down under a tree near the Vadukknathan Temple and rested. After a while, when he tried to pick up the umbrella he could not. Through a devaprasanam (ritual to find out the will of the god), they concluded that there was a divine presence in the umbrella. The ancestor decided to worship the devi there itself and a temple was consecrated. This is the Parmekkavu Temple.

3. 5 July 1875.
4. Conversation with Vikram Menon, July 2020.

Chapter 3: Exhaling the Past

1. Conversation with the late Ratnam Amma Palatt on her mother, Palghat, 1975.
2. Conversation with V.K. Aravindaksha Menon on his mother, Coonoor, 1958–78.
3. When a Nair lady left her tarwad to reside with her sambandhi, she lost her right to return to her tarwad house and she could no longer claim her portion of the tarwad property (Paliath Ravi Achan in cochinroyalhistory.org Symposium 2003 Part 4).

Chapter 4: Sambandham

1. Menon, C. Kunji Rama, *Kochi Valliya Thampuran Thirumanasu*, Trichur, Mangalodayam Co. Ltd 1918, p. 8.
2. Ibid., p. 9.
3. Menon, T.K. Krishna, *Progress of Cochin*, Ernakulam, Cochin Government Press, 1932, p. 3.
4. Menon, C. Kunji Rama, *Kochi Valliya Thampuran Thirumanasu*, p. 11.
5. Ibid., p. 12.
6. Conversation with the late Parukutty Neithyaramma, Trichur, 1958–63.

7. Conversation with the late Parukutty Neithyaramma, Trichur, 1958–63.
8. Menon, C. Kunji Rama, *Kochi Valliya Thampuran Thirumanasu*, p. 24.
9. Conversation with the late Parukutty Neithyaramma, Trichur, 1958–63.
10. Conversation with the late Parukutty Neithyaramma, Trichur, 1958–63.
11. Caste rules stated that as Nairs were considered Sudras, Thampurans could not eat with them. Should they touch them, the Thampuran had to purify himself immediately by taking a bath. Thus, Thampurans could not touch their Nair sambandhis until before they had a bath in the morning or just before they bathed in the evening or after dinner.
12. Achan, Ravi, Cochin Royal Family Symposium 2003 Thrippunithura, available at https://www.cochinroyalhistory.org. Last accessed 10 June 2021, Part 4; Pillai, Manu S., 'The Paliath Achans, a Cochin Family That Once was Richer Than the Maharajas', *The Hindu*, 2019.
13. Achan, Ravi, Cochin Royal Family Symposium 2003 Thrippunithura, available at https://www.cochinroyalhistory.org. Last accessed 10 June 2021, Part 4.
14. Ibid.
15. Ibid.
16. Conversation with the late Parukutty Neithyaramma, Trichur, 1958–63.
17. Conversation with the late Parukutty Neithyaramma, Trichur, 1958–63; Achan, Ravi, Cochin Royal Family Symposium 2003 Thrippunithura, available at https://www.cochinroyalhistory.org. Last accessed 10 June 2021, Part 4.

Chapter 5: Taking up the Gauntlet

1. Achan, Ravi, Cochin Royal Family Symposium 2003 Thrippunithura, available at https://www.cochinroyalhistory.org. Last accessed 10 June 2021, Part 4.

2. The royal precinct of Thrippunithura was exclusively for the royal family. There were Nair tarwads in the Thrippunithura township. Only the Elamana and the Mangat Panicker tarwads had sambandhams with princes and, as their tarwads were in the township, those ladies who had sambandhams with princes lived in their own tarwads. Parukutty was the first Nair woman to live in the royal precinct with her sambandhi.
3. Conversation with Vikram Menon, July 2020.
4. Conversation with the late Sankaran Palat and with the late Parukutty Neithyaramma, Trichur, 1958–78.
5. Conversation with the late Parukutty Neithyaramma, Trichur, 1958–63.
6. Menon, C. Kunji Rama, *Kochi Valliya Thampuran Thirumanasu*, p. 26.
7. Conversation with the late Parukutty Neithyaramma, Trichur, 1958–63.
8. Conversation with Vikram Menon, July 2020.
9. Conversation with Vikram Menon, July 2020
10. Menon, C. Kunji Rama, *Kochi Valliya Thampuran Thirumanasu*, p. 26.
11. Conversation with Vikram Menon, July 2020.
12. Conversation with Vikram Menon, July 2020.
13. Conversation with the late Sankaran Palat, Trichur, 1975–78.

Chapter 6: Coming into One's Own

1. Menon, I.N., *The Rajarshi of Cochin, Autobiography and Biography of Maharaja Sir Sri Rama Varma*, Trivandrum, Kerala State Archives Department, 2010, pp. 38–39.
2. Edavom 1018 in the Malayalam calender.
3. C.G. Herbert's letter dated 24 December 1931 and cochinroyalhistory.org
4. Menon, I.N., *The Rajarshi of Cochin, Autobiography and Biography of Maharaja Sir Sri Rama* Varma, p. 43.
5. Menon, I.N., *The Rajarshi of Cochin, Autobiography and Biography of Maharaja Sir Sri Rama* Varma, p. 44.

6. Menon, I.N., *The Rajarshi of Cochin, Autobiography and Biography of Maharaja Sir Sri Rama* Varma, p. 252.
7. Raja Rama Varma XV was Kunji Kiddavu's first cousin once removed.
8. The Raja Rama Varma XV's letter dated 4 February 1899 to the Diwan.
9. Menon, C. Kunji Rama, *Kochi Valliya Thampuran Thirumanasu*, p. 30.
10. Menon, C. Kunji Rama, *Kochi Valliya Thampuran Thirumanasu*, p. 32.
11. Ramachandran, R.V., Cochin Royal Family Symposium 2003 Thrippunithura, available at https://www.cochinroyalhistory.org. Last accessed 10 June 2021, Part 1.
12. Raja Rama Varma XV's letter dated 4 February 1899 to the Diwan.
13. Raja Rama Varma XV's letter dated 4 February 1899 to the Diwan.
14. Conversation with Kocha Varma, February 2021.
15. Based on conversations with the late Parukutty Neithyaramma.
16. Ramachandran, R.V., Cochin Royal Family Symposium 2003 Thrippunithura, available at https://www.cochinroyalhistory.org. Last accessed 10 June 2021, Part 1.
17. Ibid.
18. cochinroyalhistory.org, last accessed 10 June 2021; and Kocha Varma.
19. Based on a conversation with the late Parukutty Neithyaramma.
20. Shodganga National Antecedents, p. 18, available at https://shodhganga.inflibnet.ac.in. Last accessed 23 May 2021.
21. Menon, I.N., *The Rajarshi of Cochin, Autobiography and Biography of Maharaja Sir Sri Rama* Varma, p. 93.
22. Ibid., p. 97.
23. Ibid., p. 96.
24. Shodganga National Antecedents, p. 20, available at https://shodhganga.inflibnet.ac.in. Last accessed 23 May 2021.
25. Ramachandran, R.V., Cochin Royal Family Symposium 2003 Thrippunithura, available at https://www.cochinroyalhistory.org. Last accessed 10 June 2021, Part 1.

26. Menon, I.N., *The Rajarshi of Cochin, Autobiography and Biography of Maharaja Sir Sri Rama* Varma, p. 106.
27. Ibid., pp. 75–76.
28. Paanchajanya, 'Rajarshi of Cochin: A Misunderstood Dharmika', *Hindu Post*, 8 December 2016; *The Hindu*, 'Waiting for Train of Hope', 24 June 2004.
29. Maharaja's letter to Lord Pentland, Government of Madras, 19 November 1913, RAE, File No. 136 D.O. Correspondence.
30. Report on the Administration of Cochin ME 1089, 1913 to 1914, p. 1.
31. Ibid.
32. Menon, I.N., *The Rajarshi of Cochin, Autobiography and Biography of Maharaja Sir Sri Rama* Varma, p. 111.
33. This was an extensive project to transport timber from the forests around Parambikulam to Cochin, from where they could be exported.
34. Menon, I.N., *The Rajarshi of Cochin, Autobiography and Biography of Maharaja Sir Sri Rama* Varma, p. 119.
35. Conversation with the late Ratnam Amma Palatt.
36. Conversation with the late V.K. Aravindaksha Menon.
37. Menon, I.N., *The Rajarshi of Cochin, Autobiography and Biography of Maharaja Sir Sri Rama* Varma, p. 229.

Chapter 7: The Road to Destiny

1. cochinroyalhistory.org, last accessed 10 June 2021 and telephone conversation with Kocha Varma.
2. Achan, Ravi, Cochin Royal Family Symposium 2003 Thrippunithura, available at https://www.cochinroyalhistory.org. Last accessed 10 June 2021, Part 4.
3. Ramachandran, K. S., Hamlet in Monsoon, 'Parukuttykutty Neithyaramma Ruled Cochin', 10 March 2014, available at http:// hamletram.blogspot.com, last accessed 19 June 2021.
4. Chapter 6, 'Architecture and Town Planning', p. 138, available at https://shodhganga.inflibnet.ac.in, last accessed 23 May 2021.
5. Conversation with the late Aravindaksha Menon.

6. Sweet.
7. Menon, T.K. Krishna *The Days That Were (Memoirs)*, Ernakulam, Industrial School Press, 1949, p. 586.

Chapter 8: The Crowning

1. Menon, C. Achyuta, *The Cochin State Manual*. Ernakulam, Cochin Government Press, 1911, p. 41.
2. Ibid. and as described by the late Aravindaksha Menon.
3. Menon, C. Achyuta, *The Cochin State Manual*.
4. The family of Naickery Veetil Menon held the post of minister originally.
5. This family was in charge of the Customs House on the frontier and were accorded this privilege.
6. Menon, C. Achyuta, *The Cochin State Manual*, p. 42.
7. Ibid., p. 43.
8. Chapter 6, 'Architecture and Town Planning', pp. 136–137, available at https://shodhganga.inflibnet.ac.in, last accessed 23 May 2021.
9. Report on the Administration of Cochin ME 1090, 1914–1915, p. 2.
10. Ibid.
11. Telephone Conversation with Vikram Menon, July 2020.
12. Telephone Conversation with Vikram Menon, July 2020.

Chapter 9: A Formidable Team

1. cochinroyalhistory.org, last accessed 10 June 2021 and telephone conversation with Kocha Varma.
2. Report on the Administration of Cochin ME 1090, 1914–1915, p. 7.
3. Report on the Administration of Cochin ME 1089, 1913–1914, p. 6.
4. Achan, Ravi, Cochin Royal Family Symposium 2003 Thrippunithura, available at https://www.cochinroyalhistory.org, last accessed 10 June 2021, Part 4.

5. cochinroyalhistory.org, last accessed 10 June 2021; Menon, T.K. Krishna, *The Days That Were*, p. 395.

Chapter 10: A Legacy of Loans

1. Report on the Administration of Cochin ME 1090, 1914–1915, p. 1.
2. Report on the Administration of Cochin ME 1089, 1913–1914, p. 3.
3. Report on the Administration of Cochin ME 1089, 1913–1914, p. 22.
4. Report on the Administration of Cochin ME 1090, 1914–1915, pp. 42–43.
5. Menon, I.N., *The Rajarshi of Cochin, Autobiography and Biography of Maharaja Sir Sri Rama* Varma, pp. 75–77.
6. Ibid., p. 86.
7. Ullattil, Manmadhan, Maddy's Rambling, 'The Kings Railway', 28 November 2009, available at https://maddy06.blogspot.com, last accessed 15 March 2021; *Hindu Post*, 'Rajarshi of Cochin'.
8. Report on the Administration of Cochin ME 1085, 1909–1910, Chapter 2, p. 3.
9. Report on the Administration of Cochin ME 1086, 1910–1911, Chapter 2, p. 3.
10. Socio-religious trusts made up of members nominated by the Government and the community.
11. Report on the Administration of Cochin ME 1089, 1913–1914, p. 6.

Chapter 11: Manoeuvres and Outmanoeuvres

1. Menon, T.K. Krishna, *The Days That Were*, p. 586.
2. Menon, I.N., *The Rajarshi of Cochin, Autobiography and Biography of Maharaja Sir Sri Rama* Varma, p. 195.
3. Ibid., pp. 197 and 198.
4. Report on the Administration of Cochin ME 1089, 1913–1914, p. 51.

5. Menon, I.N., *The Rajarshi of Cochin, Autobiography and Biography of Maharaja Sir Sri Rama* Varma, p. 241.
6. Jacob, Alexander, *Trichur News*, 4 April 2020.
7. Menon, I.N., *The Rajarshi of Cochin, Autobiography and Biography of Maharaja Sir Sri Rama* Varma, pp. 240 and 241.
8. Ibid., p. 242.
9. Ibid., pp. 241 and 242.
10. Ibid., pp. 241 and 242.
11. Varma, Kocha, Cochin Royal Family Symposium 2003 Thrippunithura, available at https://www.cochinroyalhistory.org, last accessed 10 June 2021.
12. Braidwood's letter to Raja Rama Varma XVI, 7 May 1918; Varma, Kocha, Cochin Royal Family Symposium 2003 Thrippunithura, available at https://www.cochinroyalhistory.org, last accessed 10 June 2021.
13. Raja's letter, 11 May 1918; Varma, Kocha, Cochin Royal Family Symposium 2003 Thrippunithura, available at https://www.cochinroyalhistory.org, last accessed 10 June 2021.
14. Minutes of conversation between the Raja of Cochin and Sir Rama Varma on 6 April 1915, Rejikumar, J. (ed.), 'Archives Treasury', Trivandrum, Kerala State Archives Dept, 2010, p. 287.
15. Conversation with the late Aravindaksha Menon.
16. Conversation with the late Aravindaksha Menon.
17. Sir Chettur Sankaran Nair had, in 1897, been the president of the Indian National Congress. He is the only Malayalee to date to have held that honour.
18. The late Sankaran Palat in conversation with the author.
19. Report on the Administration of Cochin ME 1091, 1915–1916, p. 1.
20. Ibid., p. 2.
21. Menon, C. Kunji Rama, *Kochi Valliya Thampuran Thirumanasu*, p. 64.
22. Ibid.
23. Raja of Cochin's letter of 29 March 1916 to the abdicated Raja.
24. Raja of Cochin's letter of 13 April 1916 to the abdicated Raja.

Chapter 12: A Study Tour

1. Menon, C. Kunji Rama, *Kochi Valliya Thampuran Thirumanasu*, pp. 65–70.
2. Report on the Administration of Cochin ME 1093, 1917–1918, Appendix.
3. Menon, C. Kunji Rama, *Kochi Valliya Thampuran Thirumanasu*, pp. 65–70.

Chapter 13: Save and Splurge

1. Report of the Administration of Cochin ME 1083, 1907–1908, p. 1.
2. Menon, I.N., *The Rajarshi of Cochin, Autobiography and Biography of Maharaja Sir Sri Rama Varma*, p. 103.
3. Report of the Administration of Cochin ME 1090, 1914–1915, p. 44.
4. Report of the Administration of Cochin ME 1093, 1917–1918, p. 1.
5. Conversation with the late Aravindaksha Menon.
6. Report of the Administration of Cochin ME 1094, 1918–1919, p. 5; Report on the Administration of Cochin ME 1093, 1917–1918, p. 1.
7. Report of the Administration of Cochin 1919, pp. 1 and 3.
8. Report on the Administration of Cochin ME 1094, 1918–1919, p. 1.
9. Achan, Ravi, Cochin Royal Family Symposium 2003 Thrippunithura, available at https://www.cochinroyalhistory.org, last accessed 10 June 2021, Part 4.
10. Complaint of the Thampurans to Crosthwaite, Agent to the Governor General, Madras State Agency.
11. Conversation with the late Ratnam Amma Palatt.

Chapter 14: For the People

1. Jacob, Alexander, *Trichur News*, 4 April 2020.

2. Report of the Administration of Cochin ME 1093, 1917–1918, p. 52.
3. Ibid., p. 52.
4. Ibid., p. 53.
5. Ibid., p. 53.

Chapter 15: The History of a Harbour

1. Muziris in ancient times. Greeks and Roman merchants came to the port to purchase spices and ivory.
2. Chapter 2, The Cochin Port – A Historical Retrospect. https://shodhganga.inflibnet.ac.in, last accessed 23 May 2021.
3. Bristow, Sir Robert, *Cochin Saga: A history of Foreign Government and Business Adventures in Kerala, South India by Arabs, Romans, Venetians, Dutch and British Together with the Personal Narrative of the Last Adventurer and Epilogue*, London, Cassel and Company, 1959, p. 58.
4. Ibid., p. 59.
5. Conversation with the late Chondath Raman Mannadiar, ADC to the Maharaja.
6. Bristow, Sir Robert *Cochin Saga: A History of Foreign Government and Business Adventures in Kerala, South India by Arabs, Romans, Venetians, Dutch and British Together with the Personal Narrative of the Last Adventurer and Epilogue*, p. 60.
7. Ibid., p. 79.
8. Ibid., p. 182.
9. Report of the Administration of Cochin ME 1096, 1920–1921, p. 3.
10. Ibid.
11. Ramachandran, K.S. , Cochin Chronicles, 'Mysteries of History', 14 March 2014, available at http://hamletram.blogspot.com, last accessed 19 June 2021.
12. Recollections of the late Aravindaksha Menon as told to the author.
13. Menon, I.N., *The Rajarshi of Cochin, Autobiography and Biography of Maharaja Sir Sri Rama* Varma, p. 254.

14. Conversation with the late Aravindaksha Menon.

Chapter 16: Inner Circle

1. Menon, I.N., *The Rajarshi of Cochin, Autobiography and Biography of Maharaja Sir Sri Rama* Varma, p. 111.
2. Rejikumar, J. (ed.), 'Archives Treasury', p. 286.
3. Ibid., p. 287.
4. Menon, T.K. Krishna *The Days That Were*, p. 594.
5. Menon, I.N., *The Rajarshi of Cochin, Autobiography and Biography of Maharaja Sir Sri Rama* Varma, pp. 248 to 250.

Chapter 17: Fires to Fight

1. Report of the Administration of Cochin ME 1094, 1918–1919, p. 48.
2. Ibid.
3. Ibid., p. 49.
4. Menon, T.K. Krishna *Progress of Cochin*, p. 133.
5. Conclusion from the Report of the Administration of Cochin, 17 August 1918 to 16 August 1919.
6. Literally means 'Emperor of India'. This award was for persons without distinction of caste or creed who had distinguished themselves by important and useful accomplishments in the advancement of public interest in India.
7. Movement to show the allegiance of muslims to Khalifa of the Ottoman Empire, who had been deposed by the British after the First World War.
8. Jaykrishna, 'The Thrissur Riot of 1921', Varnam, 19 September 2020.
9. Shodganga, 'National antecedents in Cochin', p. 31, available at https://shodhganga.inflibnet.ac.in, last accessed 23 May 2021.
10. Ibid.
11. Jaykrishna, 'The Thrissur Riot of 1921'.
12. Shodganga, 'National antecedents in Cochin', p. 34.
13. Shodganga, 'National antecedents in Cochin', p. 33.

14. Shodganga, 'National antecedents in Cochin', p. 34.
15. Report of the Administration of Cochin ME 1096, 1920–1921, p. 4.

Chapter 18: Contingency Plans

1. Menon, I.N., *The Rajarshi of Cochin, Autobiography and Biography of Maharaja Sir Sri Rama* Varma, p. 257.
2. Achan, Ravi, Cochin Royal Family Symposium 2003 Thrippunithura, available at https://www.cochinroyalhistory.org, last accessed 10 June 2021, Part 4.
3. Ibid; and conversation with the late Aravindaksha Menon.
4. Description provided by the author.
5. When a Nair lady left her tarwad she could not ask for her share in the tarwad property (Paliath Ravi Achan in cochinroyalhistory.org Symposium 2003 (Part 4).
6. Menon, T.K. Krishna, *Progress of Cochin*, p. 98.
7. Gangadharan, T.K. *Evolution of Kerala History and Culture*, p. 282.
8. Menon, T.K. Krishna, *The Days That Were*, p. 399.
9. Ibid.
10. Ibid.
11. Ibid.
12. Report on the Administation of Cochin ME 1095, 1919–1920, p. 8.
13. Menon, A. Sreedhara, *A Survey of Kerala History*, Chennai, S. Viswanathan (Printers and Publishers) Pvt. Ltd, 2003, p. 409.
14. Menon, T.K. Krishna, *The Days That Were*, p. 98.
15. Shodganga, 'Nair Matriliny: An overview', p. 104, https://shodhganga.inflibnet.ac.in, last accessed 23 May 2021.
16. Gangadharan, T.K., *Evolution of Kerala History and Culture*, pp. 282 and 283.
17. Ibid., p. 284.
18. Report of the Administration of Cochin ME 1095, 1919–1920, p. 8.

Chapter 19: Vox Populi

1. Menon, T.K. Krishna, *The Days That Were*, p. 593.
2. Biju, M.R., *Politics of Democracy and Decentralisation in India, Delhi: A Case Study of Kerala*, Atlantic Publishers and Distributors,1997, p. 84.
3. Civil servant of rank equivalent to a district collector.
4. Menon, T.K. Krishna, *Progress of Cochin*, pp. 261 to 265.
5. Report on the Administration of Cochin ME 1085, 1909–1910, p. 47.
6. Report on the Administration of Cochin ME 1089, 1913–1914, p. 50; Menon, T.K. Krishna, *Progress of Cochin*, pp. 255 and 256.
7. Ibid., p. 256.
8. Menon, T.K. Krishna, *Progress of Cochin*, p. 257.
9. Report on the administration of Cochin ME 1096, 1920–1921, p. 9.
10. Menon, T.K. Krishna, *Progress of Cochin*, pp. 259 and 260.
11. Menon, T.K. Krishna, *Progress of Cochin*, pp. 95 and 96.
12. Ibid., p. 97.
13. Menon, C. Achyuta, *The Cochin State Manual*, p. 465.
14. Menon, T.K. Krishna, *Progress of Cochin*, p. 95.
15. Menon, T.K. Krishna, *The Days That Were*, p. 315.
16. Ibid., p. 315.
17. Ibid., p. 318.
18. Menon, T.K. Krishna *Progress of Cochin*, p. 94.
19. Ibid., p. 30; T.K. Krishna Menon, *The Days That Were*, p. 594.
20. Menon, T.K. Krishna, *Progress of Cochin*, p. 95.

Chapter 20: Wedding Bells

1. Menon I.N., *The Rajarshi of Cochin, Autobiography and Biography of Maharaja Sir Sri Rama* Varma, p. 254.
2. Ibid., pp. 254 and 255.
3. Conversation with the late Aravindaksha Menon.
4. Menon, I.N., *The Rajarshi of Cochin, Autobiography and Biography of Maharaja Sir Sri Rama* Varma, pp. 254 and 255.

5. Conversation with Vikram Menon, July 2020.
6. Conversation with the late Aravindaksha Menon.
7. Menon, I.N., *The Rajarshi of Cochin, Autobiography and Biography of Maharaja Sir Sri Rama* Varma, p. 25.
8. Conversation with the late Malathy Menon.
9. Conversation with Vikram Menon, July 2020.
10. Conversation with the late Malathy Menon.
11. Conversation with the late Sankaran Palat; Conversation with Vikram Menon, 16 May 2020.
12. The late Sankaran Palat on his drives with Maharaja Rama Varma XVI.
13. Diwan Herbert's letter to H.R.N. Pritchard, 24 December 1931.
14. Ramachandran, K.S., Hamlet in Monsoon, 'Parukutty Neithyaramma Ruled Cochin', 10 March 2014, available at http://hamletram.blogspot.com, last accessed 19 June 2021.
15. cochinroyalhistory.org, last accessed 10 June 2021; Conversation with Kocha Varma.
16. cochinroyalhistory.org, last accessed 10 June 2021; Conversation with Kocha Varma; Ramachandran, K.S., Hamlet in Monsoon, 'Parukutty Neithyaramma Ruled Cochin', 10 March 2014, available at http://hamletram.blogspot.com, last accessed 19 June 2021.
17. Maharaja Rama Varma's letter to Cotton, 24 December 1924. cochinroyalhistory.org, last accessed 10 June 2021.
18. Menon, T.K. Krishna, *The Days That Were*, p. 609.
19. Cotton's letter to Patterson, 5 February 1925. cochinroyalhistory.org, last accessed 10 June 2021.

Chapter 21: Rumblings of Revolt

1. Jacob, Alexander, *Trichur News*, April 2020.
2. Menon, T.K. Krishna, *Progress of Cochin*, p. 43.
3. Ibid., p. 147.
4. Menon, A. Sreedhara, *A Survey of Kerala History*, p. 410.
5. Menon, T.K. Krishna, *Progress of Cochin*, p. 43.
6. Ibid., p. 238.

7. Bristow, Sir Robert, *Cochin Saga: A history of Foreign Government and Business Adventures in Kerala, South India by Arabs, Romans, Venetians, Dutch and British Together with the Personal Narrative of the Last Adventurer and Epilogue*, p. 232. Wikipedia on Cochin Port, last accessed 30 May 2021.
8. Menon, T.K. Krishna, *Progress of Cochin*, p. 44.
9. Ibid., p. 43.
10. Ibid., p. 73.
11. Report on the Administration of Cochin ME 1090, 1914–1915, p. 52.
12. Menon, T.K. Krishna, *Progress of Cochin*, p. 73.
13. Ibid., p. 171.
14. Ibid., p. 172.
15. Ibid., p. 82.
16. Ibid., pp. 59 and 61.
17. Converation with the late Sankaran Palat.
18. The late Sankaran Palat on the late Parukutty Neithyaramma.
19. Bristow, *Cochin Saga: A history of Foreign Government and Business Adventures in Kerala, South India by Arabs, Romans, Venetians, Dutch and British Together with the Personal Narrative of the Last Adventurer and Epilogue*, p. 220.
20. Menon, T.K. Krishna, *Progress of Cochin*, p. 205.
21. Menon, T.K. Krishna, *The Days That Were*, p. 318.
22. 'A Century in Service', available at The Hindu.com/life and style, article 26201102, last accessed 13 December 2020.
23. 'Sree Poornathraseeya Temple Celebrates the Thulam Mahotsavam Yasado', available at www.religionworld.in, 27 October 2017 and *The Hindu*, 26 October 2017.
24. Menon, A. Sreedhara, *Cultural Heritage of Kerala*, p. 200.
25. Menon, T.K. Krishna, *The Days That Were*, p. 609; Ramachandran, K.S., Hamlet in Monsoon, Parukutty Nethyaramma Ruled Cochin.
26. Varma, Leela, Cochin Royal Family Symposium 2003 Thrippunithura, available at https://www.cochinroyalhistory.org, last accessed 10 June 2021, Part 4.
27. Conversation with Usha and Kocha Varma, February 2021.

28. Kerala Varma the 8th Prince, Kerala Varma the 15th Prince, Kerala Varma the 16th Prince, Rama Varma the 17th Prince and Rama Varma the 30th Prince.
29. Note by Diwan C.G. Herbert on 24 December 1931.
30. Note prepared on meeting with the Thampurans in 1930 for the Agent to the Governor General to discuss with Mr Herbert in Madras prior to his arrival as Diwan.
31. Ibid.
32. Note by C.G. Herbert on 24 December 1931 and note from 9 February 1929.
33. Note by C.G. Herbert dated 24 December 1931.
34. Note prepared on meeting with the Thampurans in 1930 for the Agent to the Governor General to discuss with Mr Herbert in Madras prior to his arrival as Diwan.
35. Ibid.
36. Crosthwaite's note attached to letter of C.G. Herbert, 24 December 1931; Pritchard's letter to Charles Watson. 3 January 1932.
37. Note by C.G. Herbert, 24 December 1931 on complaint of Thampurans; Note prepared on meeting with the Thampurans in 1930 for the Agent to the Governor General to discuss with Mr Herbert in Madras prior to his arrival as Diwan.
38. Ibid.
39. Ibid.
40. Note by C.G. Herbert, 24 December 1931 on complaint of Thampurans.
41. Note prepared on meeting with the Thampurans in 1930 for the Agent to the Governor General to discuss with Mr Herbert in Madras prior to his arrival as Diwan.
42. Note prepared on meeting with the Thampurans in 1930 for the Agent to the Governor General to discuss with Mr Herbert in Madras prior to his arrival as Diwan.
43. Conversation with the late Sankaran Palat.
44. Conversation with Vikram Menon, July 2020.
45. Conversation with Vikram Menon, July 2020.

Chapter 22: City Fit for a Consort

1. *The Hindu*, 20 January 2021.
2. Jacob, Alexander. *Trichur News*, 4 April 2020.
3. Report on the Administration of Cochin ME 1089, 1913–1914, pp. 48 and 78.
4. Menon, T.K. Krishna, *Progress of Cochin*, p. 305.
5. Kerala Forest Department, Part 1, available at https://forest.kerala.gov.in/images/flash/tsrzoo07122011.pdf.
6. The circular road now known as the Swaraj round extends for 2 kilometres and is the second-largest roundabout in the world.
7. Jacob, Alexander, *Trichur News*, 4 April 2020.
8. Ibid.
9. Built by the Neithyaramma's son, Aravindaksha Menon.
10. Achan, Ravi, Cochin Royal Family Symposium 2003 Thrippunithura, available at https://www.cochinroyalhistory.org, last accessed 10 June 2021, Part 4.

Chapter 23: Fighting Fire with Fire

1. Palat, Raghu and Pushpa Palat, *The Case That Shook the Empire*, New Delhi, Bloomsbury Publishing India Pvt Ltd., 2019, pp. 157–161.
2. Gandhi, Mahatma, *The Collected Works of Gandhi* [hereinafter *CWG*], correspondence with V.K. Vilasini Amma (letter of 31 July 1924), Ministry of Information and Broadcasting, Publications Division, 1958–1995, Volume 28, p. 396.
3. Gandhi, *CWG*, Volume 31, p. 65.
4. 'Fortnightly Intelligence Reports', National Archives of India.
5. Conversation with the late Parukutty Neithyaramma.
6. Conversation with the late Aravindaksha Menon.
7. Gandhi, *CWG*, Volume 40, p. 25.
8. Gandhi, *CWG*, 1914–1945, p. 69. Gandhi, *CWG*, Volume 28, p. 396.
9. Conversation with the late Aravindaksha Menon.

10. Nehru, Jawaharlal, *Jawaharlal Nehru—An Autobiography*, New Delhi, Jawaharlal Nehru Memorial Fund, 1982, pp. 271–275.
11. Conversation with the late Malathy Menon.
12. Conversation with the late Saraswathy Menon, later Ranjan.

Chapter 24: The Opposition Unite

1. Pritchard's letter to Watson on 3 January 1931.
2. Diwan C.G. Herbert's letter to AGG Pritchard on 24 December 1931.
3. Note by Diwan Herbert, December 1931.
4. Diwan C.G. Herbert's letter to AGG Pritchard on 24 December 1931.
5. AGG Pritchard's letter to Sir Charles Watson on 3 January 1931.
6. Conversation with Vikram Menon, July 2020.
7. Koji, Kawashema, *Missionaries, the Hindu State and British Paramountcy in Travancore and Cochin, 1858–1936*, London, School of Oriental and African Studies, University of London, 1994, p. 314.
8. IOR/R/1/1/1939 File 183-P(S)/1930, Selection of Successor to Rao Bahadur Narayana Iyer, Dewan of Cochin State.
9. Koji, Kawashema, *Missionaries, the Hindu State and British Paramountcy in Travancore and cochin 1858–1936,* p. 310.
10. Ibid., p. 311.
11. Ibid., p. 312.
12. Koji Kawashima, *Missionaries, the Hindu State and British Paramountcy in Travancore and Cochin, 1858–1936*, p. 312; Note prepared regarding complaint of the Thampurans that was prepared for the Agent to the Governor General to brief Mr Herbert.
13. Koji, *Missionaries, the Hindu State and British Paramountcy*, p. 313.
14. Ibid., p. 314.
15. Vikram Menon's email of 3 April 2015.
16. Vikram Menon's email of 3 April 2015.
17. Diwan Herbert's letter to AGG Pritchard on 24 December 1931.

18. Menon, T.K. Krishna, *The Days That Were*, p. 591.
19. Diwan Herbert's letter to AGG Pritchard on 24 December 1931.
20. Note written by Diwan Herbert in December 1931.
21. Ibid.
22. Socio-religious trust that managed Hindu temples and ensured their smooth operation.
23. C.G. Herbert's letter to the Maharaja of Cochin on 10 August 1931.
24. Maharaja of Cochin's letter to C.G. Herbert on 11 August 1931.
25. C.G. Herbert's letter of 13 August 1931.
26. C.G. Herbert's letter of 15 August 1931.
27. C.G. Herbert's letter of 10 September 1931.
28. Maharaja of Cochin's letter of 13 September 1931.
29. Maharaja of Cochin's letter of 16 September 1931.
30. C.G. Herbert's letter to the Maharaja of 16 September 1931.
31. Maharaja Rama Varma's letter to H.R.N. Pritchard of 18 September 1931.
32. AGG Pritchard's letter to Charles Watson of 3 January 1932.
33. Ibid.
34. Ibid.
35. Maharaja Rama Varma's letter to AGG Pritchard on 13 October 1931.
36. AGG Pritchard's letter to Maharaja Rama Varma on 14 October 1931.
37. Maharaja Rama Varma's letter to AGG Pritchard on 18 October 1931.
38. Maharaja's letter on 18 October 1931, with note from Diwan Herbert on this letter of 24 October 1931.
39. Note written by Diwan Herbert in December 1931.
40. Ibid.
41. Ibid.

Chapter 25: Checkmate

1. AGG Pritchard's letter to Charles Watson on 3 January 1932.
2. Ibid.
3. AGG Pritchard's letter to Diwan Herbert on 30 January 1932.

4. AGG Pritchard's letter to the Madras Government on 30 January 1932.
5. The Madras Government's letter to AGG Pritchard on 4 February 1932.
6. AGG Pritchard's letter to Turner in Bombay on 9 February 1932.
7. Letters dated 27 February 1932 to 16 March 1932 between AGG Pritchard and Turner.
8. Menon, T.K. Krishna, *The Days That Were*, p. 614.

Chapter 26: Afterword

1. Son of her daughter Ratnam Amma Palatt.
2. Daughter of her son Aravindaksha Menon.